An Obsession with

Carp

by Dave Lane

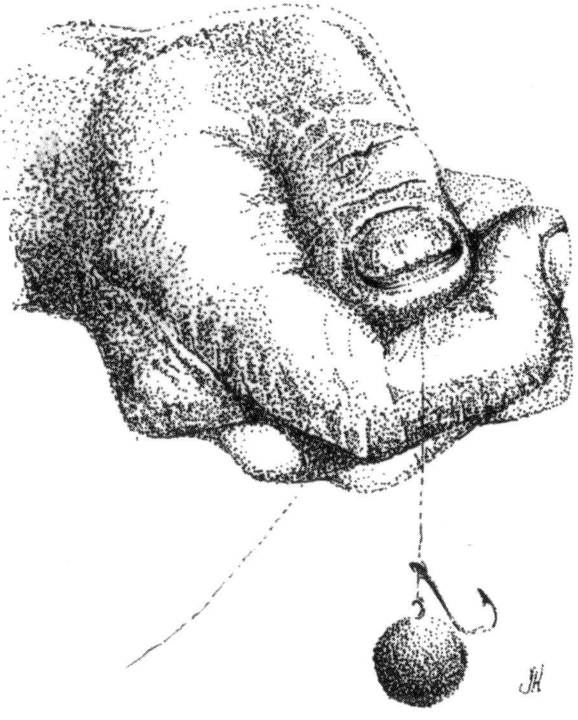

• Angling Publications Ltd •

This book is dedicated to Sam the Carp Dog, my loyal companion.

An Obsession with Carp - a limited edition book.
Published in 1998 by Laneman Publishing

Reprinted 2004 by Angling Publications Ltd, 0114 2580812

British Library Cataloguing in Publication Data

A catalogue record for this book is available from the British Library.

ISBN 1 901717 03 8

Edited by Paul Selman.
Design and production by Lane Design.

All photographs by the author unless marked.

Printed in Great Britain by
Biddles Limited, King's Lynn, Norfolk
Print management by John Mason Design & Print, Aylesbury

Contents

Introduction & Acknowledgements

In writing this book I have not tried to instruct any one of the way to fish, but more to tell of the ways of fishing. As a younger man I used to enjoy the writings of Rod Hutchinson and his prowess at setting a scene. I find his style of story-telling far more entertaining than simply reading of the technical preferences of one man. After all is said and done, carp angling is a sport ideally suited to the individualist rather than the conformist.

My story is that of my life as an angler and of the humour and heartache I have encountered along the way. It is about one man's true obsession and the lengths to which he will stretch to achieve it. I hope that you enjoy reading it as much as I enjoyed recalling my long forgotten memories and writing them all down. The making of this book, like everything in life, was made considerably easier by the help of my friends, and I would like to thank them for it.

Firstly, I must thank Sue, my devoted girlfriend, for putting up with the sound of me tapping away on a lap top every night for a year, breaking only to ask for punctuation advice, or more tea, and for her excellent sketches and paintings, without which the book would have been noticeably poorer.

My thanks to Keith for his endless proof-reading, the changing of a thousand 'of's' into 'have's' and for curing me of my comma-phobia. Also for the use of his memory as a substitute for the void that used to be my own.

Thanks also to Andy for his computer wizardry which dragged me, screaming and kicking, into the nineties and made this book a reality.

Not forgetting, of course, Sue's brother, Jon, who stepped in to supply some extra, and much needed, sketches at very short notice.

To Max Cottis at Fox International for supplying me with fishing tackle, and Steve and Kev at Mainline Baits for the constant stream of quality baits that flow in my general direction.

And to all those glorious and eccentric characters whose paths have crossed with mine throughout the years. Some appear within the folds of these very pages and others, too numerous to mention - thank you for the memories.

Finally, I would like to thank Fat Sam, for being this man's 'best friend' throughout the entire ordeal, and supplying me with a constant source of amusement and companionship. Not to mention doubling up as a waste disposal unit and dishwasher!

Foreword
By Keith Jenkins

Have you ever been in that desperate situation when, with fish feeding in front of you, you are frantically searching for that essential item of tackle you so recently purchased, but to no avail?

Have you sat, gazing over the lake, as the first rays of the sun mark the start of a new day, and relished the dipping of your last chocolate Hobnob into a steaming cup of tea - only to find no Hobnobs and no tea in your cup!

If these scenarios are all too vivid, then you've been fishing with Dave and Sam. In all the time that I've known him, Dave has never quite had the tools for the job and has, therefore, found it necessary to raid any unguarded tackle box to meet his needs but, after the crisis is over (and inevitably after the photos), you find he has more than enough - yours and his!

Dave has always said what a marvellous invention food is, and how he would dearly love to shake the hand of the man who invented it! Strange, then, that he never has any of this marvellous invention whenever he goes fishing and has to constantly eat yours, or mine, to be more precise! There will be a few people nodding sagely, at this point, but with a strange smile flicking across their lips because that is how Dave normally leaves you - strangely amused. I have been strangely amused for fifteen years now, and still put the phone down after our fourth or fifth conversation of the evening, chuckling quietly at our usual verbal jousting.

If, however, you were to ask those same people what they gained from meeting Dave on the bank, they would all relate tales of the small bits of knowledge gleaned from him that go to making an exceptional angler, and most of them would freely tell what else they gained - a very good friend, who would do anything in his power to help someone in whatever way he could, no questions asked.

So, that's Dave Lane, and I have been lucky enough to know him for many years, and for many more to come, I hope. Many of you have yet to meet Dave on the bankside and, so, do not know what to expect - I envy you that pleasant surprise.

By the way, Dave, have you still got my waders ?

Chapter 1

Beginnings

Way back in the mists of time, well 1965 to be precise, a small boy of four years old sat on the parapet of an old stone bridge over the River Mole. Skinny little legs poked out from the ends of grey flannel shorts and dangled precariously over the edge. Clutched in his hand was a four foot solid glass 'spinning' rod, courtesy of Woolworths, and hanging on desperately to the scruff of his bri-nylon shirt was his proud father. Dangling below (a clear three feet above the surface) was a chunk of Sunblest white sliced loaf, presented delicately on a hook more suited to cod fishing! So enraptured was his father by the sight of his son, staring expectantly at the gaily coloured plastic float swinging from the rod tip, that he only spotted the approaching swan at the last moment. With a quick flick on the rod butt a disaster was narrowly averted, and the swan caught his free meal as it fluttered down to the surface. The boy noticed nothing, his eyes were still glued to the plastic float as it suddenly leaped into the air.

"Come on then son, it looks like it'll have to be fish and chips again tonight," the old man chuckled as they made their way back to the car.

Six years and a few thousand perch and roach later, the same couple set-up for their very first 'night-fishing' session. Half a dozen extension leads all joined in a long line, snaked their way from a gently idling Ford Escort van, ending their journey half-way up an old willow tree. Attached to the end of the lead, and rudely illuminating the scene, was a 1,000 watt building site lantern! Sat within an island of light, father and son tentatively tried their hand at floating crusts for carp. Neither had any real grasp of the mechanics involved, but at some time in the wee small hours a ten year old boy found himself chasing his rod down the bank, as an unseen leviathan attempted to drag it off into the darkness.

The battle that followed between the boy and his quarry was momentous, until eventually beaten, the monster from the deep allowed himself to be wrestled ashore. Man and boy stared at each other in mute disbelief, for there on the ground between them, shining in the sodium glow, lay the most stupendous and colossal common carp that either had ever witnessed. The uncatchable had been caught, the totally unobtainable, obtained, a spell broken. Carp and captor stared at each other for long moments, and something that lay previously undisturbed deep within the boy's soul stirred. His fate was sealed, a carp angler was born.

During those next few years the obsession grew and every spare moment was spent in the pursuit of carp. Long nights sitting hunched over on an old wicker creel, hand hovering over the butt, waiting for that dough bobbin to start its silent and eerie ascent toward the butt ring. When dawn arrived, huge squares of crust were dunked in the margins before being hurled out into the pond, where small wild carp would play pass the parcel with them until the unlucky 'winner' would be dragged, fighting all the way, to the bank. I suppose the fish weighed around three or four pounds each, which by comparison would put that first 'monster' common somewhere in the region of two and a half pounds. There was something truly magical about those early days, not just the allure of staying out all night or the roaring fire that we'd inevitably

Dave's earliest fishing picture.

build in the darkest hours. It was something about the unknown that lay within the pond itself, something that to an extent was lost with the inception of electronic bite indicators. For those who have never sat all night staring at a piece of bread pinched on the line, the jarred candle reflecting hidden faces in its surface, have sadly missed out. Not to have experienced that exhilarating yet almost heart stopping moment when the bobbin first trembles and then ever so slowly and in complete and utter silence slides up towards the rod, pulled on the other end by the unknown. Nowadays we fish only for screaming runs from fish that are, to all intents and purposes, already hooked. To strike at a bite is a thing of the past, but memories, thankfully, are forever.

Fishing took precedence over all else throughout my teenage years. Even the truant officer could not dampen my enthusiasm. While the rest of my class struggled with the finer points of algebra, I, under the cover of a badly forged sick note, would be struggling to extract a tench from under a bank of rhododendrons, or to tempt a wildie into taking a piece of freelined sausage from the edge of a lily bed. Should the park warden venture around, I would hide in the bushes until he passed to avoid embarrassing questions (and paying, of course).

My first job on leaving school was in Tilgate Forest, chopping down trees to make way for a new golf course. So I suppose to all intents and purposes I was a lumberjack, although I didn't exactly 'jack' much 'lumber'. Within Tilgate Forest are three lakes, one of which held a fair head of carp. It was the summer of 1976, which went down on record as one of the hottest in living memory. It was obviously too hot for working so most of my time was spent surreptitiously angling. I had double reason to avoid the bailiff now though, as he was also my boss!

I fished Tilgate on and off for years, taking fish up to high doubles and generally cutting my teeth as such into the new up and coming high tech style of angling. I saw my first hair rig on there and I can still remember pointing at it and laughing out loud. I was fishing on the main dam wall at the time using a secret bait that I had invented. It was sausage meat mixed with a chicken feed called Layers Mash. I used to bury a size eight hook into the middle of a lump the size of a golf ball, and with a small Arsley bomb to add more weight, I'd hurl it out at least thirty yards, and would catch more than my fair share on it as well. Then along came this bloke with a little round and rock hard ball of bait that smelt of maple syrup, and it was hanging underneath

An 8 1/2lb common from Tilgate in 1984.

his hook!

"You won't catch bugger all on that mate," I roared. "It's not even on your bloody hook."

I could hardly contain my laughter as he proceeded to cast it out into the lake. I turned to my mate and stated categorically that he'd NEVER catch me using something as stupid as that. By the end of the day the idiot with the silly rig had caught four carp. We had never caught four in a week from here let alone in a day. So the very next week we were back, armed with hair rigs and silly baits made out of flour and smashed up cat biscuits. As the years went by the baits got slowly better and the rigs got more and more inventive, we even caught a few fish on some of them.

Winter carp fishing was pretty much unheard of in those days and, consequently, I would swap over to pike angling. We had a small pond up the road where gudgeon and rudd live baits could be easily bagged, and I used to keep them in an old loft water tank at the bottom of the garden. I was still living at home at the time (when your parents own a pub it's very hard to leave), and on a cold winter's night while they were away on holiday, I decided to keep the baits warm and bring them indoors for the night. Half way through the evening an Australian couple walked into the bar, and announced that they were my cousins, and were midway through a tour of Europe. Whether they were or not I had no idea, but I invited them upstairs to get cleaned up and told them they were welcome to stay the night.

The girl, Sheila or something similar, wanted to go straight to the bathroom to freshen up. "If you want to use the bath give a shout and I'll come and clear it out

An early set-up at Tilgate.

first," I said.

This could be amusing I thought. The Aussies are always going on about monster spiders in the 'Dunnie.' Let's see what they make of this! Two minutes later she was back and looking a bit pale. She smiled at me nervously as if I was a small alien being that she didn't want to offend. As she leant over next to her boyfriend I heard her whisper, "Jeez, Carl, there's live fish in the damn tub!"

For some strange reason they declined my fine offer of a night in a nice warm house, and opted instead, for a night in the safety of their own camper van parked in the street.

Apart from the pike fishing, I was also a keen tench angler but carp fishing was always my main obsession. I was doing well out of Tilgate and a few other local pits. I had discovered very early on that mobility was definitely the key to catching more than your fair share. I was always on the move and scored well as a result. Before long, I'd upped my personal best fish to sixteen pounds. Floater fishing had started to weave its way into my repertoire as well, and anchored Chum Mixers were providing me with some good catches.

A 16lb personal best from Tilgate.

About this time in my life, I encountered two kindred spirits who would, as it turned out, fish with me from that day until this. The first of these came from a chance meeting in a pub one bitterly cold November night. I'd been having a few pints of Guinness with some mates at the bar. A rock band was pumping out their tortured cover tunes in the function room next door and I was getting steadily more and more drunk. Every time I looked around it seemed to me that the same young female was staring at me. I ignored it at first, thinking that it must just be coincidence but when it was still happening an hour later I realised that I was definitely getting 'The Eye'.

Eventually after a few more pints, I decided I was drunk enough to make a move, so I staggered over to her table and presented her with a drink and a packet of crisps. I ended up chatting to her for the rest of the night and although I can't actually remember leaving the pub, or the walk home, I found her lying in bed beside me the next morning when I awoke. Her name was Sam and she was the nicest looking Collie-cross that I'd ever set eyes on. From then on I took her fishing everywhere I went.

It was during one of these trips the next summer (1983) at Tilgate Lakes, that I met what would transpire to be my second companion for the years ahead. I was fishing in the shallows, up against the boom, and I got chatting to a bloke who I had seen fishing a few times but had never actually spoken to before. The conversation turned after a while to other waters in the area, and eventually settled on a complex of lakes situated in Ashdown Forest known collectively as Pippingford Park. Neither of us had seen the place but we'd both heard rumours about it, and, as we seemed to hit it off quite well, we decided on a little joint reccy the next week to find out what it was all about. I didn't know it at the time but that was to be the start of a wonderful friendship that would shape my whole angling career. Now 15 years later Keith and I still fish, drink, and socialise together, usually managing to combine all three.

Back then, there was only a fraction of the tackle that is available to today's anglers, and most of our finer items were home made. On seeing my first set of adjustable bed chair legs which were marketed by Dave Preston, I thought that I'd save myself a few bob and make my own. At the time I was working as a steel erector at Gatwick Airport's new North Terminal, and periodically I would sneak off into the basement to my little hidden workshop. I had pinched a load of conduit piping and lovingly cut and drilled each piece to match the D.P version that my friend had lent me as a pattern. It was only when I came to take them upstairs for welding that I realised the weight of them. I hadn't actually lifted them all at once before. If I'd have bolted that lot on to a bedchair it would have taken a fork lift truck to get it to the lake! Keith used to call me 'Heath Robinson' after the hundreds of bodged-up pieces of kit that I used to come up with.

Keith himself was undoubtedly the 'King of the Rigs.' Every conceivable medley of nylon, tubing, hook and bead had been cast hopefully into the pond. On one occasion, I counted seven different hairs on one rig! But the main thing was that we were learning, and catching. Pippingford Lakes are a chain of four small lakes at the bottom of a heavily wooded valley with one other pond of about an acre set back on its own. This separate pond was known as the Army Lake. Although the whole estate was shared with the army training camp, it was on this pond that they would test their amphibious craft or paraglide across it.

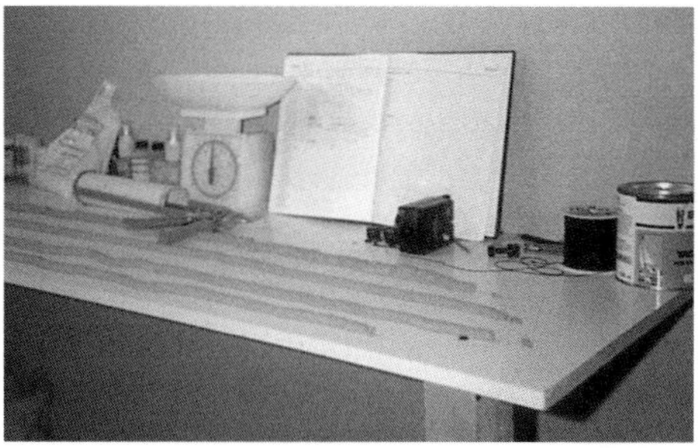

Early baitmaking!

All the close season we baited the pond with hand-rolled 8mm boilies, three times every week. We decided on a milk protein bait, but knowing next to nothing about protein bait formulation, we had to first wade through the few books that were available on the subject. Eventually, armed with bags of caseins and caseinates, soya and semolina, we set about mixing it all together with a pineapple flavouring that we'd been given the nod about. We also pre-baited the larger of the chain of lakes. We christened this The Keyhole. Into this scenic little lake we piled kilos and kilos of maple peas, heavily influenced by the writings of Rod Hutchinson, we had high hopes for our particle approach. It paid dividends, and in the first week of the season on The Keyhole we cleaned up using the maples. Fishing popped-up stacks of three peas with a shaped piece of cork on top to balance the rig, we caught fish after fish, and from standing on the high bank behind our swims we could clearly see the fish as they made their way across the shallows before dipping down and sending up large clouds of silt as they fed with merry abandon. The protein bait must have been at least semi-reasonable as well. On the first time of trying it we bagged the biggest two fish in the Army Lake, one each. We really thought we'd cracked it then, as we posed smiling for the camera with our monster carp of fourteen pounds apiece. We did quite well out of the other lakes too, and before the season was up I had upped my personal best to an incredible eighteen pounds!

Even back then, I used to move swims so many times a day that by the end of it, I couldn't remember which ones I had fished. I have never been a particularly patient sort of an angler. My thinking is that while you are sitting in one spot waiting for the fish to come along, the fish are in another spot feeding their heads off. So, why not just move to there? It certainly paid dividends on Pippingford and indeed it has everywhere that I've fished since then.

Tiger nuts also came to our attention while we were at Pippingford Park, and it didn't take long for us to realise that here was a bait that could really do the business if used correctly. I learned a valuable lesson while fishing the tigers. This was about the speed at which carp can adapt their feeding methods when they are getting a bit of a hammering. The rig I started off using was a straightforward pop-up hair rig incorporating a piece of shaped cork, placed on the hair between two tigers. This worked fine for a few months but then the 'twitch and bow wave' stage appeared. One or two bleeps on the alarm would be followed by a bow wave out of the area as a spooked fish charged away. After trying a few different rigs out I hit on the winning formula. I had figured out that by unbalancing the rig it should in theory make it that much harder to eject. This was achieved by adding a separate, longish hair to the eye of the hook, this held one large bottom tiger. On the very first day that I tried out my new 'super rig', I hooked every fish that made its way across the shallows and onto my baits. In all, I landed seven carp that day, all doubles, including the eighteen pounder which was the biggest fish in the lake. This was by far my best ever day's angling at the time and highlighted to me the importance of adaptability.

Pippingford Park Lakes, apart from offering wonderful fishing, held an absolute plethora of wildlife. Deer wandered freely around the forest and badgers, foxes and mink could be seen on a regular basis. One night, while Keith and I were driving through the woods along an old army track, a badger stepped out in front of the van. Paying no heed to the headlights or the noise of the engine, he casually sauntered along the track for a hundred yards or so, no more than twenty feet in front of the bumper. Before he disappeared into the bushes he nonchalantly turned his head and gave us the most disparaging look imaginable. The only downside to this natural beauty spot was the Army itself. At times it was as if World War Three had broken out, with phosphorous flares and mortars going off in the middle of an otherwise peaceful night. On one occasion, I was happily minding my own business, sitting behind the rods in the afternoon sun waiting for a bite, when I heard a rustling in the bushes behind me. On turning I saw a procession of soldiers approaching on their hands and knees. Keeping a straight face was the hardest part, as they crawled in steady single file past my low chair, only a few feet away from where I sat! To add reality to their little charade, they obviously had to pretend that a harmless fisherman didn't even exist in their make-believe battle zone, but you could practically smell the embarrassment oozing from their every pore as they crept past, averting their eyes as they did so.

Things were not always so amusing though, and one morning an hour before dawn as I made my way down the track to the lake I was challenged by the old, "Halt. Who goes there, friend or foe?"

"Fisherman," I replied and shone my torch into the woods towards the spot that the voice had come from. There in the beam, sat a soldier behind a tripod on which was mounted a belt fed machine gun, pointing straight at me! It's a good job I was wearing waders that's all I can say! We still fished on at the Army Lake quite a lot, and even though we had caught most of the better fish in there relatively quickly, there was still something magical about the place. It was surrounded on all sides by high ground and woodland and on a cloudy night you literally could not see your hand in front of your face. So many spooky occurrences happened there that I would need a separate book just to list them, but it would be wrong of me to turn the page on Pippingford without first telling the tale of 'The Dead Body'.

We'd had the Army Lake pretty much to ourselves for most of the season, but there was one old boy of about seventy and his wife, who used to visit regularly. He never fished the nights but was happy just to be out fishing in the day time. The old boy had a dog-eared old photo of himself holding a big mirror carp in a half-nelson. Its weight used to fluctuate in the breeze and he would proudly show it to everybody, regardless of how many times they had seen it before. Now, I don't know if you remember it from the news, but in 1985 a decapitated body was found in Ashdown Forest. The head, hands and feet, and for some reason the intestines were missing from the corpse. It just so happened that it was found in the lay-by opposite the entrance to the lake.

Keith turned up early for a weekend session on the Thursday and an incident room had been set up in the lay-by gathering information from all and sundry. On turning up at the Army Lake, he could see that only the old couple were already angling, so risking 'the photo' again, he went around for a chat. The old boy seemed a bit flustered about the body affair, and he told Keith that divers had been called in and had checked the lakes over earlier in the week. Thinking no more about it Keith went and set up on a small point opposite them. Around midday the old fella was obviously into a fish and great deal of hand waving and running about ensued. A few minutes later he appeared at Keith's side with his face as white as a sheet.

"I-I-I think I've hooked those intestines," he managed to stammer. "C-C-Can you come and have a look with me?"

Now, Keith could see his long weekend's fishing going up the Swanny if police divers and camera crews were going to descend onto this little one acre lake. So, begrudgingly, he led the old boy back to his swim. By the time they got there the poor old sod looked about ready to keel over with fear. Keith took the rod from on the floor where matey had dropped it in shock, and unceremoniously heaved the offending article back up off the bottom in the margins. As it came into view they could make out a bloated stomach and some entrails. The old fella had to sit down while Keith examined it a bit closer. There, on the underside, he spotted some feathers and lifting it up for the old boy to see announced, "That's alright, mate, it's only an old swan."

Within half an hour the old couple were packed and gone, and Keith settled in for a nice peaceful weekend.

Eventually the time came to move on, and it was with a heavy heart that we surrendered our Pippingford tickets, in search (we hoped) of larger carp. Apart from the odd return trip to Tilgate, our next proper water was a gravel pit at Chichester. It

Keith 'the Spiv' gets one from Chichester.

was the first gravel pit that we had fished and we were looking forward to learning about fishing bars and gullies, rather than silty estate lakes. Being an hour's drive away, it was the furthest we had ever travelled to fish, this cut out the pre-baiting angle, and meant we would have to learn about the lakes as we fished them.

The Chichester complex was compiled of four lakes. Two were instantly dismissed as holding only small fish, while another (The Church Lake) was a bit of an unknown, so we left that one aside to start with as well. The lake we chose for the coming season was known as Whick Lake, and was actually two lakes joined by a very narrow channel. The stock, as far as we could make out, was mainly doubles with two known twenty pounders, one of these was a common carp known as Half-Tail. They were both only scraper twenties but these at the time were very big fish for us as we had never even seen a twenty on the bank before. At first we had trouble obtaining tickets, but this was only a small hurdle and for the summer we were constantly borrowing tickets from friends who were already members. A member was allowed one guest per day and his ticket had to be bought in advance from a local tackle shop. Our usual plan was to ponce a membership from some poor unsuspecting fool and then split the cost of the extra day ticket between us. This meant that every time we fished, we would first turn up at the tackle shop and pretend to be somebody entirely different to the last time we were there. We fished it on and off throughout the summer, taking a few doubles and generally feeling our way around.

Our main plans hinged on gaining a winter ticket. In November every year the controlling club, in order to boost funds, would offer a discounted winter ticket and this was our opportunity to slide in as members, which we did with gusto. In readiness for our coming winter campaign we had (unfortunately for our wallets) splashed out on some good but incredibly over-priced protein bait from Cotswold Baits. It would, so the guy had taken great lengths to inform us, breakdown after a day and give off various attraction signals even in the coldest months. It was called Meta-Bait and we added to this, Garlic essential oil which stank something horrible. It was in all fairness a very good bait, it was just a shame that it was so expensive. For anyone who has never

Above: Taking to the water to land a fish at Pippingford

Left: The 18lb mirror from Pippingford.

Below: Half Tail - the biggest fish in Chichester at twenty and a half pounds.

Above: Dave with The Orange One at thirty three and a half pounds of sheer magic from Harefield.

Left: A lump of a twenty five and a half pound common.

used Garlic oil as an attractor, a word of warning - Don't! It's not that you won't catch on it, it is without doubt one of the better attractors that I have used, it's just that you'll lose all your friends and family as a result. One summer Keith went off on holiday leaving his bait-making gear, complete with Garlic oil, in an outside cupboard at the front of his house. During his absence the neighbours called in the Gas Board to investigate the strange smell. They, in turn, smashed his front door down convinced there was a major gas leak!

Equipped with our new tickets and smelly bait, we loaded up my battered old Escort van and set off for Chichester for our first session as full members. Winding the windows fully open in spite of the temperature, went some way to keeping the garlic aromas to a minimum, and we eventually arrived an hour later feeling only a little queasy. Keith opted for the deeper half of the lake. This was called Whick Two. I chose the little back-point at the far side of the lake. This formed one side of the gap that separated the two halves. From here I could fish both Whick One and Two at the same time, which I did.

On my first morning as a member and half-way through eating a roadblock-style fry up, I had a take on the rod that was cast into the shallower half of the lake. I had been messing about with balanced baits and stiff nylon hooklinks, and it was one of these, cast into only two feet of water that had been picked up. The fish made it easily into an adjacent bed of rushes and I had no choice other than to strip off and wade out to free it. Sticking the landing net over my head, I paddled out up to my waist and sloshed my way out to the reeds. The fish was surprisingly obliging and I netted him quite easily. The water was absolutely freezing and by the time I got back to shore my legs had turned blue. But there in the net lay an enormous common. I passed it over to Keith and started to clamber out. As I did so, the other rod that I had cast into the deeper half of the lake roared off as well, and after risking hypothermia for a further ten minutes, I landed another huge fish, this time a mirror carp. Before I could even look to see what I'd caught I had to leap back into the sleeping bag to warm up, as my teeth were chattering uncontrollably by now. After all, it was the middle of November. Keith looked after the fish while I put on every available piece of clothing before digging out my scales and weigh sling. The common was 'Half-Tail' and weighed twenty and a half pounds while the mirror was also one of the biggest in the lake at nineteen and a half pounds. All in all, not a bad way to celebrate my new permit!

We fished on at Chichester for two seasons taking a lot of good catches, and constantly experimenting with rigs along the way. One rig that was born out of circumstance at Chichester and still serves us well today was the pop-up straight off the lead. The first time that I ever tried this was due, quite simply, to running out of split shot to balance my rigs. The one rod that had to do without, and popped-up straight off the lead, produced an incredible twelve runs in one weekend! Obviously it wasn't long before this was our favoured method. I have never been able to figure out just how a rig as blatant as this can possibly keep on catching, but the one thing that you can never argue with are results, and we've certainly had our fair share of those over the years on this rig.

After our second season on Chichester had come to an end, we decided to start looking around for a new water to move on to. We had caught a lot of good fish and had a terrific time while we were at it. The local pub had been particularly welcoming throughout the cold months. Most Saturday nights would find us sitting by the fireside supping Guinness, with Fat Sam curled up on the huge pile of discarded thermal clothing at our feet. At the end of our last session on Chichester, we decided to give it a fitting send off. We started early in the Five Bells and by chucking out time we were more than three sheets to the wind. After a very wobbly short cut through a graveyard, we reached the lake and launched our baits out in all directions before tumbling into bed. At some time in the night I must have had a run, as in the morning I awoke to find a mid-double sacked up in the margins. Keith was unconscious and

Sam the Carp Dog.

groaning a lot, so leaving him to it, I photographed and weighed the fish with a couple of other lads and slid him back. Keith didn't appear until about two in the afternoon and he looked like the walking dead. All the way home in the van he was moaning about his head, and growing steadily paler by the mile. With only five miles to go he could take it no longer and frantically winding down the window, emptied the contents of his stomach onto the hard shoulder of the dual carriageway.

"Stop the van," he screamed, waving his hands maniacally. "My toof, my toof!"

I pulled over and watched in absolute amazement as Keith staggered back up the road, searching on the ground as he went. A couple of minutes later he was back, clutching his sick and grit-encrusted prize. We set off again, and to my horror, Keith spat on the offending tooth before wiping it once on his jumper and popping it back into his mouth.

"That's better," he announced. I just shook my head in disbelief and drove home.

The sort of water that we were after now was something with a decent head of twenties and maybe even a thirty pounder. We drew up a short list of waters that we felt it might be possible to obtain membership for. But as is often the case, we never got to fish any of those.

Chapter 2

The Obsession Grows
Harefield

At the start of the close season, Keith and I went to one of those Carp Society slide shows. The sort where everybody stays in the bar getting pissed, while the poor sod presenting it waffles on to himself in the other room (I know, I've been that poor sod). While we were there we got chatting at the bar, to a bloke who fished somewhere called Rodney Meadow. He waxed lyrically on about it for ages, telling us all about the twenties and thirties that dwelled between its tree lined banks. We were more than a little interested at the sound of this, and by the time he left, we had managed to get the name of the owners, William Boyers and an address out of him.

Keith was set the task of phoning around from work, to see what he could find out about the whole affair. A few days later, in the middle of the afternoon, the phone rang and it was Keith. He sounded all excited and pleased with himself. He'd managed to get through to this John Stent fellow at William Boyers, and although there were no tickets left for Rodney Meadow there were a couple of places available in the Harefield syndicate. This meant as little to me as it had at first to Keith, but according to Mr Stent the lake held everything that our little hearts could possibly desire. Not being total plonkers we instantly halved his estimate of a dozen thirty pound carp, but even then that still left six more than we had ever fished for in our lives up until then. Keith informed me that there was an absolute shedful of twenties also residing in this sixty acre pit, and did we want tickets?

"Of course we want bloody tickets," I yelled back down the phone.

"That's handy as I've already ordered them," he replied. "We pick them up at the weekend."

After I had put the phone down I started thinking, Harefield? That name rings a bell somewhere. I flicked through a few magazines and then the penny dropped. Grabbing Hutchie's book, I turned quickly to a guest chapter by Paul Gummer and there it was. I must have read the article a hundred times in the past, all about the horrendous gravel bars that could cut through twenty pound line as if it were cotton! The account of him swimming halfway along the pit in an effort to land an upper twenty now left me slack-jawed and wondering what the hell we had let ourselves in for. The picture on the adjoining page, however, of a fish far and above anything in the league we had been used to fishing for, reminded me of what could be in store for us if we braved it out. Oh well, I thought, he who dares wins. I phoned Keith back at work.

"Jenkins," I said, "We seriously need some bigger tackle."

The following weekend after a trip down to Farlows to pick up our new tickets from John Stent, we decided we might as well go down to Harefield and see just exactly what we had got in exchange for our hard earned dosh. After a brief detour to look at the famous Savay Lake, we pulled into the Horse and Barge which is situated opposite Harefield Lake. Following our hastily scribbled directions down an asphalt track, we came across a large gravel workings to our left. Huge trucks laden with various aggregates slowly filed their way through, as mechanical shovels darted to and fro, loading and unloading with merry abandon. All the while a crane swung an enormous steel bucket back and forth to the rhythmic beat of the clanking conveyor belts. It looked like a modern day re-enactment of a dinosaur ballet! A vast open gravel pit could be seen as a backdrop to the scene. Then the awful truth dawned, all this was actually taking place on one bank of our new lake! We looked at each other in horror before hurrying on through a small copse of trees at the end of the track which brought us out onto the long north bank of Harefield. The wind that day was a howling north westerly, and waves more suited to Brighton beach charged across the surface. Looking across to the far bank the first thing we noticed was another crane, this one was situated right in the middle of the bank and made it blatantly obvious that they were still digging the damn place. The bank that we were standing on though, was actually quite pretty with large, well established trees along the whole length and a small point which jutted out three quarters of the way along, this put within casting range a series of three large islands. The far end of the lake on this side was dotted with smaller islands and, being on the back of the hooligan wind, looked quite fishable. The other side, by comparison, was the most inhospitable piece of ground you could imagine. As we made our way towards the crane I saw something odd by the water's edge, on closer inspection it turned out to be a dead cat (or at least what was left of one.) Its back was broken. I surveyed the surrounding scenery, sixty foot crane, wind lashed pit, gravel workings, and the dead cat, and then slowly shook my head at Keith in total disbelief. I carried on walking along the bank in silence.

You tend to build up a mental picture of a lake before you visit it, but never in my most bizarre nightmares had I imagined it would look anything like this.

We were now on the windy side of the lake and the further we walked along the bank, the higher the waves became and halfway along, it became hard even to stand upright. Heading off towards an old rusting gravel 'Hopper' that adorned the bank, I stopped on one of the rare pieces of grass and, bracing my self into the teeth of the gale, I gazed out across Harefield Lake!

Something bobbing about in the undercut margins caught my eye, I looked down and there at my feet was a Jack Russell dog! It was bloated with water and looking decidedly dead. Keith came walking up the bank, and, following my incredulous stare, also looked down in the edge.

"What the bloody hell is that?" he said.

"I think his name's Bob," I replied as I strode away towards the pub. I was suddenly in dire need of some alcohol.

We sat in the bar absolutely shell-shocked. The worst part was that we'd already paid our money! By the time the second pint was history, we had managed to play up the lakes 'high points' and pretended to ignore its many 'lows,' to the extent that it didn't seem half so bad on reflection (it's funny what effect a couple of beers can have). We decided to come back on a nice hot day and give the place another chance.

We went back and we saw fish, and then we went back again and saw even more fish, and the stamp of fish we had seen left us in no doubt at all. This was the place for us, regardless of the cranes and its assortment of deceased domestic pets. The whole close season was spent making glorious plans and rolling baits. We had changed back to making our own base mixes again after spending far too much on bait the previous winter. We used to use the same basic mix for most of our bait. It comprised of sixty percent of assorted milk proteins, to which we would add forty percent of either fishmeal or birdfood to create whichever bait 'type' we required. We decided on the fishmeal for Harefield, and like the masochists we are, stayed on the garlic oil, though we had managed to find a cheaper supplier by now.

People were practically queuing up to warn us about the savage bars that peppered the bottom at Harefield, and would slice our lines like a knife through butter. After a large intake of breath they would then inevitably say something like "What you need is parachute cord," or "Wire line, that'll sort 'em out." Our brains went into overdrive considering all the possibilities. I even made a twelve foot beach rod up with just a tip ring cut in half and a 'breakaway' casting button on the butt. The idea was that I could prop my normal rod up, pointing skywards, leaving the bail arm open, and using some hideous leader material on the end that would not normally 'cast', I could hurl it out into the pond using the 'launching rod'. Thankfully this was one of those inventions that never left the sanctuary of the shed.

We approached it in the end much as we had any other water but just used heavier nylon leaders.

After what seemed like an eternity, the new season was imminent and we made our way down to Harefield, fully laden with tackle, food, bait, and Carp Dog. We'd show 'em!

It was all still a bit daunting, and a total change of fishing for us. It felt, for some reason, akin to being the top dog at junior school, and then going up to secondary school only to become a little squirt all over again. But we met a few of the other lads in the car park and they seemed like a decent enough bunch. Apparently, a draw for swims was to be held later that afternoon and the general consensus was to retire to the pub and wait. This sounded like a wonderful idea so we trotted over for a swift one (just to be sociable).

There we were in the Horse and Barge, waiting for the draw, surrounded by big hairy anglers all giving it large, thirties this and thirties that, fishing at a hundred and twenty yards, parachute cord for leaders! etc.. etc. We'd had the fishing experience in terms of years, so we could 'talk the talk' but when it actually came down to it, with fish of this size and gravel bars of this magnitude, would we be able to 'walk the walk?' Only time would tell. One thought helped keep my sanity, I kept reminding myself that I had previously thought twenties were unobtainable until I'd fished a pit that had actually held some. At the end of the day the Harefield carp were only fish, just bigger that's all. Lots bigger!

When the draw eventually took place we were praying that we didn't come out first as we hadn't a clue where to go. As it was, our numbers surfaced from the hat about halfway through the draw and we ended up fishing on the Causeway Bank. There was a period of a few hours before we could cast out and we used this to try to get to know some of the lads. The afternoon was spent sipping cold beer and leaping from tall trees into the cool waters of Broadwater Lake, situated behind the Causeway Bank.

One of the first people I got to know was Bernie Loftus and, over my time at Harefield, we were to get on like a house on fire. He told me about the Richworth Tutti Frutti's and about how they were dividing the lake's anglers into two separate camps of thought. Apparently the 'Purists' abhorred the use of ready made baits, claiming that they were less than 'proper angling' while the Tutti brigade were catching a far greater number of fish and really couldn't care less what anybody thought. Bernie was firmly in the Tutti camp whilst other anglers like Ian Booker and Paul Klinkenborg were more of the 'real baits' and soapbox brigade. Most of it was taken in good humour and everybody seemed to get on well enough, especially in the pub. I myself was a bit sceptical about the ethics of just buying a bait, having always rolled my own, but I decided to sit on the fence and see what transpired throughout the season. A lot of the other lads, as it turned out were also on their first season and were as intimidated by the size and nature of Harefield as I was. As it happened, I actually had the very first take of the season, but for some reason my nylon hook link parted as I struck, a very strange occurrence and thankfully one that was only ever to be repeated once more. A few people around the lake bagged fish, but none that we saw, and then Don Hipkin fishing further along the bank had a twenty six pounder just as we walked into his swim. As it lay on the mat before us I looked up at Keith and there was no need for words. We wanted some of this, and one way or another we were going to get it. I must have moved swims half a dozen times in that first week in an attempt to catch one of those Harefield Whackers but we remained fishless for our efforts. Just as we were leaving we bumped into a couple of guys who had been fishing opposite us on the Road Bank, near the hopper, and had fared a bit better than us. The fish, so they told us, had been showing well over the last couple of days and they had bagged two twenties.

All the way home we plotted and planned for the next session, reasoning that the fish had moved away from the more popular north side of the lake. We intended to set up in the Dead Dog area, and fish at range, beyond the deep boat channel that we had found when plumbing during the close season. Apparently, when the crane was working digging out the pit, an old steel tug would periodically chug its way along the margins of this bank to pick up any full up barges of gravel. We just prayed that it wouldn't happen whilst we were angling there. On the way home we stopped off at a small pond of one and a half acres that we had also joined. We only fished for an hour or so, but I hooked one carp which I lost when the hooklink parted again. I had been trying out a new low visibility nylon for hooklinks and it was obviously not up to the task. I tied some to the scales and pulled but it seemed strong enough. The problem was, that with a sudden jerk it would part like thin cotton, it became apparent that it was some form of pre-stretched mono and really should have been labelled as such. It was my own fault for not testing it out properly at home first. Pre-stretched lines although nice and thin in appearance, have no tolerance to sudden movement, and because of this are not entirely suitable for carp angling, especially not at somewhere like Harefield. It goes without saying that when I got home, this particular batch was in the bin before the front door had closed behind me.

The next week saw us back at Harefield for another try, it was still fairly busy and the Dead Dog was unfortunately already taken. Between the Dog and the entrance gate is a bay, backed off by the gravel workings. Two large sets of lily pads were situated three quarters of the way across the bay. As luck would have it both swims in this area were free and the pads being only sixty five yards out were well within even Keith's casting range. Pretty soon we were set-up and angling. A cross-wind made baiting-up a bit tricky, but the far bank belonged to the gravel company and we planned to sneak round there after dark and bait up a bit more accurately. As the evening approached a steady procession of anglers made their way past us on their way to the pub. The gate was only forty yards away to my right and banged incessantly as a result of the exodus. As it clanged shut for the umpteenth time I noticed a swirl appear from right in the margins at the foot of the gate. I wandered up for a closer inspection but the water here was so murky from the constant washing of gravel, that I could see nothing. I sat and waited for the next parched angler to pass, and as he did so I bade him good evening and watched the water as the gate squeaked open and then clanged shut again. Sure enough, a sub-surface boil slowly flattened the surface above it, as a fish reacted to the sudden noise. The area here would not usually warrant even the briefest of glances. The lake just sort of slowly ceased to be, ending in a small swampy puddle below the gate. Just over the edge of the marginal reeds however, in what appeared to be just a couple of feet of muddy water I'd found myself at least one carp if not more. The problem was that the light had all but faded, and what with all the angler traffic up and down this section of bank, I decided to sprinkle a few chopped baits in the edge and fish it at dawn, when hopefully the rest of the anglers would be sleeping off their hangovers.

The sun had hardly even started its ascent into the sky when, complete with rod and net, I crept stealthily through the dew soaked grass to 'my' little corner. I could just make out a few tiny pin prick bubbles breaking the surface in the half light. Silently, from a kneeling position behind the reeds, I lowered my freelined boilie

The first fish from Harefield at twenty four and a half pounds made Dave the happiest man alive.

onto the spot, hardly daring to breathe. I watched as the top lobe of a carp's tail gently broke the surface. A new patch of bubbles peppered the surface, only momentarily before my line gave a little twitch, and then ever so slowly coiled its way through the small hole in the surface film. I wound the handle once to eliminate the slack and jerked back the rod tip, but instead of the expected fireworks the bait flew neatly out of the water and over my head. I sat back on the damp grass and took a deep breath, it seemed like hours since my last one. I was sure I hadn't ruined my chances and as if to labour the point a fresh patch of bubbles appeared in the edge. This last patch was no more than one foot from the reeds and I carefully replaced the bait. I did not have to wait for long before the line once again snaked silently across the surface. This time the strike met with an entirely different result, the rod hooped over as the fish shot off to my left on its way out of the bay. I shouted up the bank to Keith to get his lines out of the way, as I couldn't even slow this one down let alone stop it. Keith obliged with his rods and then ran down to help, for some reason he brought one of his rods with him. I can't imagine why! There was a small tree directly to my left which made playing the fish a bit tricky, so stripping down to my underpants, I waded out a few yards until the water reached my waist and played it in from there. Compared to the battles we'd been used to on the smaller estate lakes this was a monumental affair, these fish really made the most of their environment and it was ages before I managed to get him anywhere near ready for netting. I backed up a bit until I was standing in the reeds, this way Keith could reach with the net and he did an admirable job first time.

That first Harefield carp was without doubt a major turning point for us, for it confirmed what we'd always thought, that no matter where they lived or what size they may be, they were at the end of the day all only fish, and ultimately catchable as a result. This wondrous specimen swung the Avons around to twenty four and a half pounds and made me the happiest man alive. While we were photographing him a few bleary eyed anglers wandered along to have a look, a couple of them were visibly 'gobsmacked' when I told them where and how I'd caught it, which only added to my glee. One of the guys who had obviously had more than his fair share of the liquid life-saver the previous night in the Barge, staggered off back to bed looking like the walking dead.

"Take a good look Jenkins," I said. "For tomorrow that's exactly what we're going to look like."

As if to reinforce the fact, Keith managed to drag a seventeen pound common out from under the far bank bushes later that day. While we were in the warmth of the pub that night my legs started to itch like mad, and on inspection in the loo's I found that I had been bitten, not once but somewhere in the region of a hundred times over both legs. It must have happened when I'd waded in for the fish, and by the end of the session, my legs had swelled up to half again their normal size. I ended up having to take anti-histamines to relieve the swelling.

I haven't mentioned it up until now, but this would be a good time to explain about insects, and the strange and almost obsessive affinity that they have for me. Everybody it seems has a different level of attraction, where mosquitoes and midges are concerned. Some people can go for months without a single bite, while others are peppered as soon as their shirt comes off, and then, at the far end of the scale, are people like me. I can get multiple bites under full thermal clothing in the middle of February. I'm like a magnet to every proboscis-waving invertebrate this side of Malaya. Why this should be so I have no idea, but believe me there is no comfort in the myth that it's because you taste good!

I was woken on my first morning by the sound of a fog horn blaring out. . .

The more I fished at Harefield the more the lake grew on me, and I ended up seeing beauty where before I'd seen only a bleak and desolate pit. I would be lying however if I said that it had the same effect on Keith. Big pits were not his forte, and I think he would admit that he never found the same affinity with the place as I. One thing that I never did quite come to terms with though was the tug boat. The first time that I fished on the Road Bank on a mid-week session, I was awakened on my first morning by the sound of a fog horn blaring out, and on staggering out of my bivvy I was greeted by the sight of a row of anglers all holding their rods above their heads keeping the lines high above the water. The reason for this soon became apparent, as the tug chugged along underneath the lines. All except mine of course. I was to busy wondering what the bloody hell was going on! I soon realised though, when both alarms screamed out in unison and I was briefly connected to a few tons of steel. I ended up losing both sets of end tackle as a result. From then on, I was always first out at the sound of the horn!

Some excellent times were had throughout that summer, and some good friends made along the way. Many a night was spent in the car park after the pub, seriously socialising. I owned a V.W transporter van at the time and the sliding door would be thrown open to allow Pink Floyd to blast out as we partied the night away. We managed to catch a few fish in-between times as well, and in September of that year I banked my very first thirty pounder from the Point Swim.

I'd arrived after dark and in the pouring rain, and for anyone who hasn't witnessed Harefield mud it has to be seen to be believed. The Causeway was knee-deep in black cloying mud that managed to cover everything within a few yards of walking. As I approached the entrance to the Point en route to the top bank, two anglers were just emerging from the bushes. They stopped for a chat and it turned out that they had just vacated the Point after having caught three or four fish each. Apparently, so they said, there were still fish present but they had to leave. This was too good an opportunity to miss and I was in there like a rat up a drainpipe. I pulled the rods out and checked the rigs, they still seemed o.k from the last session. I was using a pretty standard hair rig at this time with eleven pound Sylcast as the line and a size six Super Specialist hook, the only added refinement was a short piece of tubing that I used to push over the eye of the hook. Using a baiting needle, I'd pull the hooklink through the front of the tube and the hair through the back to offset the hook in a similar style to the line-aligner that Jim Gibbinson publicised.

The Point Swim, like most areas at Harefield, has a series of bars running across in front of it, the difference being that from here they are a gentle lob as opposed to a full blooded, banshee-yelling chuck, as they were from a lot of the swims. A section of log had drifted into the swim and grounded itself on the second bar. Even in the dark and pouring rain it still acted as a marker and I put one rod in front of it in the gully and one just past it on what I hoped was the base of the bar. Before I had even got the brolly up I had a take on the short rod. The fish didn't put up much of a scrap at first, but refused to be netted. Twice I thought he was in the net only to find it empty when I checked. The second time I was so convinced that I'd netted him I dropped the rod on the floor and prepared to drag my catch ashore, it was only when the rod shot off across the gravel that I realised my mistake. The rain and wind did not let up for a moment and bits of bivvy and tackle swirled around the swim as I tried once more to net the fish. The problem, apart from the darkness, of course, was that the water under the rod tip was inordinately shallow and there was no room to sink the net properly. Wading out a few yards though, saw him slide into the net on the third attempt.

As long as I live I'll never forget the sight that greeted me as I shone my torch into the folds of the landing net. The very first thing that struck me was his eyes, they were so far apart. I'd never seen a carp that was so wide before. I could spread my fingers as far apart as possible and it didn't even span the top of his head. I felt, to an extent, as if I'd captured something that I wasn't supposed to. I'd known from the moment of that first Harefield capture back in June that one day in the not too distant future I would catch a carp in excess of thirty pounds, but standing there in the dark on the end of the Point in the pouring rain I was totally overwhelmed by it all. Laying out a mat at the back of the swim, I hoisted him up for a better look, the hook was firmly embedded in the bottom lip and looked pathetically small in comparison to his cavernous mouth. I stroked his flank and told him how much I loved him before gently zipping the sack up around him. Finding an area of deeper water I carefully sacked him up before running around the lake to tell anybody who'd listen about my good fortune. Everyone seemed genuinely pleased for me which made the event even more memorable. On the bank in the morning the regulars identified it as The Orange One, and we weighed him in at thirty three and a half pounds of pure magic. The rest of the session was spent in celebration and I hardly even cast back out, I had no need of another fish just yet.

By the time the winter arrived, I'd landed a fair few Harefield carp and lost a couple to cut-offs on the bars. I had no intention of stopping now, just because the weather had turned a bit nippy, but by about Christmas, I'd begun to realise that this could be one very cruel pit in the depths of winter. Not a single angler had captured anything. In fact, I don't even think one run had been had in total. The social scene thrived however, and many a night would be spent at a car park party or in the warmth of Sabu's in Harefield village. Anglers could be found scattered around the lake like bowling pins the next morning. One particular morning, Bernie awoke to find himself laying on the Causeway in a partly frozen puddle, with bird watchers carefully stepping over him! The season ended with a fizzle rather than a bang, and before we knew it we were renewing our tickets for the next year.

I stood up to my knees in the reed beds and watched as they swam around me.

I'd decided to put a bit of bait in over the close season and by early spring I was spending more and more time at Harefield. I'd taken to driving up there twice a week to pre-bait, more for an excuse to go than any concerted effort to turn the fish on to my bait. More and more anglers had converted onto Tutti's as the last season had progressed and caught well as a result. I knew I could not compete with this, but it was nice and comforting to watch those big mirrors shovelling my lovingly prepared baits down their throats anyway. On one occasion I turned up while they were preparing to spawn, and stood quietly up to my knees in the reed beds of the Car Park Bay and watched as they swam around my ankles occasionally brushing up against me as they passed.

By the end of the close season there were fish permanently residing in the bay, and every crumb of bait that I introduced was immediately devoured. At the draw that year, I was praying for a good result as I really wanted to fish this shallow area, but as it turned out I ended up at the other end of the lake. Two other anglers fished in the Bay Swim before I got a chance at it. I could not believe that they hadn't caught as the fish were ripping into the bottom sending up great big clouds of mud and silt. I stood behind Ian Booker as he came to the end of his session in total amazement at the stationary bobbins. I was gagging to have a go myself. Eventually he gave up, cursing the lake, the fish, the silt and anything else that got in his way. This left me free to try my hand. What followed was the most frustrating two days angling I have ever known. At times there were half a dozen or more fish all with their heads down over my baits. The lines twitched constantly as fish bashed into them, and every conceivable rig known to man was tried. Slow sinking 'Fledgers' were constructed by wrapping solder wire around a cork until it barely sunk, and these fished with a neutrally balanced bait were presented on top of the silt. I tried fishing a bolt rig buried deep into the muddy bottom, float fishing, freelining, and every type of anti-eject method that I knew, but when it came to time to pack up and leave I was cursing as loudly as my predecessor had done. I'll never know how or why we all blanked, as the fish were obviously feeding their heads off. In the end, I just put it down to experience and went and caught them from somewhere else.

Stumpy.

Arriving for a session in July I realised to my horror that I'd left all my baits in the freezer at home. After a quick detour to

Weighing the twenty pound mirror at the base of the gravel workings.

Harefield Tackle, I purchased the base mix that most resembled my normal bait. As it turned out Nutrabaits Enervite, was very similar indeed and armed with a dozen eggs and a new mixing bowl and bottle of garlic oil, I was soon back at the bankside rolling them all up. I'd managed to get into the Workings Swim which had been very popular up until then, and I sat there in the sun surrounded by gaseous odours and an over-friendly goose with one leg called Stumpy. I forget what his other leg was called. I had no end of problems getting the bait to roll up properly due to the mix drying out too quickly, and no sooner had I got half a dozen baits made than Stumpy would hop over and pinch them. Once Fat Sam realised that there was a free meal in the offing, it was all I could do to fend the two of them off. After half an hour, I was still baitless and Stumpy could hardly even hop anymore he was so stuffed, the mix had gone rock hard and I finally cracked under the pressure. Leaving the goose to guard my gear, I took the garlic-breathed dog and drove back to Harefield tackle to buy some Tutti's. I felt so guilty as I left the shop with my little brown paper bag clutched in my hand, complete with its tell tale round damp patches from the frozen baits inside. I tried to bury it deep within my bag of shopping, in the same way a teenager would try and hide a copy of Playboy inside the Beano. Once back at the lake, I tied up two stringers and launched them out to the back of a large bar that ran across in front of the swim. I then hid the rest of the evidence at the bottom of my rucksack. During the night I had a run on one rod and landed a twenty pound mirror, and in the morning I had a run on the other. After a hectic battle which at one stage had me thirty feet up on top of a stockpile of gravel, I landed my personal best common of twenty five and a half pounds. I wasn't the only one who had runs either, the swim was completely littered with garlic flavoured goose shit! I decided that the Tutti's were indeed cheating, and I vowed not to use them again (for a while at least).

The fish were still using the Car Park Bay, and I decided to have another crack at them. From the main swim it was a bit tricky to cast right down into the bay, but due to the hot weather and falling water levels I figured it could be possible (just) to fish from the workings side. The water usually came right up to the gravel but as it had receded it left an area of mud flats. They were a bit soft and sinky but I pinched a load of old rubber mats from the workings and made stepping stones across the mud to reach the water's edge and set-up the rods. I had to set the bivvy up at the base of gravel, about twenty yards back from the rods.

At sometime in the middle of the night I was woken by an alarm and looking out across the flats I could see an L.E.D. shining. Using this as a guiding light, I hop-scotched my way across the matting and out to the rods. The fish charged about in the shallow water throwing off silver bow waves in the reflected moonlight. Everything was going well and then suddenly it all came to a halt. The fish was only about twenty feet out now but it had grounded itself on the shallows. I hadn't even considered the lack of depth in the edge, and now I was in a bit of a stalemate situation. Picking up the net, I started to squelch my way out into the mud, but within a few yards I was starting to sink into the mire and when my knees disappeared into the thick mud I realised another plan of action was needed. Sinking the net into the silt beside me and holding it down with big clods of mud, I backed off to the nearest mat. The fish was stuck about fifteen feet behind the net and I could see the top of his back poking out of the water. The net was only covered by about 12" of water and the only thing I could do was to hand-line the fish on its side across the shallow mud flats and into the net. Moving the fish was surprisingly easy and, as it reached the net, I threw down the rod and charged once more into the ooze. Scooping

Extracted from 50lb of mud.

A stunning looking twenty seven pounder.

Fishing off the mud flats at the Car Park Bay, Harefield.

There on the mat, lay a big dark mirror carp which I had never previously set eyes on. He weighed just over 27lb and was just one more pleasant surprise from Pit Four! Main picture: The sun sets on another day.

Dave with Rob's Thirty from Pit Four. "The season was only a few hours old, I'd already achieved my ambition, and with a single roar I let the whole of the Colne Valley know about it!"

A breath of fresh air!

up the carp and about fifty pounds of mud, I attempted to get back to firm ground, but with the added weight of the fish I was just sinking even deeper. Eventually, I sat in the ooze with the net full of carp and mud in my lap, and using my feet, I propelled myself backwards towards dry land. By the time I arrived back at my bivvy I was completely encased in mud, even my underpants were full of the stuff. Looking on the bright side I'd bagged a twenty two pound mirror from a very difficult swim, and eventually got my own back on the Car Park Bay. After returning the fish in the morning, and a total change of clothes, I decided to take a walk around with a plumbing float at the other end from the Car Park Bay and see what I could find.

The topography of Harefield has to be seen to be believed. Enormous flint-laden bars stretch along most of its length and break the surface in many places. The larger dry spots have sprouted trees and become islands. From off the Point Swim, as I mentioned earlier, you are so much further out in the lake to start with that the bars seem a lot closer. Opposite The Point is an area known as the Stick Bar, because imaginatively enough someone stuck a stick in the top of the furthest bar, which is probably just over a hundred yards out. From The Point the two main bars are at forty and seventy yards, which still leaves a fair chunk of water untapped in-between the two. After charting down the positions of these more well known bars, I took a plumbing float down to the Bottom Bank. From here it is possible to cast up the bars and gullies rather than over them. The plan was to try to locate the end of any bars that may exist in between The Point and Stick Bar. It didn't take long to find what I was after. Half way along the Bottom Bank, and equidistant between the two swims, I found a four foot deep bar about sixty yards from the bank. The grass on the bankside here was a good two feet long and there was no evidence at all that it had been fished. I scattered a six egg mix of bait on the bar and planned to fish it the next week.

My next trip down was on the last Thursday of July and I was due to fly to Turkey on holiday on the Saturday afternoon. I loaded up the barrow and pushed my gear straight up to the top bank. Usually I'd take a wander around and see if anything was showing, but I'd got a plan and I was going to stick to it for once. Getting the baits out was easy, as the bar ran perfectly along the reflection of a large poplar tree on the far bank. It was novel at Harefield, having to flatten the grass before you could set-up, but I got eaten alive by the millions of homeless insects as a result. On Friday morning, I had a belting run from atop the bar but as soon as I tightened down, the line cut clean on the mussels beds that adorned the sides. I was of mixed emotions, I had high hopes for the new 'spot', but at the same time I was gutted about losing one. I re-spooled and added ten yards of twenty pound line to the end, in an attempt to cope with the bars. I'd been messing around with rigs a lot since the Car Park incident and at the moment I was using a camouflage braided hooklink with a size ten, fine wire hook. With this I was fishing a double bait, one sinker, and one buoyant, balanced so as to just slowly sink. The hook size may seem a bit on the small size for Harefield, but I'd found when using them in the past, that they penetrate a bit like a small splinter and bury in quite deeply. About eleven that morning I was in again off the top of my new bar, the twenty pound line seemed to do the trick, and a twenty one pound common soon lay beaten in the net.

The next morning I was hovering over the rods at the hot time, convinced that I still had time to bag another one before my flight in the afternoon. But despite hanging on until two and a half hours before my departure time I had to be satisfied with what I'd already caught. I left the lake at a flat out run to try and make it in time for the plane. A few hours later I was back at Harefield but this time at 5000 feet, and as the plane banked around, I could have sworn that I saw a fish roll just on the back of the bar!

Two weeks later the plane touched down on home soil, and I staggered off, clutching my stomach in a carrier bag. I went straight home and rolled a few baits up as I was planning a swift return. Unfortunately for me, and anybody near me, I'd contracted some strange Turkish stomach bug that must have been a stand-in for Dysentery on his days off! Half of the things on the barrow as I hurried up the bank the next day were various medicines and bog rolls. It was nice to be back in the company of Fat Sam again though. I hadn't told her that I'd been to a country were they probably eat dogs, I didn't think she'd be too impressed with all that. With only a couple of emergency stops along the way, I was soon set-up in the new swim again. It looked totally unmolested since my last visit. My first cast out to the shallow mark fell perfectly in the reflection of the tree. As I pulled the lead up the bar into position there was a little tug as it snagged momentarily, before ending up in perfect position. I left it there for a while, but for some unknown reason there is always a horrible nagging doubt about a perfect first cast, and after a few minutes, I knew that I just had to try and get it even more perfect. I swung the rig up and saw to my amazement, that four inches of braid were missing, cut clean through. Now either some sad individual, desperate for my rig secrets was sitting out there with a Stanley knife and an aqualung, or those bars were even worse than I'd imagined!

The next day dawned and ran like a carbon copy of my last session, two runs on the shallow rod but this time I landed them both, the first one was a stunning looking twenty seven pounder. A big long fish with a totally scattered scale pattern, no two scales were alike. The second fish fell mid-morning again, and after a strange battle in which the fish never left the surface, I netted the very same fish that I'd seen in that old Paul Gummer chapter of Hutchie's book. I really felt that I'd achieved something that day. I'd looked through a book written by experts, and seen a fish that I was so in awe of, and from a lake that I'd originally found so intimidating. To then, two years later, be holding that fish for the cameras at thirty three pounds, I couldn't really imagine how it was going to get much better than this. My only regret was that my old mucker Jenkins wasn't there to see it. I knew that he would be down that afternoon but it was too hot a day for sacking fish and there was no shortage of photographers around. When Keith finally arrived he was almost as happy for me, as I was myself, and we partied the night away in the time honoured tradition. He even cooked a curry on the bank and we sat there under the stars toasting Harefield with mugs full of fine red wine.

The rest of the season passed with a couple more fish falling to both our rods. Keith, unbeknown to me sneaked out a Tutti one night and bagged a nice twenty - the crafty git. That season we'd decided to spend the winter on another water that we'd joined just over the road behind Savay. It was called Pit Four and, although I didn't know it at the time, it was to enrapture me over the next two years.

We returned to Harefield for the last few weeks of the season, but I'd already been smitten with Pit Four and knew my days at Harefield lake were coming to a close.

Paul Gummer's fish from Hutchie's book at thirty three pounds.

Chapter 3

Keith's Story

. . . We returned to Harefield for the last few weeks of the season, but I'd already been smitten with Pit Four and knew my days at Harefield lake were coming to a close. The saga, unbeknown to us, was not quite over yet though and before the Fat Lady had a chance to sing Harefield's final aria, Keith had one more very important task to perform. Over the years Keith has, metaphorically speaking, played the bridesmaid far more often than the bride, so for this final session - when eventually the bell tolled in his favour - it would be unfitting of me not to let him tell the story in his own inimitable style.

Unlike Dave, I had found it difficult to come to terms with Harefield. The transition from fishing an estate lake, where the furthest cast was a thirty yard flick to the edge of the lily pads, to a huge windswept gravel pit, where it was sometimes necessary to cast further than you could see, had seriously damaged my confidence. The fact that Dave had slipped effortlessly into the guise of 'gravel pit man' made it increasingly obvious that I was missing a large part of the puzzle. It wasn't until a few years later that the piece of the puzzle became evident to me - then somebody changed the puzzle!

By the end of our second and final season on Harefield I had a mere two fish to show for my efforts, the biggest being just over twenty pounds, taken on a pub chuck after a wobbly return from the Horse and Barge. I had fished as hard as possible from then until the end, but had failed miserably, so the looming finale to our Harefield sojourn did not cause me to shed many tears. We had fished the penultimate weekend of the season the previous week, on the Causeway Bank and Dave had lost a fish within minutes of casting out. After that, however, nothing further transpired but we did note that a couple of fish were caught on the opposite bank - the Road Bank - a mere quarter of a mile away!

It was to this area that we were headed the following Thursday and we were pleasantly surprised to find the area vacant on our arrival. We set up a couple of

Going for the 'big one' on the Road Bank.

hundred yards from the gate and gazed in trepidation across the North Atlantic in front of us. The water was being whipped into a frothing frenzy by a big north-westerly blowing from our left which made plumbing, baiting up, casting, and bivvying up all a tad stressful. We knew that there were two or three gravel bars in front of us, and from a mix of experience and information gleaned, we knew that we needed to be casting in excess of one hundred yards to pass the second bar and put ourselves in with a chance of a carp. However, being hampered by the wind, we were falling a frustrating few yards short. Due to the severity of the bars, light line was not a logical option so we had to sit on our hands and wait for a change of conditions.

Then, on Saturday morning, we suddenly became Mother Nature's favourite sons and, deciding that he had infringed once too often, she showed The North the red card and left The West in total control of the wind direction. Being a good old cove, West decided that the wind should blow straight over our heads and, in doing so, add another ten or fifteen yards to our casting, landing us, hopefully, straight into Mr Carp's kitchen. The downside was that we needed a further dozen six inch nails to keep our bivvies attached to terra firma but, for the first time in many months, I was fishing this inland sea with more than a cupful of confidence. The sun had set a few hours earlier and Dave and I sat in my bivvy consuming a recently constructed curry when the most bizarre of things occurred - for the first time in over six months I had a run! Due to the distance involved I gave it the usual Jenkins 'welly' and hung on for dear life in order to get whatever it was over the bar. As was usual in the initial stages of a run to my rods, Dave just stood cringing and shielding his eyes from what he always assumed would be the inevitable line-parting. As was also usual this never happened and I commenced winding furiously as the fish ran strongly towards me. At this point I had no idea what was on the end - it could have been a roach or a conger eel! All I knew was that it was lessening the distance between us rapidly. I had the benefit of a very deep margin and so it wasn't until about five minutes or so after the run that we eventually glimpsed the fish looming up from the depths.

"That's a bit of a lump," said Dave, casually. What marvellous things these verbal enemas are for the anally challenged, of which I had never been one - until now! Seconds later, another equally effective laxative drifted across the night air.

"It's a whacking great common carp," he gasped. This revelation, along with the fact that my previous best common was well into low doubles, gave me severe problems in the nether regions. Then it was in the net and Mr Lane confirmed his suspicions. It was indeed a whacking great common carp! At twenty six pounds and ten ounces, not only was it a whacking great common, but it was also a personal best for yours truly. After all the heartache on this most unforgiving pit, what a way it was to end my torrid affair with Harefield! We celebrated grandly in the Horse and Barge and photographed proudly in the morning. Not to be outdone, Dave had a last gasp double before North got reinstated into the wind team and returned with a vengeance, demolishing my bivvy hours before my departure! What a way to end it all. I couldn't have scripted it better and, probably due to that ending, I now view my time on Harefield with affection rather than gloom.

"It's a whacking great common carp!" Keith with his personal best.

Chapter 4

Pit Four

When we had originally discovered Pit Four during our first season on Harefield, the stock had been reputedly fairly high, with doubles and low twenty's making up two thirds of the fish with high twenty's up to a lake record of 36lb accounting for the rest. On the strength of this, Keith and myself along with another mate from Crawley, Mick Bridgeman, had acquired tickets in the April of 1987. Half way through that close season however, total disaster struck, when, due to weeks of torrential rain the Colne Valley flooded!

Tales of huge mirror carp swimming up Staines High Street were rife, and it wasn't long before the source of these escapees was tracked down as being Pit Four. We phoned about and eventually spoke to Mark from Essex, who we had met during a visit to the pit the previous year. He had personally seen two or three of the bigger

A breath of fresh air!

known mirrors battling unsuccessfully to get back into the outlet stream from their new impromptu home in the River Frays. Powerless to assist, he had watched as the surging flood water had eventually swept them off downstream. After the flood had subsided, estimates of the losses from the pit varied from half the stock upwards. As a direct result of this decimation, most of the existing members dropped their tickets for the coming season and Pit Four became even more tranquil and serene than normal. Keith and I had already paid for our tickets and decided, therefore, to fish Harefield for the summer and chance our arm at Pit Four during the winter, by which time Mick, who held no other tickets apart from Pit Four, would have discovered if there were any fish left to catch. As it transpired Mick had a blinding season, taking twenty carp from the pit and practically having the entire place to himself. The biggest carp that he landed though, was only 22lb, which seemed to bolster the theory that it was the bigger fish that had escaped in the flood.

We pulled on to Pit Four in late autumn, and instantly fell in love with the place. We knew straight away that this could have been the lake for us, but at the same time being very apprehensive as to the amount and size of the remaining carp. After the harshness of Harefield, this beautiful little pit with its individually sculpted swims and heavily wooded banks, came to us as a breath of fresh air. Unfortunately, by the time that the season drew to a close, we had come to the conclusion that the remaining fish stock didn't realistically offer us the size of fish that we were after. Having bagged four or five fish all of a similar size to Mick's we reluctantly decided, after careful deliberation, not to renew our tickets for the following year. We were absolutely devastated at the loss of such a picturesque little water that we'd been so looking forward to fishing, but life goes on. We quickly acquired tickets for Rodney Meadow and a large gravel

Mick with a typical Pit Four twenty.

pit near Reading called Burghfield. All thoughts of Pit Four were put out of my mind as I threw myself into the preparations for the coming season. At least three times a week I would drive over to Burghfield and bait up likely-looking spots, but despite seeing some very good fish in there it failed to grab me the way that Pit Four had done. As for Rodney Meadow, we knew that it would be incredibly busy throughout the summer months so we left that to one side for a while.

The season eventually kicked off and we spent a disastrous long weekend at Burghfield during which time speedboats ploughed merrily through our lines for most of the daytime, and over-enthusiastic pleasure anglers bombarded our swims with groundbait or cast spinners out and dragged in our perfectly placed baits! To cap it all off, after swimming out into the pit with a bucket full of particles, I managed to contract severe poisoning in a cut on my left leg, swelling it up to over twice its usual size. Keith ended up taking me down to the local surgery where a nurse with arms like a gorilla, told me that if the proffered antibiotics failed to shift it in two days, she would have to lance it with a hyperdermic needle and syringe the poison out that way!

I may have been unable to walk when I limped into that surgery, but I could sure as hell run when I came out! Luckily, sheer will power managed to reduce the swelling enough for me to be able to drive home the next morning, never to return.

The next week saw us arrive at Rodney Meadow only to be greeted by the most cliquish bunch of anglers that we'd ever come across. The progress of our first walk around the lake was charted through countless pairs of binoculars, although dropping my trousers and doing a little jig went some way towards deterring the voyeurs! We'd expected the place to be busy, but this was a joke. Only two swims on the entire lake were free, both of which were in tiny corners next to the car park. Having no other options we set-up in these. The swim I chose actually looked quite good as the wind was pushing into a large overhanging tree in the margins. I sprinkled a few baits around the branches and flicked a light running lead set-up just on the edge of it. No sooner had I done this, than a voice behind me piped up.

"Nothing ever gets caught under there mate!" I turned round to find a bush-hatted angler slowly shaking his head with an incredulous gesture.

"I thought it looked quite inviting," I ventured by way of reply.

"No, nobody ever fishes under there," he said.

I resisted the temptation to point out that this was probably why nothing ever got caught from there and carried on about the business of setting up my tackle. Three quarters of an hour later, I was slipping the net under a 19lb mirror from under the tree. I shortly followed up with a common around mid-doubles! Strangely enough, nothing more was heard from Bush Hat that evening!

Later that night, Keith almost completed the coup after hooking a fish from the margins in his own little corner. Unfortunately, a hook-pull robbed him of a quick

result and in the morning Keith and I decided that Rodney Meadow wasn't exactly the new spiritual home that we were searching for. We hurriedly packed up and left. Somehow that evening we ended up in the Horse and Barge at Harefield. I think we must have taken a wrong turning on the way home or something and by the time we realised it we were too drunk to drive anyway, so we stayed on for the social. We bumped into Mark from Essex at the bar and it turned out that he had kept his Pit Four ticket. He insisted that he had already, that season, seen a fair number of the bigger fish still residing in the pit and, seeing as we had nowhere else to fish, he told us we'd be mad not to at least have a look.

It was exactly the tonic we needed after such a poor start to the season, a chance (however remote) of a water to fish and a good old Harefield party. It started in the pub, moved temporarily to the Indian and eventually ended in the wee small hours when we collapsed on the grass outside somebody's bivvy on the Road Bank. If the the evening was Heaven - then the morning was surely the inner circle of Hell! I felt as if a whole herd of elephants had danced the conga across my cranium, and then all lined up and urinated in my mouth! I could barely walk, let alone drive back down the M25 so, after copious amounts of tea, we decided to go for a walk around Pit Four. Even through eyes like pickled onions, the lake looked more beautiful than ever as all the trees were out in bloom and tall banks of rushes fronted most of the swims, only two of which were occupied by anglers. The nicest surprise, however, was still to come.

We made our way around to the Point Swim on the East Bank behind which lies a small secluded bay, ninety percent of which is inaccessible due to marshland and tall bullrushes. A fallen willow extends out over the bay at a forty five degree angle, and is so easily climbable that even Fat Sam wandered out half way along its length beside us. There below us, with their backs barely breaking the surface, was a shoal of at least twenty carp, the biggest of which was probably around the thirty pound mark. As we watched, half a dozen or so more drifted in along the treeline on the far bank to join in the sunbathing party in front of us. There were clearly fish here far in excess of our meagre estimations at the end of last season. Everything about the place had felt right from the moment that we set foot in the car park and here, being dangled in front of our noses, was the final carrot. Neither of us spoke for a moment and then suddenly we were both babbling inanely at the same time. Tickets, we needed tickets right now! And bait and floaters and some time off work, and how big was that one, and who was going to fish what swims etc, etc. This carried on, barely pausing for breath, all the way home down the motorway and, with the aid of a fax machine, we were full members again within a week!

Life was suddenly a bowl of roses once more, and at last we had ourselves somewhere to fish. Pit Four was, and probably still is, a classic 'spots' water as the entire bottom is peppered with sharp gravel humps and bars but only certain spots produce fish with any regularity. It took us a while to track down the more congenial areas but as we did so, the results started to get better and better. Such attention was paid to detail that even now, ten years later, I can still remember which trees provided back markers for casting to in nearly every swim. Two of my favourite areas that year

Pit Four - the Pads Swim.

were the Point Swim which sported one of the most lethal bars in the lake, and a small and practically unfished swim on the nature reserve bank known as The Bricklayers, although quite why it was called this I never did discover. The bar off The Point could be fished from two swims along its length, the most popular being under a set of lilies from The Pads Swim, but I much preferred the next swim along where the bar came to an abrupt halt just to the left of the swim about forty yards out. It would seem that most mornings the carp followed this bar down into the lilies where they would happily bask in the sunshine, but a bait placed just on the end of this bar would usually produce a take about seven o'clock in the morning as they came through, the main drawback was cut-offs. Even compared to Harefield, these bars with their vast zebra mussel populations were devastating. I tried using front rod rests of four feet in length, in an attempt to keep the line clear of the bar, but unless you were on the rods within seconds of a pick-up, it was only a fifty-fifty chance of success. Obviously, this was not acceptable, and something had to be done to even up the odds. After a bit of thought, I started putting pilot floats of the sort sold for pike fishing, onto a long snagleader made of twenty pound line. I left the float free-running, and added a small rubber bead above it to stop it passing too easily over the leader knot. On the cast, the float would travel back up the leader line to the knot and, by fishing a slack line, hold everything clear of the bar.

The first time that I tried this new method out was most unsuccessful. This was due - unfortunately - to other circumstances which were beyond my control. I was fast asleep in bed when a single tone wrenched me into consciousness. As I looked out, the rod tip, which was still being fished beachcaster-style, whipped up and down as line poured from the open bail arm. I attempted to leap out of bed but received only a mouth full of gravel for my efforts. The zip on my mummy-style sleeping bag had jammed solid, and both my arms were firmly pinned to my sides. It must have been hilarious to watch as I thrashed around helplessly on the ground like an oversized maggot, as my spool was emptied of line before my eyes! Short of grabbing the rod between my teeth, there was absolutely nothing I could do to prevent it. Just at the exact moment that I eventually managed to rip the zip free of the bag, my main line snagged and cut clean on the mussels! I persevered with the method though, and managed to land some immaculate-looking mirrors using it. One morning, I took a brace of 23 and 26lb. This confirmed that not all the better fish had disappeared down the river.

Other spots within the swim also used to produce, but at totally different times of day to the bar. As the swim was on the end of a point, I tried fishing one rod at night tight under the tree on the tip of the point, as I had found these areas to be productive in other similar situations in the past. To present a bait in the right spot involved a very complicated manoeuvre. Standing on the small stump at the front of the swim to gain height, twenty feet of line had to be pendulummed to and fro, until the correct momentum could be gained before swinging the rig on a long arc out and around the branches of an overhanging tree tight to the left of the swim. The second that the lead hit the water, I had to release the line and plunge the rod tip under the branches to allow the rig to sink unhampered to the bottom of the marginal shelf. If this rigmarole was successful, a take was practically guaranteed at some time in the middle of the night. Obviously, a re-cast was totally out of the question, but for some strange reason I only ever caught doubles from this little margin spot.

Pit Four was an incredibly social lake due in part, I think, to the small number of members that had kept their tickets. There was never any backstabbing or jealousy and most evenings would be spent around the communal barbecue or, as often as not, at the bar of the Horse and Barge. To get to the pub involved a drive up a dangerously pot-holed lane of about half a mile, that ran along the banks of two other lakes, ingeniously named Pit Two and Pit Three. Quite how nobody ever ended up actually driving into either on the way home always amazed me. However, the plethora of spare parts that littered the bushes on the other side of the track bore testament to the very poor standard of alcohol-induced driving skills on this perilous return journey.

We were, as always, still locked in an endless struggle to find the ultimate bait. As well as the fishmeals, whose flavour we had changed to Shellfish with added Mexican Onion Oil, we had decided to go in heavily with tiger nuts this season, as we knew that no one else was using a particle. I was working in Fulham at the time, and on a couple of occasions every week on my way home, I would pop over to the pit and swim out a bucket containing about ten or fifteen pounds of tigers. The main area that I chose was The Bricklayers, as from here about thirty yards out is a small gravel hump that it is possible to stand up on. I would swim out to this hump and then scatter tigers all around me. Nobody else ever fished over in the back two swims which made them ideal for a baiting campaign. The problem with tigers, is that you can never disguise the fact that they are being used, and half way through my preparations, Mark caught a twenty from the other end of the pit that passed about half a pound of crushed tigers out into his sack. As a result, he ended up catching two fish on the nuts before I'd even cast

One morning, I took a brace of 23 and 26lb.

Steve Allcott with a mid twenty from Pit Three.

one out! The first time that I tried them I sat patiently behind the rods for twenty four hours with no action, and then during a much needed trip to the bushes, I had a run on both rods at once on the gravel hump and suffered two cut offs as a result! Tigers quickly became the 'in' bait, and accounted for quite a few fish that summer. The allure didn't seem to last long and as the autumn arrived, the boilies started catching again.

Up until now I'd caught somewhere in the region of a dozen fish, half of which were twenties, but only the 26 came close to the stamp of fish that we'd seen on that first visit of the season. We knew now that they were there, but catching them was proving to be a little more tricky. I was fairly sure that the key lay in the precise positioning of hookbaits, as even the smaller fish were so fastidious when it came to picking up the bait that I would cast a dozen times to make sure that I got it perfect.

It was about this time that I first got to know Steve Allcott as he was fishing Pit Three on a fairly regular basis. Over the weeks we got to chatting about this and that and he told me of his affinity for Ball Leads and their excellent bolt rig properties. When he showed me one I wasn't in the least surprised that the fish bolted as the bloody things weighed five and a half ounces! I certainly wasn't willing to cast one of those things out, but I did manage to get hold of some three and a half ounce versions. I found straight away that apart from any extra bolt effect they may give, their ability to 'feel' the bottom, was far greater than a normal shaped lead. Now these were, at the time, a pretty new concept and while I would not insult anyone's intelligence by suggesting that a change of lead is all that's required to put fish on the bank, I will say that the extra feel when using them helped me to identify features in a lot more detail, which in turn led to better results.

I also changed from the braided hooklinks that I'd got into using on Harefield and started using a short length of multi-strand tied direct to a large Murutu Kinruyi hook. These hooks had a large gape and were incredibly sharp and reliable. So, armed with my new style outfit and a few pounds of freshly rolled baits, I set-up in one of the Canal Bank swims that I'd regularly seen fish topping in over the previous sessions and pulled about with my new feature finding leads. It didn't take long to locate a couple of rock-hard clear patches on the back of a bar that ran through the swim at sixty yards range. Eventually happy with my positioning, I sat back and took in the special atmosphere of Pit Four. Autumn has got to be one of my favourite times of the year, as the leaves turn to a burnt copper and the sun sets in a spectacular array of shades of red, it becomes a pure joy just to be present on the bankside. It was a mid-week night so, resisting the pub, I sat back with a cup of tea and a cigar to watch the sun sink over the horizon before eventually turning in for the night.

I awoke the next morning to an absolutely perfect carp fisher's dawn. Silver mist coiled spectre-like from the calm surface and the rods, hung with the early morning dew, stood sentinel before the autumnal scene. There was a feeling of stillness, as if the pit and everything around it held its breath in expectancy and, as if on cue, the tip of the right hand rod shook and droplets of dew showered from the taut line into the margins. I was halfway toward the rod, before the first bleep split the still morning air and, on the second, I swept the rod back over my shoulder and a fish was on. I had to hold the rod high to clear the line from the sharp bar and not an inch was given until I was sure he was out of danger. All alone on the pit, I switched from one ploy to another in an attempt to outsmart my opponent, until finally the margins boiled as I acquainted him with the net. There on the mat, amongst the red and gold carpet of fallen leaves, lay a big dark mirror carp who I had never previously set eyes on. He weighed just over 27lb and was just one more pleasant surprise from this glorious little water!

I hoped that maybe the change of tactics and the extra little attention to detail had helped toward providing me with my biggest Pit Four fish to date - but only the test of time would tell.

A few more of the elusive bigger mirrors fell foul of anglers' baits that year, including two over the magical thirty pound barrier. One of these was a spawnbound fish that sadly died later in the year but the other was a scale-perfect thirty and a half pounder that fell to Rob, one of the Essex regulars. I was lucky enough to be present on the day and instantly set my sights on this fish as it was a beautiful-looking specimen. It was probably the biggest fish in the lake at the time, although a few of the lads had reported seeing a much bigger fish with an unmistakable grey scar across one shoulder. If it did indeed exist. I would have been a bit surprised that I'd never seen him myself, taking into account the amount of time that I'd spent up trees watching these carp at such close quarters.

Strangely enough, Keith was still to bag a twenty pounder from the pit. Every time his bait was picked up the culprit, it seemed, would be determined not to weigh more than 18lb. How or why I've no idea, it just happened that way. He even brought his

A perfect carp fisher's dawn at Pit Four.

A new day - a new lake - a new challenge

friend Porky along from work, for a winter's guest session, and watched as he pulled out a twenty two pounder on his first night. I guess some things are just not meant to be!

Rob with his solid looking thirty pounder.

The social scene which had been excellent at the pit in the summer, went into overdrive throughout the colder months and although there were fewer anglers present, you certainly wouldn't have known it at chucking out time on a Friday night. All the regulars were instantly amiable, which makes a nice change on established carp lakes and I think the total and absolute lack of bailiffs went a long way to creating a nice and relaxed atmosphere. Sam, for some strange reason known only to her own doggy mind, decided to hound one poor chap on a regular basis which was strange as he was a thoroughly nice bloke. He had earned himself the nickname of 'Nutty as you like,' as it was one of his favourite sayings and he worked as a chef in a London hotel. Every weekend he would arrive straight from work at about three o'clock in the morning and, although nobody else ever heard him arrive, Sam would sneak out of the bivvy as the car coasted into the car park and lay in wait for him in the bushes behind whichever swim I was in at the time. 'Nutty as' would creep along the path on tip-toe in search of a swim and determined to make it past Fat Sam undetected. However, as regular as clockwork, right at the last second she would come flying out of the bushes, barking at the top of her voice and snapping at his heels. He remained convinced that she held some pathological hatred for him, but I knew she was just

Keith returns another carp determined not to be a twenty.

having a bit of a laugh in her own strange way. One big advantage of his job was the obvious access to prime cuts of meat, and on one particular winter's morning, when I'd been having nightmares with the tufties and coots, he walked into my swim and proceeded to cook up duck and steak sandwiches for breakfast. Now that is what I call mighty fine angling!

All in all, Pit Four, had turned a potentially disastrous season into a memorable one and by the time the season came to its inevitable close, we were over the moon that we'd decided to renew our tickets. Although the fish were not as big as those that had resided in Harefield, everything else about the place had knocked it into a cocked hat. In fact, we drove straight over to Hillingdon Council Offices and renewed our tickets for the next season.

We had learnt an awful lot about gravel pit angling in general, over the previous three years, but Pit Four had brought home to us the need for accuracy on these topographically complex type of pits. It was a different ball game from the silty estate-type lakes on which we had originally cut our teeth. But, to me, the learning can be as large a part of the enjoyment as the catching. It's always incredibly satisfying having learned something. I don't care who you are or how much you think you know, there is always more to learn. After all, that is the basis of successful angling, taking a situation and creating a solution. The exciting part being that all solutions are only temporary due to the fact that fishing is a sport that revolves around a living creature, capable of its own process of thought. This ensures that the rules are constantly changing and this in turn keeps the angler mentally active.

I for one, could not wait to put some of this new found experience into action during the coming season. We'd decided to carry on with particles but for reasons

The social scene at Pit Four.

that I can no longer recall had changed from tigers to peanuts and, in an attempt to place these with the necessary accuracy, I'd invested in a second hand remote control bait boat. I was, unfortunately, under the misconception that this wonderful device would be the answer to all my problems but I'd learn the truth soon enough.

The first night of the 1989 season apparently coincided with a football match of some degree of importance. I think it may have been a cup final. Not being a great lover of the sport, my attitude towards it was that if they had played it in my back garden I would only have glanced out of the window once, and that would have been to tell them all to piss off! Unfortunately for me, I was seriously outgunned in the anti-football department and as a consequence, come the opening night of the season, I was forced to endure the whole debacle on a portable T.V. What made it worse was, being set up in The Pads, which just happened to be the most sociable swim on that side of the lake. They all decided to watch it at the back of my bivvy! Obviously, there was a penalty to be paid for this pleasure and my own crate of lager never even left the safety of the van all night. I also bombarded them with annoying questions throughout the whole game such as: "How come the wicket keeper can use his hands?"

"Why doesn't that pratt with the whistle ever get to have a kick ?"

I don't know who was more relieved at the end of the game, the winning side, me or the Pit Four supporters club...

The Pads Swim, where I had opted to start the season, offered three realistic options in terms of potential spots. There was the obvious bed of lilies on the left, that sprouted from the top of the bar running through the swim forty yards out, and further right along this same bar I had found a small deviation in height. This spot rose a foot higher than the surrounding ground, and was covered in zebra mussels which made an interesting area to present a bait. During the high winds in the close season, a tall poplar that had stood to the right of the swim had sadly given in to the relentless battering and toppled into the margins. Newly fallen trees always seem to offer an irresistible draw to carp, although I have in the past heard the experts state that a certain chemical on the fresh leaves acts as a repellent to fish! Notwithstanding this, I have a stack of trophy shots that tell a different story entirely. Using the tree as a 'tightrope' I had (before the lager) balanced my way precariously along to the end of the main limb from where I could easily catapult some peanuts around the two bar spots and, whilst out there, I dropped some crushed baits amongst the furthest trailing branches. A delicate flick with a 1oz lead, put a single peanut neatly under the branches and two Ball Lead set-ups with heavy leaders were cast onto the bar.

By the time the sun set on the fifteenth everything was set for the new season. We sat around late into the night toasting our conquests to come. I, of course, remained totally convinced that I would bag Rob's thirty pounder before the season was over, and the more I drank the more convinced I became, until eventually, when I staggered off to bed, it came as quite a surprise not to find it curled up in the sleeping bag waiting for me! The very next thing I remember was laying on the gravel swim at dawn with the sleeping bag wrapped around my ankles and the margin rod buckling over in my grasp as the water under the fallen tree erupted in fury. I wasn't aware of the alarm waking me, or the obviously failed dash to the rods. One second I was sound asleep and the next I was engaged in battle with a big old mirror carp! Keeping the carp inside the distance of the bar and out of danger was a lot trickier than I'd first imagined, but with a little luck and a lot of brute force I was soon gazing down on the recumbent form of Rob's Thirty upon my unhooking mat. The season was only a few hours old and I'd already achieved my ambition, and with a single roar I let the whole of the Colne Valley know about it!

By the afternoon, a drastic change in conditions had taken place and a low pressure area had moved in from the south west, pushing a strong wind over my head and into the opposite corner. Winding in the rods, I took a walk around to the windiest spot and climbed up a large oak tree on the water's edge. The pads were directly opposite me and I could just make out the dark shadows of carp a few feet below the surface as they drifted slowly further out from the bar toward the open water. I stayed just long enough to make absolutely sure they were headed in my direction. As the first fish appeared below the waves at the back of the swim I ran back to the pads to get the rods and within two minutes of casting out in the new swim I had a 27lb mirror on the bank!

That season was to see a drastic change in the average size of the fish. It wasn't that they had grown, in fact the Big'un was down to twenty nine and a half, but an entirely different set of fish were caught. We'd known all along that there were better fish

Dave baiting up the bars from his 'tightrope' walk.

present, but until now they had been keeping a very low profile.

By the second week I'd managed to get the bait boat working after a few teething troubles, Keith and I set-up once more on the small point where we had started the season. The weather had become hot and the fish behind The Pads looked as if they may be tempted off the surface, although Pit Four had a very poor reputation as a floater water. The problem was that the fish were out of range of free offerings and the wind, although only light, was determined to blow in every direction apart from the one needed to carry the Chum Mixers out to the fish. Luckily the answer lay before us in the shape of one very crudely- constructed remote control bait launching boat. The actual launching device was constructed using two sawn-down plastic tubs, spring loaded and mounted onto the deck. They fired by way of an over-steer to either the left or the right - or at least that was the theory. One rod I flicked out under the pads (just in case) while on the other I tied up a floater rig and loaded this on to the 'Titanic' along with half a box of Chum Mixers. Keith had the task of holding the rod and paying out line whilst I, from my vantage point thirty feet up a neighbouring tree, directed the boat out to where I could see the fish idly milling about in the middle. As I'm sure you can well imagine, carp have a particular aversion to being sneaked up on by an electronic monstrosity full of dog food, and the result was nothing short of a high speed pursuit! When the boat reached a range of sixty yards however, a new and previously undetected problem arose. Suddenly, and with little or no regard for the supposed control box, the Titanic fired off both of its scoops full of bait at random and then banked sharply to one side before charging off in a series of massive circles spooking everything in its path! As if this wasn't problematic enough, the other rod that I'd cast to the pads and then placed on an alarm thirty feet below me suddenly burst into life. I don't think I could have descended that tree any quicker if I'd fallen! I had the remote control between my teeth as I leapt from one branch to another, eventually arriving in a tangled heap at Keith's feet and, after wrestling the rod back from him, I proceeded to land the smallest known carp in the lake. This was a common of eleven pounds. Needless to say, the boat, (when it eventually ran out of batteries) was dragged out of the far margin and hurled unceremoniously into the back of the van where it stayed for the rest of the season.

Keith somehow managed to avoid the upsurge of bigger fish and continued to catch eighteen pounders with an alarming regularity. He even brought his young son Vincent along one weekend and had the pleasure of holding the landing net while Vince steered the Big'un, at a shade under 29lb, into it!

As well as the carp, a handful of very respectable perch lurked in the waters of Pit Four, and during one particular session on the Canal Bank, Keith and I noticed a disturbance in the reeds at the front of the swim. Peering into the margins we saw two of these impressive hunters, fins erect, standing sentry over the reeds. Within the reedbed at my feet, we could just make out a small and very wary-looking roach that had been forced into seeking refuge. Whilst we watched, the roach, no longer able to contain himself, decided very unwisely to make a dash for freedom. As he shot out of his cover, the two perch, with a speed that defied the human eye tore into their prey and a few seconds later all that remained of the scene was a handful of shimmering silver scales fluttering slowly down to the bottom. I tried every conceivable spinner and lure to tempt one of these prehistoric-looking beasts but they steadfastly refused to be outwitted.

Even pulling the scales can't make a twenty pounder!

On one occasion in early September, I came close to catching a fish that until then I had assumed was merely mythical. I was stalking a few fish in the small outlet stream at the southernmost end of the pit, and for once they were showing more than a little interest in floaters. The lake here is only ten yards wide and I had spent fifteen minutes on my hands and knees crawling into position behind a small bush. Underneath this, four or five fish had been swirling lazily at the odd swollen Chum Mixer that had drifted down with the flow. A light scum helped to obscure their view as, painfully slowly, I parted the branches and peered down onto them. There below me and not three feet away sat the mythical Grey Scar. In two years of searching, it was the first time that I had ever come across his formidable bulk. He was noticeably larger than the normal Pit Four fish and the large grey scar along his back was in plain view. As I watched,

Vince with the Big'un.

he turned and, as if staring straight at me in defiance, lifted slightly to drink a soggy dog biscuit off the surface before my eyes. I hardly dared breathe as, slowly, I closed the curtain of branches and shuffled backwards to the waiting rod and net in the bushes behind me. He was too close to the bank to risk another look so, laying prostrate in the grass, I fed the rod forward until just the top few inches protruded over the edge next to the bush. As slowly as possible, I lowered a free-lined mixer onto the surface. I could just see the slight ripples emerge from the back of the bush as a fish turned on the surface and then, with a loud slurp and a tightening of the line, I was in. The rod hooped round and, leaping up from my hiding place with a, "Ha, ha, I've got you now," I victoriously heaved him straight into the net before he had a chance to realise what was going on. Quite what had occurred under that bush I'll never know, but there in the bottom of the net lay the smallest mirror carp in the lake, all thirteen pounds of him. From that day on, I never set eyes on Grey Scar again.

Throughout the autumn, I managed to bag a few more carp up to 26lb, along with a couple of doubles. A few of these came in quick succession from one particular swim on the Canal Bank situated, conveniently enough, right next to the car park. A laboriously handwoven willow fence secreted the swim from the path, and overhanging trees shielded you from the elements. It even had a little cut out section at the front to house the rods, but its main advantage was a large gravel hump straight out in front at fifty yards range. Beyond this hump lay a deeper area that Keith and I had both caught fish from the previous autumn, whilst fishing from the Oaks on the bottom bank. The fish seemed only to pick up hookbaits from the hump if they were presented tight against the back of the gravel at the bottom of the far slope. In retrospect, this was probably also the area that all the freebies I catapulted out, ended up rolling into. By overcasting the hump and swinging the lead down on a tight line, I could feel it crash into the base of the bar with a resounding thump. If it should land soft, then I had over cast and if the line entered the water at too high an angle then the lead had landed short and was laying on top of the hump. Once in perfect position though, this one rod produced five carp in the space of three weekends until the first frosts came along and put paid to my little run of success. During this time I had no action at all on the other rods, which just reinforced what I'd always thought about the importance of accuracy on this sort of gravel pit.

Mark from Essex was doing particularly well this year and was striving for his tenth twenty of the season as winter approached. He had an annoying habit of fine tuning his Delkim converted bite alarms until the resulting pitch and volume of a run could bring down passing planes and shatter glasses in the Horse and Barge half a mile away. One session in the autumn I turned up at the pit on a Thursday. As usual, I was loaded up with Keith's gear as well as my own, seeing that somehow he had still managed to avoid the reality of learning to drive! I was due to pick him up from Denham station the next afternoon after he had finished work for the week. As I started to set-up in my swim near the car park, I realised - to my horror - that I'd left my bite alarms in the airing cupboard at home, drying out from the previous week's session. This wasn't too much of a pain for the first night as I could borrow Keith's,

A somewhat knackered Dave with one of his run of five carp.

but when he arrived the next day I would be faced with the old method of balancing fifty pence pieces on the spool and placing a saucepan under the reels. I didn't fancy this idea much, so when Mark arrived at lunchtime on Friday, I tapped him up for a loan of his spare buzzers. As I've already said, Mark was fanatical about his alarms and I had to swear on penalty of death that I would in no way alter the tone controls as it had taken him hours to reach the highest possible decibel per eardrum rating, even with the volume on its lowest setting they were frightening. I caught two fish that session, a double figure common and a dumpy little mirror of 22lb, nearly suffering a heart attack both times that the alarms screamed their piercing battle cry. Come the end of the session, I slowly packed away all my kit into the van leaving, as always, the rods until last. I laid them on the ground while I put everything else away. Keith was already loaded and waiting to go, so I placed the two borrowed Delkims on the roof by the driver's door to remind myself to give them back before I left. Begrudgingly, I reeled in the last rod and, slinging it into the back of the van, we set off for home. The lane at Pit Four had grown steadily worse over the last two years and we bumped our way along until eventually we were out, and onto the dreaded M25. Half way back to Crawley, whilst travelling down the centre lane at about seventy, I heard a clatter across the roof. Thinking I'd hit a bird, I glanced in the rear view mirror just in time to see a black plastic thing fly off the roof and disappear under the wheels of the car behind.

"What was that?" Keith asked, having heard it as well.

"I'm not sure," I replied. "It looked like a piece of plastic trim of some sort. It was black and square and... OH SHIT!"

We stared at each other in horror as the penny finally dropped. Mark's alarms. I'd killed Mark's little soldiers, his pride and joy crushed to death on the motorway.

"I wonder if the tone controls have been altered," I quipped.

"Well, if not, he probably heard them die from the lake," came Keith's reply.

Joking aside, I knew that I would never hear the last of this one. In the end that little blunder cost me three Stevie Neville roller buzzers and the rest of the season spent grovelling pathetically. Luckily, soon afterwards, Mark finally caught his tenth twenty which went some way towards cheering him up, and took the heat off the buzzer incident

Mark from Essex doing OK.

for a while.

The Pit fished poorly throughout the early part of winter that year, and we soon lost our enthusiasm and drifted back to Tilgate for a few short day sessions. At least we could hope to get a bend in the rod on there. At some time during January, Keith phoned me from work to tell me, he'd seen in the angling press, that Horton was turning into a syndicate water, and what did I reckon on trying for tickets? Having fished with a few lads who were unfortunate enough to have lost their fishing, when the old Longfield lakes had been netted to create the new Horton fishery, we had obviously been affected to some extent by the bad feeling that surrounded this decision at the time. After some deliberation, we decided it wouldn't hurt to put our names down, if only to postpone the decision until it may or may not become a reality.

We returned to Pit Four for the final few sessions of the season, wanting to pay our respects to the water that had given us so many fond memories, before setting off once again in search of monster carp. We spent the last weekend in full Colne Valley party mode. The Horse and Barge was rocking, and although we didn't manage a last carp, we certainly said farewell in good style, before eventually clattering our way along the bumpy track for the very last time. It was only on the drive home that the disturbing truth sank in.

We had absolutely nowhere to go to!

Sam relaxing in winter. It's a dog's life!

Chapter 5

Horton

The First Season

By mid April, we were still not any nearer to a new water, although we had been invited up to Frampton in Gloucestershire for an initial look around. I decided to ring up Leisure Sport to see if I could get any early indications about Horton. I was informed that we were numbers fifty two and fifty three for a proposed syndicate of fifty members, and that if we phoned again on the first of May after the ticket deadline had passed, they would give us a definite answer on whether we had scraped in or not.

The first of May turned out to be a major turning point in my life. Mid-morning a phone call from Keith confirmed that, after years of playing chauffeur and tackle

The Reeds.

taxi, not to mention having to abstain from alcohol while Keith was, "Juz dwinking yore share meyowd mukka!" Keith had finally passed his driving test! I immediately suggested a celebration at a nice country pub I knew. It was miles from anywhere, but what the hell? It certainly wasn't my turn to drive for a few years yet! Later that day I also heard that we'd been offered tickets for the Horton syndicate, so I phoned Keith back up and told him he could drive us over there on Saturday for a look. I offered to get him a few beers at the local Horton pub at lunchtime in return. What was I thinking of? He was driving wasn't he? Oh well, maybe a couple of cokes! I was going to milk this new found passenger status for all it was worth.

Keith dutifully picked me up on Saturday morning and, I must admit, with a little trepidation on my part, he drove us up the dreaded M25 to Berkshire. Our first impressions of Horton weren't exactly what you would call favourable. It looked just like a typical trout fishery and all the branches had been pruned from the trees to a height of about ten feet from the ground. It was basically just a plain rectangle with a little point at one end, forming a small bay on either side. An old trout fishing lodge adorned the car park end. The tree cover was a bit poor, especially after Pit Four, but then most lakes would look meagre by comparison. Unsure as to how we felt about the place, we decided on a little stroll around the neighbouring Kingsmead pit while we weighed up the pro's and con's of joining Horton.

The fish were present, there could be no doubts on that score, but the lake was a bit lacking in character and I suppose the bad feeling generated by the Longfield netting still swayed us to some extent. Eventually though, we came to our senses and realising that this was the only way we were ever going to get to fish for these historic leviathans now, we consented, and the next day we waved goodbye to a total of four hundred pounds as Postman Pat chugged off with our application forms and the usual convict-style passport photos. Just to be on the safe side, we took up our invitation to Frampton and after a good look around we handed over even more of our ill gotten gains to join that syndicate as well. I must admit to liking the look of Frampton a lot more than I had Horton, but the two and a half hour drive was more than a little off-putting and it offered no comparison in fish stocks.

With two new waters to fish, we decided that a new bait was also needed. We hadn't had one for a while and there were so many different ideas still to try out. Mick Bridgeman had told me of an aviary and bird seed merchant's in a village not far from us and apparently it was a veritable grotto of bait ingredients. I just had to go and have a look at it. I was not disappointed either, as both walls of a large wooden farm building were lined with open sacks containing more potential ingredients than you could shake a stick at.

One Wednesday evening, Keith and I were to be found sitting around his living room table which was covered in crisp packet-sized plastic bags filled with samples of every type of birdfood that could conceivably be crushed, mashed, or sieved into a base mix and, after numerous 'sniff tests' and even the odd tentative tasting, we settled on two ingredients that we thought were worth a try. The first was called Gold Pate and was a coarse yellow feed with little red dots of carophyll in it. Its main attraction was the fact that it was soaked in a type of honey and was so sweet and sticky that a handful squeezed together would bind instantly into a ball. I had no idea if this constituted a good ingredient or not but it had already managed to catch Keith and myself. The second and final birdfood we decided on was, if my memory serves me correctly (which it seldom does), called Bogina or something like that. It was a coarse powder made from crushed insects and such-like, and anything that involved the mass slaughter of mozzies and flies was just fine by me. It had a totally unique smell and, we assumed, taste. Having made our minds up I drove back over to the aviary the next day and purchased half a sack of both of the birdfoods. All that remained was the laborious task of grinding it all up into a fine powder.

At the end of every close season I have traditionally held a party for all my non-fishing friends. It's sort of a farewell party for people that I wouldn't be seeing again for about six months. This year we'd decided on a barbecue at Keith's house instead of the usual house-wrecking affair at my place. In between the burgers, and regular doses of embalming fluid, Keith and I managed to roll up our new season's bait. We added the ground birdfood to our regular carrier bait and included a strange smelling flavour/appetite stimulator-type thing, that we had acquired from somewhere and the whole resulting mess was lovingly transformed, into what we considered at the time to be a shedful of bait. In reality, about a thousand boilies lay spread on the towel next to the barbecue to dry, but after hand rolling them all it certainly felt like a whole lot more!

Fat Sam taking it easy before the off!

A decision was made to start the season on Horton and, ignoring the close season rumours that were circulating about most of the better fish having died, we turned up at lunchtime on the day before the season kicked off. This left us a good thirty six hours to acquaint ourselves with the place prior to actually angling.

The gates to the lake were firmly locked on our arrival, and we parked in line behind the two cars already present. Sometime during the afternoon, a Leisure Sport representative turned up and opened the outer gates before directing the now substantial traffic queue into a makeshift car park where, we were informed, we would be spending the night before the inner gates would be opened the next

I ended up in The Reeds.

morning. An interesting night was spent getting to know the other new members. Everybody was in the same boat as it was the first year of a new syndicate so none of the usual hierarchy existed and a full blown party was soon in operation. As is usually the case in situations like this, the true characters immediately shone out from the crowd. Like a moth to a flame I found myself drawn to the back of a large white van, where I made the acquaintance of two local Slough lads, called Chrissie and Robbie. A more down to earth and amiable pair you'd be hard pressed to imagine. Sloughisms rolled off their tongues in an endless stream of banter that made short work of the long hours spent waiting for the gates to open. Copious amounts of alcohol were consumed and coils of smoke drifted out of the back of the van as we drank, smoked and chatted long into the night. Everybody had a tale to tell, but without doubt the most discussed topic was which method of swim designation would be employed come the magical hour. So much so that the sentence, "Are we having a walk off, or what?" became a mini legend overnight, and the mere mention of it now brings memories charging back to amuse me. As the penultimate day finally dawned, I was woken by the gentle pitter-patter of rain on my head as, unbeknown to me, at some time during the night, my brolly had launched into orbit and I was left sleeping under the heavily laden skies on a bedchair in the middle of the car park!

When eventually we were allowed into the main car park later that morning, a gentleman's agreement was reached, and hastily scribbled tickets designating your order of arrival and subsequent walk off spots were handed out. Although we were numbers three and four, Keith and I ended up fourth and fifth, due to the late arrival of a young kiddy who insisted he had been sent home from the main gates two days earlier! For this feat he was awarded a corresponding ticket and the nickname of 'Zero'.

As Horton was totally new to us all, there were no preconceptions of hot areas, so the day was spent wandering around the banks, figuring out how best to utilise our early departure in the much discussed and eagerly awaited walk off. The Church Bay situated at the north west corner of the lake looked like an interesting area, as fish were very evident in there already. We came across Chris Ball in the bottom of the bay and he was practically hand feeding two of the most colossal carp that we could have possibly imagined. They were, so he informed us, The Parrot and Jack the Net Ripper!

The sight of these gargantuan warriors held us spellbound. Nothing previously experienced could have prepared us for our first sight of a carp in excess of forty pounds. The Plateau area at the other end of the lake near the club house also showed signs of fish, and from what we could make out, was one of the most fancied areas. So it transpired at the walk off, as Zero and the following three anglers occupied both the Plateau and Church Bay swims, I opted for the small point swim on the mouth of the Church Bay and Keith fished just behind me into the Dog Bay. On plumbing around, I was horrified to find an average depth in front of me of eighteen feet or more, and I assumed that I'd chosen the deepest area of the lake as Keith's swim was only thirteen feet! However, on talking to Chrissie and some of the other lads it appeared that Keith was practically in the shallows and sixteen to eighteen feet was the average!

With the new season only ten minutes old, a cheer went up from the bank to my right as somebody scored first blood for the new syndicate. What a way to start! Johnny Moult had landed Jack at forty four pounds! This capture made me realise that the reality of catching a fish of this magnitude in the not too distant future was far more than just a futile dream.

With the early morning bombardment of leads out of the way, the fish, not surprisingly, started to show out in the middle of the lake and from the vantage of my little point Keith and I had seen three fish show in roughly the same area. That was good enough for us we just had to move. I'd never been one to sit put in an inactive swim and I had got the business of moving down to a fine art by now. So a very short while later, the pair of us were standing side by side on the North Bank behind two (amazingly) vacant swims, quibbling over who would fish which one. After a gentlemanly flick of a coin, I ended up in the left hand swim called The Reeds with Keith on the right. No sooner had we tipped our respective piles of tackle on the deck than, as if working from a script, a great big mirror carp rose from the pond in between the two swims about seventy yards out. I say in between the two, but in all fairness it was firmly in front of Keith's pitch. But what the hell, we were mates weren't we? Suddenly, bits of tackle and bait were flying in all directions as we maniacally charged about trying to win the race to get a bait into the water. Almost in unison two single bottom bait rigs arced out across the water to land side by side in the dying ripples. After adding one more rod each to the assault, we sat up on the grassy high bank behind the rods and cheered like little kids as the fish continued to show over our new area.

I was fishing the rod tips high at the time and, as we watched, my right hand tip nodded once and then slowly pulled down towards the water. As the line pinged out of the clip, the rod tip bucked back in the air as line flew from the spool. We were spared the added effect of a screaming bite alarm as I had somehow in the excitement forgotten to turn it on! From the moment that I set the hook, I knew that this was a very big fish. The sheer power being transmitted up the line left me in no doubts about that. He effortlessly defied my attempts to prevent him kiting down the lake into the margins beyond Keith's swim and we had to employ the time-honoured method of hurling bricks, logs, and small children into the overhanging branches before we could persuade him to leave this new found sanctuary. With a bit of gentle persuasion, I soon had him back out in front again and slowly the leader knot broke the surface. A few feet more and we would have had our first glimpse. Then he was gone. The hook and fish had simply parted company, no last second surge of power or dramatic crack of broken line, just one second there and the next, gone! I can still remember that exact feeling to this day. I don't think you ever get over the loss of a really good fish like that and I was determined to get my own back even if it meant catching the entire Horton fish population to ensure that I did so.

Over the next twenty four hours, I managed another two carp from Horton, a common of eighteen pounds and a strange-looking mirror of twenty pounds who was almost white in appearance. These fish were landed with such comparative ease that it only strengthened my opinions about the size of the previously lost monster. One thing was apparent though and that was that the bait and rigs were working well. All we needed now was for Keith to join in and catch a couple of Horton carp to make the party complete. On the following session, a week later, he did just that.

I had arrived the day before Keith and found to my delight, and utter amazement, that the three swims along the North Bank that covered the area we had caught from the previous week were all free. I decided eventually to go into the one that Keith had fished last week as, although it had been me who received all the action, I knew that I'd been casting well and truly in front of Keith at the time. When

A strange looking mirror.

Keith arrived the next day, I was amazed that I was still fishless. Great big mirror carp had been performing aerobics out in the middle section of the lake at regular intervals. Keith set up in the closest swim to my right and, due to a very localised cross-wind, accidentally dropped both his hookbaits bang in the middle of my swim! I couldn't shout too loud after the blatant poaching that I'd performed the previous week so I politely pretended not to notice!

The following morning dawned bright and sunny and the carp showed their appreciation by staging an aerial display for us. At times they were crashing out of the water directly above our baited area, almost as if they had eaten so much birdfood that they were under the illusion that they could fly! The display was punctuated every few minutes by a splosh as one or the other of Keith's hookbaits was frantically recast in a futile effort to induce a take. Only after a monumental effort on Keith's part to leave everything put for more than ten minutes did a take eventually occur. After a short and uneventful fight I finally slipped the net under Keith's first Horton carp, a mirror of just over nineteen pounds. After all, these were Keith's forte! His prowess at extracting doubles from lakes crammed full of twenties was second to none!

We sat full of confidence throughout the day, but the main period of activity seemed to be from first light up until about ten o'clock. Around lunchtime, I became aware of a rustling from the tall grass behind my brolly and, on closer investigation, I found a tiny swift that had crash-landed in the grass and was unable to take off again. The wind had built up into quite a strong blow, so carefully scooping the little bird up in my hands, I placed him on top of the umbrella. With one flap of his wings, he was lifted up on the air flow and soared away across the lake to rejoin his friends who were busy feeding on mayfly hatches. I spent the rest of the day convinced that my benevolent deeds would somehow, in the great scheme of things, be rewarded by the gratuitous capture of a great big mirror carp. Sadly, it was not to be. We decided around tea time that Keith's first capture from a new water was more than worthy of a small celebration. As evening approached, and with no further action on the fish front, we made our way across to the local hostelry for a couple of pints of embalming fluid and a pickled egg.

One of my pet hates in pubs are television sets. They are bad enough at home, but in pubs they have the art of killing all forms of conversation stone dead. My first reaction was one of contempt until we remembered that tonight was the first meeting of Chris Eubank and Michael Watson for the world middleweight championship belt. This I could suffer! Making ourselves comfortable, we ordered a tray of beers and we cheered and booed at all the appropriate spots until eventually, long after the final bell, we tottered off across the fields and back to the lake. We had stayed a lot longer than we'd intended and as a consequence drank a lot more beer than we needed to. Such is the way of carp anglers and who were we to break with tradition? I can only assume that the next morning dawned gloriously, as I wasn't there to see it. In fact, the first realisation of morning came in the form of Keith's puffy-eyed and beer-bloated face looming in through the door of my bivvy bleating out words that my addled brain couldn't understand. It all sounded Belgian to me. Hiding behind an empty cup I kept repeating the word, "Tea!" He finally went away. No sooner had I drifted off again than he was back and after a few sips of the liquid life restorer and with my hearing returned to normal it became obvious that Keith had bagged another one.

"How big?" were the first intelligible words that I managed to utter. "At least a mid-twenty," came the very excited reply. I stumbled out of bed and dutifully followed Keith back to his swim with a set of scales and my camera. The fish looked wonderful, especially in comparison to the company it was keeping at present! From the scales we took a weight of twenty five pounds and ten ounces. Unfortunately, I only had four frames left on the camera and once these were used up we returned him to his home where, with a flick of his tail, he disappeared into the depths.

Back home in Crawley, I dropped the film off into the local developers and twenty four hours later we sat astonished at the size of the twenty five pounder. It looked far bigger than the nineteen - almost twice the size in fact - but I assured Keith that this was due to my amazing proficiency with a camera. A Hall of Fame had started to form in the lodge at Horton, and the following week we proudly added our photographs to the steadily growing array. Even after a procession of anglers had quizzed Keith as to the weight of this impressive-looking carp we still failed to realise the extent of the cock-up that had occurred during the weighing ceremony. It was to be a full sixteen months before we realised that this fish was in reality probably the biggest carp either of us had ever seen on the bank before!

Keith's twenty five pounder. . . or was it?

Although the lake held somewhere in the region of fifty carp, there were a small band of historic old warriors who were known collectively as The A Team. Among these were some of the lake's largest residents, headed by Jack the Net Ripper, they formed the essence of dreams. Without doubt, these fish were revered above all others. In subsequent years, when other fish eventually surpassed some of the original A Team members in terms of sheer size, they were still regarded by those in the know as pretenders to the throne. I knew in my heart of hearts, that the fish I had lost during the opening week had been one of these much coveted prizes. I also knew that I would be unable to walk away from Horton until I had redressed the balance in full. With this goal and determination, I threw myself, mind, body, and soul into the pursuit of the A Team. I would stop at nothing until the very last member was mine.

For some reason, the next week I decided to give Frampton a crack. I braved the two and a half hour drive and arrived on the Pine Tree Point about ten minutes after the lake record of forty pounds had been returned. The lucky captor was Lee, and the first half of my session was obviously spent assisting in the celebrations that followed. I was horrified as to the number of anglers on there. I hadn't realised just how popular the place was. Although a lot of the lads were also in their first year, it seemed as if a concerted effort to boost membership had occurred throughout the close season. I liked the lake a lot, but it soon became clear that a well established clique of regulars and bailiffs looked disparagingly at all newcomers. Regardless of this a good time was had at Frampton and although I only ended up doing a few sessions on there I look back at it with fond memories. The main drawback for me was the driving involved, as I was travelling over one hundred miles. This was past some of the best waters in the land. I then had to queue for a decent swim when I arrived. Because of that, I decided to turn all my attentions to Horton for the rest of the season.

Of all the fish that resided in Horton the one which took my fancy more than any other was a chunky mid-thirty called Shoulders. What a set of shoulders he sported! They made his head look too small for his body by comparison and gave him the appearance of a body builder amongst the carp kingdom. I had decided in my infinite wisdom that he and his A Team friends would much prefer our old fishmeal bait to the new and obviously highly successful birdfood that we had been using. In retrospect, this was an absolutely bizarre decision, taking into account the fact that we had hooked five carp in our first two sessions on the birdfood, but somehow I convinced not only myself but also Keith that a change was needed. We left the new Gold Pate ingredient in, but swapped back to the fishmeal with shellfish flavouring. After noticing that hardly anybody was using particles we also reverted to our old favourite from the Pippingford days, maples.

I knew from those early days that carp could, if the fancy took them, consume vast amounts of maples and my own favoured type were the mini-maples. Care had to be exercised when buying them to ensure that they were fresh and unaffected by damp in any way. As a rule of thumb, if the peas appeared light in colour with a defined mottled finish and were rock hard then they were usually o.k. It is possible to use them after only a short period of boiling, but I much preferred to soak them for two days and then boil the granny out of them until they turned a dark, almost black colour, and could be pulped in the fist by gently squeezing them. The smell and taste of maples prepared in this way is totally different, and for my money, far superior than their lightly cooked counterparts.

Although Horton has a noted deficit of topographical variations, there is one large feature situated at the eastern end of the lake, where a large plateau bisects the lake rising from ten or twelve feet up to an apex of four feet at the shallowest point. The small area of water trapped beyond this plateau plummets away sharply to over twenty feet deep in places making the feature an obvious warm weather area for the inhabitants to visit. Two swims give access to the plateau and are situated opposite one another. One is on the South Bank and inventively named The Plateau, the other is on the North Side and called The Spindley Tree. It was in the latter area that I first decided to give the particle approach a serious trial.

Using an old Burco boiler that I'd bought second hand for forty quid, I soaked and cooked a twenty five pound sack of maples, which, when prepared, filled a large fermenting bucket and weighed somewhere in the region of forty pounds. I'd picked a mid-week day to start my session as the lake was a lot quieter then. This gave me more chance of a swim within casting range of the plateau and, taking into account the scorching hot conditions, this was where I'd decided I wanted to be. Luckily enough, The Spindley Tree was vacant and I sweated buckets dragging the bait and tackle around there.

I'd never been of the persuasion of pre-determined swims or setting up before a good look about. In fact, a look around before setting up in a fancied swim usually resulted in moving before even casting out! But today was a definite exception. Not only had I arrived armed with a plan and the bait to match, but the swim I'd chosen to execute my master stroke in was absolutely heaving with carp. As I looked out across the shallow bar, the backs of mirror carp with dorsal fins akin to sails, criss-crossed the area with great bow waves. As a plane from nearby Heathrow airport soared overhead, they would all spook at once, erupting the surface of the water into a turbulent frenzy. The temptation to flick a single hookbait or floater out onto the plateau for a quick kill was practically irresistible, but somehow with a level of abstinence that would have shamed a monk, I stuck to my original plan with the mass baiting of maples. Any reference linking mass baiting and monks is purely coincidental!

I ripped the lid from the large yellow bucket and was instantly knocked back by the acidic gasses of maples that had been sitting in the sun steeping in their own milky fluids. The bubbles and froth of a healthy fermentation were fully evident across the surface. Using a beach casting rod and a home made spod that, in true Blue Peter fashion, utilised an old washing up liquid bottle and some sticky backed plastic, I launched the best part of twenty pounds of cooked maple peas out onto the top and shallow side of the bar. Fish scattered in all directions as the spod repeatedly shattered the calm surface but I was confident that they would soon return. By the time I had finished my assault, sticky maple juice covered everything within a ten yard radius of my swim and a plethora of winged insects swarmed around my head. The surface of the water above the bar fizzed and bubbled, as various oils and particles of food were released from the carpet of bait that now covered the bottom. Before long, larger patches of bubbles appeared as the first fish returned to make tentative inquiries of this new food source that had appeared like manna from the heavens.

I was trying out a new rig that I had concocted for fishing particles in popped up stacks. This rig presented the hook at the top of the stack rather than underneath, and unlike threading the baits along the hooklink as I had done in the past this new method made rebaiting a lot less complicated. A clip had been incorporated into the counterbalance weight allowing a long hair to be doubled back and fixed along the hooklink leaving the hook exposed to do its job at the top of the stack.

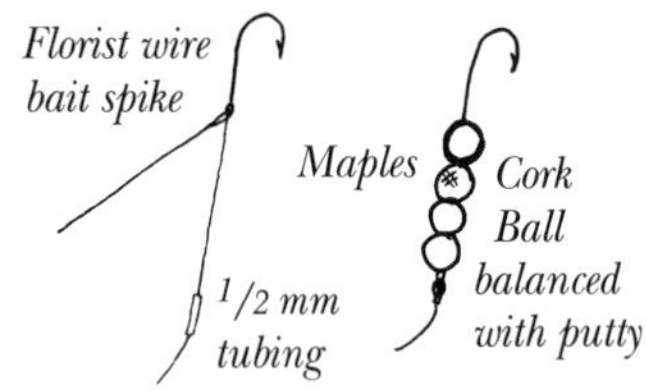

The level of activity rose throughout the evening, and I was confident of a result at some time during the next twenty four hours. As is often the case on shallow areas like this, the fish appeared to drift away as the temperatures fell during the night. As long as the weather held, I knew that come the morning they would return. Further down the lake to my left, in the corner swim, another angler was setting up for the night. Although I did not know it at the time, he was to become a good friend and fishing companion over the next few years, but for the time being he was just 'some bald bloke' fishing in the corner. I wandered along for a chat and was pleased to see that I wasn't the only angler left using what was commonly considered to be out of date tackle. The bloke's name was Phil Thompson and his old Mitchell reels and Sportex rods made even my ten year old Tri-casts and Cardinal reels appear state of the art by comparison. After a brief chat I left him to it and returned to my swim.

First thing in the morning, as I sat on my low chair drinking tea whilst waiting for the fish to return, I absent-mindedly watched as Phil reeled in to go off to work after an uneventful night's angling. Suddenly it appeared that Phil was playing a fish and my first thoughts were that a pike must have grabbed his boilie as he reeled in. But the fight was becoming very protracted and another angler had appeared on the jetty next to him and they seemed too interested for a pike to be the culprit. Eventually a huge eruption

A 42lber for Phil. He really ought to stop doing that with the fish no matter how large it is!

on the surface left me in no doubt as to the species involved and as it went into the net I called over to enquire as to the size of it.

"Forty pounds," came the immediate reply. Unsure as to whether he was winding me up or not, I took a wander round for a look. Phil was a bit embarrassed as to the method of capture as it transpired that he had indeed been reeling in to go to work and had quite simply found the fish on the end. Regardless of this with a fish of forty two and a half pounds he was suitably elated and I was more than a little impressed! After the fish was photographed and returned, and Phil had gone off to work, I returned to the low chair at the front of my swim and pondered the morning's events.

I had never seen a fish of those proportions on the bank before, and how easily the capture had occurred left me wondering about the validity of my own current approach. I need not have doubted myself, however, as shortly after midday my right hand bait cast to the slope off from the bar was picked up and I watched as the line tightened to the tip before being pulled from the clip as the fish panicked on feeling the hook. The calm water boiled as he made off across the lake, despite my concerted efforts to persuade him to the contrary. After he had put about sixty yards between us, the charge became less manic and I soon had him under some measure of control. Ten minutes later, and he was back where I'd originally hooked him and trying with all his might to bury himself in the thick weed that covered the top of the bar. Exhausted from his earlier efforts at escape, it was no real problem to roll him over on the surface and gently steer him into the net. As soon as I peered in, I knew that the first fish in my quest for the A Team had succumbed, as there in the net lay none other than The Lady, all thirty four pounds of her. At a recorded age of around forty years old she was surely a slice of angling history and I treated her accordingly. The sun beat down relentlessly as I layed her down on a damp unhooking mat in the potato field behind the swim, and we photographed her there in all her magnificence before hurrying her back to the cooler waters below.

Keith was obviously over the moon for me and was only gutted that he couldn't have been there to witness the capture. As he held down a normal job that required his presence five days a week, this was one of the penalties that he paid. I was at the time self employed, in the loosest sense of the word, and was currently spending more and more time mid-week at the lake. Weekends were proving to be a bit busy throughout these summer months so I usually returned home to continue with real life, returning about Tuesday or Wednesday. It was during one of these real life breaks that the phone beside my bed slowly broke into my alcohol induced coma, and with one out of focus glance at the clock, which frighteningly read five o'clock in the morning, I knew before I'd even picked it up that Keith had bagged a whacker! I'd spent the early part of the night in the pub drinking anything that would stay still long enough to grab, and then when fully tanked up and feeling particularly gregarious I invited anybody who could still stand back to my house for 'afters' and unfortunately they all came. As a result I had only crawled into bed on my hands and knees at half past three in the morning having drunk everything in the house including the industrial strength floor cleaner! The last thing thing that a man in my condition needed was to be screamed at down the phone and ordered to drive forty miles up the M25 motorway without delay, but that's what I got anyway.

One hour later I staggered along the banks of Horton to a small swim on the causeway that separated Horton from Kingsmead to find Keith waving his arms like a demented windmill and babbling, "It's massive, it's huge, it fought like this and I hooked it there and you should have been here etc, etc." As this is indeed Keith's tale it would be inappropriate for me to relate it myself so I hand you over once again to the competent prowess of Mr Jenkins' pen. . .

Keith's Story

The earlier news of Dave's capture of The Lady had left me with mixed emotions. I was elated for him especially as our idea of a particle attack had paid off admirably, but it was evident now that our paths would cross less and less as Dave was to take full advantage of the lack of midweek pressure on Horton, inevitably leaving the lake hours before my Friday afternoon arrival - such is life. As the season progressed, however, this arrangement proved advantageous to both of us as we constantly kept each other appraised of recent events, and the lake's latest moods and tantrums.

A week or so after Dave's success, I was making my way along the South Bank, intent on reaching the Dog Bay before anybody else - and also before my arm dropped off from the weight of the bucket of maples I was carrying. Pausing for a breather, I met Chrissie Pearson coming in the opposite direction having had the same area in mind. He'd seen nothing that took his fancy so was going for a look along the North Bank. He did, however, inform me that he'd put quite a few tigers into the area over the previous couple of days so, thanking him most kindly for the information, I renewed my journey with a swagger, arriving minutes later at a very empty Dog Bay - empty of anglers anyway. As was often the way a big south westerly had blown most of them to the far end of the lake - the carp, as usual, went wherever they bloody well pleased! I was very happy to have the area to myself and set up half way between the Lookout Point and the Gate Swim.

Using my new found knowledge, care of C.P. I refrained from depositing a further ten kilos of maples on top of the already present tiger nuts, but I did think that a few pultfuls might be an appetising change of diet for Mr Carp. But what of a hookbait? I had maples, I had boilies, but what I really wanted was tiger nuts, of which I had none - or did I ? Back in May, I'd been at Zyg's for a week and had bagged a few fish, mainly on tigers. Quickly extracting my tackle box from the bottomless rucksack, I began rummaging around in the 'discarded stuff' compartment and there, in a furball of nylon, hooks, swivels and fluff was just what I required - two de-hydrated tiger nuts and a shaped piece of cork. Swiftly transferring them to a slightly more usable assortment of line, swivel, and hook, I flicked the obviously deadly concoction twenty five yards to the back of the dense marginal weedbed and in amongst the small scattering of maples. The other bait was a more conventional pop-up boilie and was cast a further ten yards. I remained undisturbed for the rest of the evening and night but, as the first rays of the sun glistened off the mirror like surface of the lake, disturbance became a major issue as the tiger nut rod was picked up at pace and the relevant bite alarm demanded immediate attention. The rod hooped over on the strike but, within seconds, my initial hope of a carp was replaced by the certain knowledge of a tench on the end as there seemed to be little resistance, just a steady kiting from left to right at the back of the weed jungle. I stopped the fish fairly quickly, and proceeded to ease it towards the weed bed, ten yards out. When the fish wallowed at the back of the weed, I revised my estimations upwards to a double figure carp. The problem was how to manoeuvre it across the weed in front of me? The water here was eight or ten feet deep and the green tendrils had reached the surface weeks ago forming an almost impenetrable barrier, my only hope was to drag the fish across the surface.

The first couple of yards went sweetly, but then the fish just wallowed on the top

Shoulders - the business end.

and I now realised that I needed a bit of help from the carp. I let the pressure off a little bit and, within seconds, the fish got the idea and kicked forward, creating a hole in the weed which I coaxed him further into. By now my estimations of the carp's size had risen again, this time into the mid- twenties, and I really wanted to land it. The next couple of minutes were excruciatingly slow, but I managed to gain a few more yards until everything went solid. The fish was clearly visible, encased in a weed cocoon, but frustratingly inches out of netting distance which meant I had no other option than to take to the water. Due to the deep margins I was only able to gain another yard, but that was all I needed and, dropping the rod, I managed to drag the carp/weed towards me with the fully extended net. Somehow, seconds later, the whole lot was in the net and I dragged the bulging net ashore and onto the unhooking mat.

As I began tearing away the weed the carp became visible and the more weed I tore away, the more carp became visible. This looked like a big carp and I was starting to think in excess of my P.B. - a twenty six pound common from Harefield - so, quickly wetting the sling I slipped her in and grabbed the Avons. Up she went and round and round went the needle, past twenty, then thirty, and beyond! The scales had bottomed out and I went into orbit. After lowering the carp back into the net, I ran along three or four swims until I found a couple of anglers who were just setting up, and containing my elation the best I could, I uttered the coolest line.

"Have you got any scales? I've just caught a carp and my scales only go up to thirty two pounds!"

After some spluttered exclamations, one of them came along with a set of fifty six pound Happy Hooker scales and we weighed my prize at thirty eight pounds and one ounce. I had no idea what the fish was but didn't give a damn, it was mine, I'd caught it and it was in my carp sack. Safely securing the latter, I floated off down the bank in search of a telephone. The day was still in its infancy, probably no later than five am, when I reached the phone box and dialled my home number. Linda answered with sleep muffling her voice, but that soon disappeared when I screamed the news down the phone to her and she was soon screaming her elation. The next call had to be to Dave but, knowing the hour and Dave's love of his bed, I doubted that I could get through to him which made the sound of his voice on the other end after just two rings, very surprising. After blurting the news to him, he informed me that he'd only just gone to bed - but he'd see me in forty five minutes!

True to his word, forty five minutes later he strolled unsteadily into my swim, handed me a bottle and, warmly shaking my hand, said, "Bloody well done, boy, where's my cup of tea?"

After a few cuppas we photographed the marvellous beast which was identified as Shoulders, and my tonsils danced their usual conga as she swam strongly away. It was then that Dave and I realised that we were hooked as strongly as any carp - we wanted them big'uns real bad. So it was then, that The Shoulders Swim was christened and became one of my favourite swims on the lake, from that day to this.

Seeing that fish on the bank had completely blown me away. I had decided before we'd even wet a line in Horton that this was to be my target fish but now I craved for him with a vengeance. There are not many carp that exude the kind of stature that this impressive beast manages to effortlessly wrap around himself and one day I was convinced I'd be the one that it was directed at as I held him for the cameras. But for now I could only dream.

There was also a more pressing matter to be taken care of, as Keith's capture of a new personal best also just happened to mean that for the first time since we had been fishing together Keith had now caught a bigger fish than I had. That would have to change, as I was unsure if I could take the stick that would surely follow for too long. As far as we knew there was only one fish in Horton that could better this thirty eight pound target and that was the much celebrated Jack, and although I didn't know it at the time, my chance at this historic leviathan was to come sooner than I thought.

September has long been a favourite month of mine for angling, and a lot of my better catches - including my first thirty - have been taken in the early half of this month. I think a lot of it is due to the drop in temperature from the notoriously poor month of August and the rise in rainfall that goes a long way towards re-oxygenating the water and subsequently encouraging the fish to feed with a little more enthusiasm.

It was the beginning of the second week of September when I arrived in the Horton car park and was amazed and delighted to find only one other car already present. Halfway along the North Bank was the unmistakable twin bivvy set-up of Snowy, the proud owner of just about every item of fishing tackle known to man. The second bivvy was there to park his trolley under and house the outside cooking equipment while the main dome was fully equipped with everything from a remote control television to a portable gas fire!

Armed with a rod, net, a shoulder bag full of stalking gear and a couple of cold beers I wandered past, on my way to the Church Bay in search of carp. The weather was still in summer mode and the sheltered water in the bay looked like as good a place as any for a few fish to be laying up in the sun. On climbing the small twisted willow on the entrance to the bay, it became instantly apparent that I'd made the right choice as there at the bottom of the bay, just below the surface, lay abut a dozen fish lazily circling below the first batches of fallen leaves and early flotsam that heralded the approaching autumn. From the small and unfished swim at the bottom of the bay, I could get a much better view of what was on offer and, after just a few minutes of watching, I had singled out one particular fish as being far bigger than the others. At first I estimated him to be in the mid-thirty pound bracket. There was a very slight breeze drifting into the bay which petered out just shy of the fish but the surface movement was still enough to drift Chum Mixers in from the swim on the mouth of the bay. I chose this approach rather than risk spooking the fish by firing baits directly onto their heads. It seemed to take an eternity for the bait to reach them, but my patience was rewarded when a small common rose instantly at the first drift of Mixers and as is often the case the other fish, not wanting to miss out on a free meal, soon joined in. The bigger mirror could easily be distinguished from the others, even from ground level, due to the enormous hump on its back that preceded each disappearing Mixer. He seemed so gentle and demure in his approach to this floating buffet, unlike the smaller commons on the outside of the pack who snatched greedily at the baits as they drifted into range, even breaking formation to intercept them before their larger and more ponderous cohorts could get in on the act. It was going to be very tricky separating this fish from the rest of the pack, so I decided not to cast out for a while but to keep feeding them and to wait for the right opportunity to arise. After what seemed like an eternity the smaller fish, in their eagerness, had moved closer to the mouth of the bay leaving the big fella and a couple of slightly lesser mirrors at the bottom of the bay plodding around looking for any missed titbits and I figured that this was the best chance I was likely to get.

Cutting off the supply of bait sent the smaller fish off in search of more, and a few carefully placed freebies at the bottom of the bay kept the bigger fish interested while I tried as quietly as possible to get a hookbait out into position. For some reason in situations like this, the ability to cast in a straight line deserts even the most accomplished of anglers let alone a plonker like myself. The first cast sailed perfectly up the tree above my head, two more equally crap casts later, and I was faced with a badly tangled hooklink. Originally six feet in length, it was now reduced to ten inches of spaghetti in my lap. The fish were beginning to look a bit bored of waiting to be caught, so I figured that the quickest way was to bite it all off and start again. Just as I pulled the seven pound line tight in my teeth the whole tangled mess miraculously unknotted itself and apart from a slight flat spot where my gnashers had been, looked fairly serviceable. The bait was still intact, so throwing caution to the wind, I launched the whole lot out into the pond and by some last ditch miracle

it landed perfectly and directly in the path of the biggest of the bunch. Once again that colossal hump rose from the water as he eyed this new arrival to the banquet. With a sense of purpose that left me in no doubt that I was going to hook him, he surged forward, that cavernous mouth parting at the last second and I watched as his lips closed around the hookbait before sweeping the rod around low to the water to set the hook.

A brief moment of truce followed as the fish, unsure of what was occurring wallowed on the surface, and then as the harsh reality struck him he took up the battle with a display of power that left me shaking in my boots. Suddenly the seven pound Sylcast seemed incredibly inadequate as weedbed after weedbed was defiled with frightening ease. By the time everything came to a halt the spool was considerably lower than a few moments previously and the fish was well and truly buried in weed. No amount of persuasion would budge him and, eventually, the only option was to point the rod at the fish and walk slowly backwards praying that the line held. Somewhere just short of breaking point the whole mass started to slowly move under the pressure and after about ten minutes a massive bed of weed came into view deep down in the clear margins. Luckily, with a little shaking, the bulk of the weed fell clear of the line, putting me back in contact with the fish. Before he had a chance to realise what was happening, I managed to coax him up and half over the net cord. I was holding the net at full stretch and the first half of the fish was in the mesh but I couldn't lift as the cord was under his middle. The point of balance was slightly in his favour, the rod was bashing against the branches above me which prevented me pulling him any further. I could clearly see now that I was attached to none other than Jack, the largest carp I had ever seen let alone hooked. This did little to ease the situation! Just at that moment he came to his senses and erupted from the net in fury, showering me with water as he did so. It had turned into a real 'bicycle clips' job now, as I knew I had in excess of forty pounds of mirror carp connected by a length of seven pound line that was further weakened by a bite mark and half an hour of being dragged through every snag and weedbed in the bay! Ten minutes of kid-gloves treatment later and once again he was approaching the net cord. This time I was taking no chances and, as he crossed the cord, I jumped straight into the margins and scooped the net up underneath him before physically wrestling my prize up onto the bank.

I had no scales large enough to weigh him on but I knew a man who had, so I sacked him up and floated along to see the man who had everything.

"Snowy, I've just caught Jack off the top have you got any big scales I can borrow?"

"That's not fair," came the amazing reply. "You've only just got here and I've been here for days," he grumbled while searching out some scales from under a mountain

The Lady for Sticky.

of tackle.

"There you go," he said and left me to it. I ran back to my swim, a bit confused by his attitude to it all, maybe if I'd said that I'd got the very latest in bite alarms or something he'd have come along for a look. Oh well, I thought, everyone to their own. Up on Snowy's brand new scales, Jack pulled the needle around to forty pounds and two ounces, and in a complete daze I sacked him up and went off to the phone to try and summon some photographers. In the car park I bumped into Martin or

'Sticky Bean' as he'd become known due to his Charles Atlas 'before picture' physique. Let's face it, anybody that I can accuse of being skinny must be pretty damned thin! Sticky was in possession of a brand new video camera and I had just the thing to try it out on! A couple of quick calls on his mobile had Keith and a few others on their way down to the lake and pretty soon Jack and I were facing an entire battery of photographers. Of course, I couldn't resist pointing out to Keith that the tables had turned once again on the personal best front!

That two week period proved to be the best by far of the season. The day after my capture of Jack, the weather cooled and an area of low pressure moved in which resulted in the fish shoaling up in the middle area of the lake in between the Ski-Slope, so named for its treacherous banks, and the Captor Returns on the opposite bank. I was in the former and Sticky was opposite in the Captor. Over the next couple of days, I had two runs resulting in one lost fish and a low twenty mirror, while Sticky helped himself to one of the prestigious A Team members in the form of Heart Tail at thirty three pounds. The following week fishing the same area he captured The Lady also around mid-thirty's as part of a brace. Apart from the fish that were transferred from the famous Goose Pool at Longfield, a number of smaller carp from the Road Lake on the same complex had been introduced and were growing at a very healthy rate. One of these fish, known as Moonscale had been put in at mid-doubles and had already reached a weight of twenty nine pounds and was the other half of Martin's impressive brace. After his departure I managed to stay on another night and moved into the Captor myself, and half an hour before I was due to leave, a dour fight on a single bottom bait produced the famous Split Tail common at a shade over twenty five pounds. This rounded off a fortnight to remember.

The rest of the season passed with comparative calm. Although I did manage to bag another twenty pound common at the beginning of December to take my first year's total to a respectable seven fish. In fact, only one angler had more fish that first year and that was a guy called Pete, but due to the fact that all his time and results were concentrated on one swim, The Weedy Bay on the South Bank he soon became known as Weedbed Willy. He took an impressive nine carp from Horton that year.

One other capture that stood out on that first season was The Parrot at a staggering forty two pounds. This usual mid-thirty pounder had gone the way of a lot of the Horton residents and stacked on the weight since their stocking from Longfield.

All in all, it had turned into one of the most enjoyable seasons' angling I'd ever had and some wonderful friendships had been forged along the way. There was the charismatic Chrissie and Robbie and former Bald Bloke Phil Thompson, Sticky Bean and his cohort Wing Nut, so named for obvious ear related reasons. There was Tony Badham from Chingford and the effervescent Johnny Moult, who, if talking were

The Lady - thirty four pounds, forty years old and a slice of angling history.

Shoulders for Keith at 38lb.

Jack the Net Ripper. Dave's first forty and below, being returned to Horton.
Main picture: Sunset at Horton.

A December common is returned.

Braving the winter at Horton. Inset: Split Tail common.

made an Olympic event, could win gold medals with an alarming regularity. The list really went on and on, but the most noticeable thing was the lack of any counterproductive bad feeling or guardedness, as everybody it seemed would go out of their way to help somebody else catch a fish, whether by information pooled or simply jumping in to free a tethered carp. It was indeed a year to remember.

The few of us that stayed on to fish the winter months created a social scene that would rival that of any lake, due in part to the lodge house that was situated at the car park end of the lake. This throwback from the old trout fishing days was equipped with freezers and a fully fitted kitchen and, after a bit of a clean-up we all brought in bits and bobs from home to make it a bit more comfortable. I donated an electric blow heater and all the spare kitchen utensils that I could lay my hands on and before long, tables, chairs and sofas were appearing on a regular basis. The cupboards were equipped with spices and pots and pans, and in the depths of winter we would take it in turns to cook roast dinners or big curries, which, when washed down with copious amounts of alcohol, made those long cold nights a lot more bearable.

It was about this time that Reg appeared to us. He had always been there but under the guise of mild-mannered Richard Howell, but this year, after apparently slipping into a phone box somewhere along the way, he metamorphosed into Reg Bampton captor of carp to over forty pounds and self confessed Party Guy. Quite how he evolved so suddenly from the mere snip of a lad that he previously was, into the Reg that we now know and love, is beyond me. Incidents, however, such as leaping up at four o'clock on a winter's morning to hit a run, with his trousers mysteriously around his ankles, and having no

Reg - Party Guy.

memory at all of how or why, definitely signified a change in attitudes. Hardly a social event went by without, at some stage of the proceedings, the appearance of Reg clutching that tell-tale yellow carrier bag.

During one of these late night soirees, a plan was hatched to start a concerted effort at pre-baiting throughout the coming close season in an attempt to wean the Horton carp onto a particular bait. As everybody seemed to have being doing their own thing up until now it seemed like an incredibly feasible plan. Eventually the number of interested parties whittled down until only four remained, along with myself and Keith, just Phil and Chrissie would be there to follow this wonderful plan through to fruition.

Chapter 6

Horton
The Second Season

The formulation of our new Super Bait was left up to Keith and I, as somewhere along the line the other two had got the idea that we knew what we were doing in the bait department. In reality we hadn't got a clue.

A couple of ingredients were high on the list for inclusion and green lipped mussel extract was one that we really fancied trying, along with the birdfood that we'd used all that season. I knew that Zenon Bojko, who we'd met at Harefield, was something to do with a comparatively new bait company called Mainline Baits, so I decided to give him a ring and see if we could get any sort of a discount for bulk buying. As it turned out he put us in contact with the management and bait expert who ran Mainline and, to cut a long story short, we ended up striking a deal whereby all our bait was rolled for us and at a price that we could all afford.

They even managed to trace the active ingredient within the G.L.M as being a substance called betaine, which he included in the finished mix along with an exceptional plum flavouring. Basically, the bait was a fishmeal but it incorporated some milk protein ingredients and the rolled baits arrived in two sizes, being 16 and 18mm. A strict pre-baiting rota was arranged, with everybody being allocated certain days to bait up on, and to start with we decided on about a couple of kilos every other day. As soon as the weather warmed up enough to enable us to watch the carp's reaction to our new bait we immediately upped the amount being put in and fed the carp as often as possible. By the end of that close season we had introduced 120 kilos of bait and although a lot of people may find this excessive it is worth noting that hardly any of this was put in just on the off chance that it was being eaten. The carp could be found on a daily basis and we watched as they devoured everything that we threw at them. Sometimes, known and recognisable fish would practically follow us around the lake turning up in a new spot as soon as the bait started going in. With this kind of confidence under our belts we could hardly wait for the season to start and, in our own minds at least, we had already caught everything with fins that resided in Horton.

We were allowed to plumb during the close season and it soon became evident that the weed would be a lot heavier that year as it was taking a hold all over the lake by the beginning of June. The Plateau Swim seemed particularly bad and on one midweek visit, when nobody else was around, I decided on a closer inspection. Donning a diving mask that I always keep in the van, I stripped off and swam the length of the shallow feature starting in the Plateau Swim and ending up opposite in the Dead Tree. I'd pulled a rig over the whole area the day before and found nothing that I'd be particularly happy to fish on but when seeing it up close I realised that it was not half as bad as I'd first imagined. There were two different types of weed present, the Canadian pondweed that would eventually grow in thick beds up to the surface and another lighter coloured weed that covered the top of the feature. Although this second weed was also fairly long, it lay flat to the bar in big swirls like tight curly hair. If you were to pull some in on a rig or plumbing float it would give the impression of a long and unfishable weedbed, but through the mask I could see that a light lead set-up would present a bait neatly on top of what resembled an Axminster carpet! I decided to keep this little gem of information tucked away for future reference and towelled myself down and dressed before anybody happened to show up.

This year, to save all the early arrivals and queuing at the gate of the previous season, a draw for swims had been planned for the start and we all gathered outside the lodge for a barbecue and the obligatory pulling of permits out of a hat to decide the pecking order. The fish were highly evident in the R.I.P. Corner, as it later became known, and all and sundry trooped round there to watch open-mouthed as they paraded up and down the margins. Keith and myself had a plan based on the events of last year and were desperate for a swim that fished out to the middle section of the lake as we were convinced that the fish would end up there as soon as the leads started thudding into the lake bed. Everybody was in high spirits, due in part to the massive amounts of embalming fluid that had been consumed in an attempt to wash down the cremated sausages and burgers, although I think that Fat Sam ended up eating more of those than anyone else. As the first name came out of the hat we could hardly believe it, Chrissie Pearson, or 'Numero Uno' as he called himself all weekend and, after some deliberation, he chose the Weedy Bay. Keith pulled out number eight and myself number eleven, so we were all well pleased and were soon ensconced in our first choices of swims along the North Bank.

Like dogs marking our territories, we were straight out with the marker floats and before long a veritable banquet had been laid out on the lake bed awaiting the arrival of the guests of honour. Phil had decided to avoid the crowds and fish elsewhere for the first week and, as it turned, out he missed nothing as the season started very poorly indeed, although Chrissie lost a good fish after only fifteen minutes had elapsed. The fish had miraculously disappeared and, having not read our script properly, they failed to show up in the middle as we'd bargained for. A few were caught, but nothing of note, and after a few days we disappeared back down the motorway with our tails firmly between our legs.

We were both in my old van, along with Fat Sam, half a ton of fishing tackle and an unfeasible amount of empty beer bottles. The day was bright and sunny so we were both wearing shades, and due to an ever increasing need for volume, I'd wired up a couple of seventy five watt house speakers in the back of the van. Halfway back along the M25, a peculiar smell filled the van which, if you take into account the competition, must have been an incredibly noxious beast.

"Have you farted, Jenks?" I inquired.

"Not me pal," came the reply.

The further we went, the worse it became until, eventually, I peered over the shades for a closer inspection, only to find the cab full of black smoke. On turning down the booming rock music, a hideous clanging and bashing could be heard emanating from under the bonnet and I just managed to get my foot on the clutch in time before a deafening bang signalled the end of yet another carp mobile. Luckily, I knew somebody in the AA and, after pretending to be with them on the emergency phone, we managed to get a lift home with a very nice man in a big yellow breakdown truck, but unfortunately it meant splashing out another one hundred pounds on a new mode of transport.

The very next week I was back again in an old beaten-up Datsun from Honest John's Motors and ready to do battle with the denizens of the deep. Once again, though, I skillfully managed to avoid getting my landing net all slimy, but Phil opened the Mainline account with a double figure common that he quickly followed up with The Lady at thirty one pounds. This was a very low weight for this particular fish, and went some way to explaining the absence of big fish so far this season. Obviously they had spawned, and although I realised that our bait may have been good it was still nothing when compared to a once a year mass orgy of sex. As if to bolster the theory, The Parrot was caught the following week at thirty six pounds, which was a drop of six pounds on its last capture. I was beginning to wonder where my next fish was coming from and, more than anything, I was eager to be in a situation whereby I could offer the fish the bait that they had been so keen to accept throughout the close season.

After Phil's results, I had unashamedly examined every inch of his terminal tackle and deciding it was a disgusting sight, I'd turned my attentions to his rigs instead. The first thing that was apparent was the length of the hair he was using. It was as if he was trying to compensate for his own shortcomings in the Vidal Sassoon department, by using the longest hair rigs I had ever seen. There must have been at least five inches between bait and hook, and although I was unwilling to go quite that far, I could see the advantage of a confidence rig when dealing with shrewd fish like these. It was with this in mind that I re-evaluated my rigs and their effectiveness for my next session. It was not that I doubted my own approach, but I always like to be a little different from the norm when it comes to presentation. After all, if you use the same as everybody else then you can only expect to catch the same as everybody else. I liked to set my sights a little higher than that. The weed was also a major factor this year as it had taken a much stronger hold than previously and the bays were already choked with Canadian pondweed. Lighter leads and longer hooklinks seemed to be the way forward, and eventually, I ended up resorting to the type of presentation that I'd used way back in the Chichester days.

A one ounce tri-lobe lead was placed free running on the line, and a hooklink of about two feet in length sported a size six Super Specialist hook. The bait, a single bottom bait, was attached by a two inch hair pulled through the back of a small piece of tubing pushed over the eye of the hook. The tri-lobe lead, although being very inaccurate to cast, seemed to settle a lot more delicately on the bottom weed and, on the retrieve, rose instantly to the surface, reducing the amount of crap that was brought in on every cast.

My next session started on a Tuesday morning and the temperatures had soared by the time that I arrived. I pulled out a rod, net and rucksack and, dragging Fat Sam's head out of the rubbish bin in the lodge kitchen, I set off for a walk about. I'd only got as far as the first causeway swim, though, when Concorde ripped through the morning air, spooking a number of fish out on the plateau at about forty yards' range. A large tree sits to the right of the swim and from the highest branches, about thirty feet up, I could clearly see a fair head of fish all milling about in the shallow water over the bar. This was all the encouragement that I needed. Leaving the stalking gear to mark my swim, I ran back to the car for the rest of the kit. I'd brought a fair amount of bait with me and this was the perfect opportunity to see if they were still as keen to demolish it now that the season was under way. The Canadian pondweed had grown visibly since my little pre-season dip, but as far as I could see the other weed was still compacted onto the top of the bar. From up the tree, I could make out the position of the three large beds of Canadian that marked the back and sides of the area that I wanted to present my baits on and, using a marker float and a dozen trips up the tree, I eventually had everything mapped out against the features of the far bank. At first I was a bit hesitant to bait up right on top of the fish, but I figured that they would be pretty inactive while it was this hot and now was the perfect time to prepare everything for later on, in the hope that as the temperatures dropped a little they might be tempted to get their heads down a bit. Two kilos of bait was soon flying its way out onto the plateau and, using the weedbeds as goalposts, I could be fairly accurate with the catapult. The fish didn't seem to mind the disturbance too much either, but I suppose if Concorde couldn't scare them off then I had no chance! With the hookbaits in position and the cold lagers retrieved from their brief stint in the freezer, I sat and watched as the action hotted up over my baited area. Sticky Bean turned up in the afternoon and, seeing the amount of fish that were crashing and rolling in front of me, he hastily set up next door to my left. I wandered along with a cold can of beer for him as he was looking a bit hot and bothered having just suffered the motorway for an hour. Just as I set foot in his swim, my left hand rod burst into life. I was on it in a flash and a massive bow wave left the plateau as I leant into a good fish. A big grey back stuck out of the water like the fin of a shark as he forced his way through the weed and out into open water, but there was no way I was letting this fella get away and steady pressure brought him inch by inch closer to the net. A crowd had suddenly materialised from nowhere and, as he went into the net, I had to clamber over the onlookers to see exactly what it was that I'd bagged. There in the net lay the unmistakably ugly form of The Parrot, with his bulbous eyes looking up in amazement at the array of anglers all peering in at him. I let out a full volume victory cry across the lake as another member of the A Team was notched up in the log book next to my name. I felt that the only truly sociable course of action was to reel in the other rod and drive round to the Thresher off licence to fill a couple of carrier bags full of Kronenburg for a little celebration. Pretty soon a full scale carp party was in full swing

Returning The Parrot.

in and around my bivvy, and just to keep the troops happy I went and dragged out a twenty eight pound mirror just after dark as well. The fiasco that I had in landing it provided the evening's entertainment and ended up with me stripping off and wading out up to my neck in an attempt to free it from a weedbed. This seemed to go down well with the extremely rowdy crowd of onlookers and drunken reprobates.

The new rigs had performed well over the weed and gave me great confidence for the summer ahead although the tri-lobe leads were terribly inaccurate on the cast due to their un-aerodynamic shape and I eventually scrapped them in favour of more standard shaped 1oz bombs.

Over the next two weeks, I managed to catch another four twenties. These were two mirrors and two commons up to twenty seven pounds, the biggest of which was making his once only ever appearance on a bottom bait. Taking into account how well he fought, I would imagine that he had been hooked and lost at some stage of the proceedings.

The weed went absolutely bananas over the next few weeks and the vast majority of anglers struggled as a result. For my money, it just made the job in hand that much easier. After all, if ninety percent of the lake bed is unfishable then that only leaves ten percent of the lake that the fish can feed in. Once all the clear spots have been identified it's just a case of moving round and round the lake constantly checking them for fish. I've always been partial to a move of swims, but that summer I made it into a new art form. I even scrapped the rucksack in favour of a large plastic box which bore the legend 'Stolen from Halfords' across the sides. I mounted this on an old match fishing trolley and that way I never had to unpack. I could simply fish straight out of the box and hurl everything back in and be off again at a moment's notice should the need arise. The night fishing kit, like bedchair and sleeping bag etc, spent the day in the van and I retrieved it all every night when I'd settled into the day's best choice of swim. A lot of my captures were coming within a few hours of moving into a swim and, after having one fish from a small hole in the weed, quite often the spot would be blown for a while so a move straight after catching one was usually the best plan. During this period, I think I must have spent as much time up trees as I did on the ground, in an attempt to identify the feeding areas as, due to the amount of weed present, they were becoming very localised. New areas of clear, though, were appearing all the time as the fish moved in on certain natural food sources, ripping the weed up as they did so. Unfortunately, for some reason, they were unwilling to behave in this manner to obtain unnatural food such as boilies. It was from one of these newly harvested areas that I had my next encounter with a member of the A Team.

I had been off the lake for a few days and on my return I noticed a large round hole in the otherwise solid Canadian pondweed that peppered the surface in front of the point near the mouth of the Church Bay. It was only four or five days since I'd last checked this area, and found it practically unfishable but now a clear area ten feet across was clearly visible. Tetley was fishing next door in the Church Bay and I stopped off for a chat. According to him, a few days previously a group of very large carp had been patrolling the bay but he'd seen nothing for a while and was considering a move. I shinned up the nearest tree for a look and at first I thought that maybe Tetley was pulling a flanker by pretending the fish had moved off so as to keep the area all for himself. He seemed genuinely surprised when I informed him that Jack, Shoulders and a host of other big fish were milling about in mid-water right in front of him. Had I been a bit more on the ball I should have just said that there were no fish for miles and waited in the bushes until he moved out! As it was, I had to settle for the little point with the new clearing to his right. One cast with a 1oz lead into the hole confirmed that the bottom had been stripped of weed, so one hookbait went out on each side and about fifty baits got scattered around the clearing. As an added precaution, seeing as I was fishing over the top of a surface weedbed, I moulded a lump of lead putty onto the lines about four feet back from the lead and fished slack lines so as not to spook any fish moving through the swim. Tetley's swim was well equipped with a crate filled with stubbies of French lager and we spent the evening sitting in the long grass on the high bank behind the swims, sipping ale and praying for the great carp god to be gracious to us. Just as the sun sank over the horizon in a spectacular array of reds, a big dish-shaped mirror carp slid silently out of the water up to his tail root above my left hand bait and somehow managed to re-enter without making a sound. If not for the spreading ripples, I could well have believed that I'd imagined it. At nine o'clock the next morning, that same rod ripped into life as eventually he had made his mistake. With an absolute jungle of weed to choose from, I expected the fight to be a bit one-sided in his favour but he allowed me to lead him, like a dog on a lead, across the clearing and through the small channel that I'd made to sink my lines in. It was only when he was underneath the jetty that he finally woke up and buried himself into the lake bed at my feet. Tetley went to the front of the platform with the net and I heaved the fish off the bottom and up through the clear water, spinning all the way into the landing net and, as we lifted the net, an enormous banana-yellow carp lay in the mesh. Its perfectly heart-shaped tail gave away its identity and, at a new high of thirty five pounds, Heart Tail was mine.

This was my tenth fish of the season so far and things were definitely looking good. It was only the end of August, which still left my favourite month of September. Due to being self employed, in the loosest possible sense of the word, I'd managed to put quite a lot of time at my disposal for the coming weeks.

The next day, while fishing a swim on the other side of the bay, I had my first encounter with a Horton 'tornado.' I had just returned to my bivvy after a hectic tea

Dancing on air after catching Heart Tail.

drinking session with Chrissie and Tony in the Ski Slope when a strange whooshing sound drew my attention to a disturbance out in the open water to my left. As I watched, a section of the surface was quite literally sucked up into a small water spout that spun furiously and grew in height as it gained momentum while heading in my general direction. It only took a few seconds to reach my swim, and was a clear three feet high as it charged past my rods with an audible hiss before crashing into the reeds at the bottom of the bay!

I leapt out of the bivvy and ran back to Chrissie's swim blurting out what I'd seen. As soon as I arrived I wished that I'd kept it to myself. The looks on their faces left me in no doubt that I was going to get a severe piss-taking. I was not disappointed. No matter how earnestly I tried to convince them of the indisputable reality that a whirlwind had just passed through my swim, they just laughed all the louder and informed me in no uncertain terms that I'd totally lost the plot! Luckily, though, my already dubious reputation of sanity was salvaged to some extent a few weeks later when Chrissie himself witnessed one of these bizarre occurrences.

They soon became commonplace and seemed to be caused by the downdraft of passing planes clashing with an opposing wind. Sometimes they could be heard whipping around in the air above your head or seen to pass through tall trees like a whirling dervish. Sometimes small fragments of chaff or leaves would be picked up from surrounding fields, and on one occasion in the middle of a beautiful summer's day, a sudden downpour of straw appeared from out of a clear blue sky and settled all over the surface of the lake. There is, at Horton, an elderly lady called Kate who lives in one of the neighbouring houses and walks around the lake every day to feed the swans and geese which she treats as if they were her own house pets. (She also used to bring a handful of custard creams around for Fat Sam as well). Kate appeared in my swim near the lodge just as the straw started to settle and inquired as to what all that stuff on the lake was.

"Look it's raining straw," I said in amazement holding my hands up toward the skies.

"What do you mean raining straw?" she replied unable for some reason to see the falling strands.

"Look in the skies," I cried. "There's straw just falling out of the skies!" She just told me I was mad and walked off shaking her head.

At the end of the Causeway Bank that leads from the lodge is the Weedy Bay, where Weedbed Willy had his excellent results during the first season. This year it was totally choked with weed and more or less unfishable. It is not really so much a bay, more of a small depression in the bank contours that harbours a shallower section of water than either side. As a result it is a favourite area for the carp to bask in during the hotter months. Keith and I decided in our ultimate wisdom to drag out a section of weed in the Weedy Bay and bait it regularly, in an attempt to encourage the otherwise disinterested carp into feeding here. They would visit the area at some stage of most hot days but were always quite content to sit above the forest of pondweed and ignore everything that we threw at them. Hopefully, this would be the way to tempt the odd one or two to forage around a bit.

I've noticed on more than the odd occasion over the years how carp seem attracted rather than repelled by large splashes in the water and can only assume that it is linked to the jumping fish and communication theory. Swim-raking seems to be a prime example of this and even those big old mirrors of Horton couldn't resist the curiosity factor.

It was a baking hot afternoon in late August when we arrived under the willow, armed with a twin-headed rake attached to a length of rope, which actually consisted of a great many lengths of rope joined together with an even greater amount of granny knots. There is not an awful lot of room under the overhanging willow branches for a full blooded pendulum-style chuck of the sort we had in mind, so trousers off and into the margins we waded. Keith was up first and with a blood-curdling cry and a grace of movement that would have shamed Geoff Capes, he launched the offending article skyward. Twenty yards out, the water erupted as splashdown occurred and we heaved on the rope as the equivalent of a forty foot trailer full of weed hung onto the other end for dear life. The food that lived within this mass of greenery was incredible, and I was tempted to lash it to the tree in case it leapt up and made a dash for it back to the lake. It was no wonder that the fish were doing so well in here, and such astounding weight gains had been recorded. There was more than enough natural food to go around even without the constant influx of high quality baits. After half a dozen pulls, the loads became more manageable and I discreetly disappeared up the tree to give orders as to which way and how far to chuck the rake. The first thing that I saw from aloft though was two fish sitting only twenty feet away from the clear channel that we had just dragged and I told Keith to wait up and not move, I was assuming that they had just that second arrived. After ten minutes or so, we got bored of waiting and decided to carry on regardless and I sat up the tree as the next rake flew out, expecting to see fireworks from the fish as it crashed through the surface. I was amazed to see that they hardly flinched and after a few more chucks another two fish appeared beside them. They were all lying just out of range of the rake and staring straight at the epicentre of the disturbance. Although we never plucked up the courage to try it out, it certainly made us wonder about the feasibility of using a large rock on a rope as a form of attractor when actually fishing!

We fished the bay on a couple of occasions over the next few weeks, but all to no avail although on one hot afternoon I thought I was in with a chance. I was sitting up the willow peering down onto our little clear 'runway' among the forest of Canadian pond weed when a common carp of about eighteen pounds appeared at the entrance and slowly made his way up the clearing. Luckily, I had already placed a single boilie on the small exposed piece of sand where the rake had bumped the bottom on the retrieve. He glided effortlessly up toward my meagre offering and drew to a halt about six inches short of it. I was convinced he'd take it but he just sat staring at it intently as if willing it to move. After at least twenty minutes had elapsed, the only change in the state of play was an acute cramp in both my legs and the common had still not moved a muscle, so much so that I thought it might have nodded off for a while. I slid down the tree as quietly as I could, considering I'd lost the use of my legs, and hobbled off up the bank in an effort to revive them. When I returned five minutes later to the tree, the common had moved back to the entrance ten feet away and was still suspiciously eyeing the bait. It is little moments like these that make me wonder just how the bloody hell we ever actually hook anything!

September seems to be a month that repays for those tormenting times that August throws at us so relentlessly, and as the temperatures slowly start to drop then so do the defences of the wary carp. The weather however, becomes a more formidable beast and entirely unpredictable.

All the way down the motorway the wipers swept torrents of water from the windscreen, as the rain beat a tattoo upon the roof, deafening out the stereo within. On my arrival in the car park I was pleased to see that only two motors were already there and I found both owners drying out in the lodge house, drinking tea and huddling around the heater. Chrissie Pearson, or C.P. as he was more commonly known, and Tetley had both been on the lake since the previous day and were soaked to the skin by the big and extremely wet south westerly wind that was coursing down the lake. The fish had apparently started showing on the wind that morning and, from the comfort of the lodge, I saw at least three carp crash out in an area two swims further up the lake from where C.P. was fishing, Tetley was set up in the R.I.P Corner, fishing into the teeth of the gale and, as soon as the rain eased off a bit, we all bundled round to the North Bank to get some baits in the water. The swim where I'd seen the fish was The Reeds and I just managed to make it there in time before the heavens opened once more. Peering out from under a hastily thrown up umbrella, I saw a fish launch itself skywards just a few yards from the bank. He was so close that we had eye contact for a split second before he toppled over sending a spray up into the wind. Rain or no rain, I had to get a bait into the water as quickly as possible. The only problem was that in my rush for the swim, I'd left all my boilies in the van. Pulling my jacket over my head, I legged it down to Chrissie's swim. Shouting to be heard over the weather, I begged a hookbait and a hand appeared through a crack in the door holding the sum total of one single boilie. Still, one was better than none, so I grabbed it and ran for shelter!

Huddled under the brolly, I slipped the bait onto a long hair rig and holding just one arm out in the elements I somehow managed to cast it out to the spot where the carp had just shown. As the next

A twenty four pounder for Tetley.

break in the clouds appeared so did C.P. with a much appreciated cup of tea and, while we stood there drinking, a strange whirring noise begged for our attention.

"Can you hear something?" I asked.

Before he could answer, the penny dropped and we looked down to see the spool on the rod that I'd left laying in the mud spinning like crazy as a fish made off with my single hookbait, or more accurately Chrissie's single hookbait! A stream of abuse came from Chrissie as I bent into the fish, and I could tell that no more bait was going to be forthcoming that day. Unfortunately, the fish soon became heavily weeded, and eventually slipped the hook. The next twenty four hours produced a total of five takes between the three of us resulting, sadly, in two lost fish for Chris, a twenty four pounder for Tetley, and the next morning I recaptured The Lady at a shade over thirty four pounds. It was not often that the lake gave up its prizes with such merry abandon, and full advantage had to be taken when the mood was right. The Reeds swim could be a no-hoper for a large percentage of the year but in the correct conditions it took a lot of beating. One low point to this otherwise wonderful session was a heron that I found sitting under the bushes along to my left. At first I thought that he simply had not heard me approach, and I crept closer on hands and knees for a better look as it was rare to get within such close proximity to a heron in the wild. As I grew nearer to him, I could see that all was not well. His beak seemed to be stuck downwards tight to his neck and this rendered him unable to fly. I could just make out a plastic loop around his neck and he was obviously in need of some urgent attention. Creeping under the bush, pushing the landing net in front of me, I manoeuvred into a position from where I could easily and gently lower the net over him. This, I thought, would be a better plan than chasing him wildly around the bushes and further stressing him out. Even as the net settled over him he never flinched a bit, resigned to his fate and probably suffering from shock. Around his neck was one of those plastic straps that hold four beer cans together. It firmly pinned his lower beak to his neck preventing him from taking off or feeding. I carefully snipped the plastic from behind his neck and he stretched a much needed stretch but he still showed no signs of flying off. I returned him to his perch under the tree and sliced up some bacon into thin strips, laying it at his feet, in case he was too weak to fly. After a few hours had passed I re-checked him and although the bacon had disappeared the heron showed no signs of having moved a muscle. I repeated the process, but it soon become obvious that rats or voles were scoffing the bacon and poor old Harry heron was not looking too well at all. I decided to leave him undisturbed as the stress of my being there could not have been helping matters. Unfortunately, when I next checked on him he had given up the ghost and lay lifeless in the margins so I scooped him out and buried him. Having seen the effects of these non-biodegradable death traps, I can't stress strongly enough the need to snip or break each loop open the moment they are removed from the can. I'm sure this one was not left purposely and, once they are 'disabled,' at least you can rest in peace that you personally have caused no possible harm to the wildlife that help make our sport so aesthetically pleasing.

Chrissie was the only member of our little baiting team who hadn't caught as yet and it certainly wasn't for lack of trying. A few turns of bad luck had denied him landing the three or four that he had already hooked, but events were about to take a turn for the better. Shortly after the big wind session, the weather returned to normal and he bagged his first carp of the season, a twenty five pound mirror, from underneath the pontoon outside the lodge house. It was the next week that everything deservedly fell into place.

At the end of the Causeway Bank leading from the lodge to the Weedy Bay was a swim that up until now had not produced a single carp. It was known as the Salt Circle. It had acquired its name due to an insectophobic angler who had placed a ring of salt around his bivvy to keep out unwanted creepy crawlies! The grass had died under the salt, leaving a perfect circle burnt into the ground. This area of bank was also populated by slugs in the mornings, and if you were up at dawn you could find them plastered all over particle buckets and water bottles and, on one particular morning, orange juice cartons. Keith always has a carton of orange juice next to his bed. He awoke early one day after a particularly heavy night and with a mouth like a dog's armpit. Gasping for a drink, he tipped the carton up, gulping as he did so, only to feel a large wet slimy lump slide down his throat before he could do anything about it! Amazingly, he still has an open carton next to his bedchair even now, I think most anglers would be using a bottle with the lid firmly welded into place after that!

I, like many others, had tried my hand in this swim many times and we had all failed miserably. In fact, only a week earlier I had spent two hours unsuccessfully looking for a spot to present a bait among the weed after seeing numerous fish crashing and rolling there after dark. I was set up on the opposite bank on this particular morning and looked across to the Salt Circle and saw C.P. bent into a fish. Eager to assist in any way possible to help him land what appeared to be a good fish, I reeled in and raced Fat Sam around to the causeway. By the time I arrived, the fish had managed to bury himself into the thickest weed that he could and eventually there was no other option than to launch the boat in an attempt to free it. The boat, a fourteen foot flat-bottomed punt, had been called on quite a few times recently as the weed had become a major problem when landing fish. Luckily, it was an incredibly stable craft and fully equipped with life jackets. Chrissie stood at the back and I crouched over the front ripping weed from the line as we traced the path of the still unseen fish. The lead came to hand quite quickly but the fish was still a long way out so, clearing it of weed, I had to reluctantly slide it back down the line where it caused a few more problems before we eventually found ourselves directly over the fish. It was still out of sight at the bottom of the thick weed and I slowly broke the bed apart with the oar until, with a wrench to the rod, the fish was out and fighting. Chrissie was taking no prisoners, and in short order we could see a big mirror carp rolling over deep below the boat as C.P. piled on pressure and heaved him up towards the net. From my vantage point I could see that it was definitely going to be his much anticipated first thirty pounder and, as it slid into the net, I screamed thirty pounds at him even though he was only two feet away. He was so excited that he grabbed me and kissed me on the top of the head before spitting, disgusted at the realisation of his actions, into the lake!

As we paddled back to the swim we passed over the area from where he had hooked the fish and, peering down, we saw that it had been stripped of weed by feeding fish over the last week or so. Neither of us recognised the carp at all and it was only with the use of the photo gallery in the lodge that we identified it as a fish that had been stocked at twenty one pounds and captured the year before at twenty nine, but it was considerably larger now, pulling the scales round to thirty six pounds and fourteen ounces.

Everybody was over the moon with this latest capture, not just because the fish were obviously piling on the weight in their new home, but we all knew how hard Chrissie had tried since the season started and this was a well deserved result.

It seemed that I could do no wrong this year on Horton and a brace of twenty pound commons the next week, including a new personal best of twenty seven only

C.P. and a right result at thirty six pounds.

Dave with Lumpy at a massive 41lb 12oz.

A very happy Robbie with a common from Horton.

The glorious PB common from Horton. Main picture: Looking across into the Dog Bay.

Above: A family affair - C.P. with the long one. Main picture: Keith lands a whopper at Horton.

32lb worth of superb common from Horton is carefully returned.

Another major result, the magnificent Koi.

went further to confirm the fact. Both the commons came from the Ski Slope which had not been fished for a while up until then, due to the incredible banks of weed that choked the entire swim. Careful plumbing accounted for both of these fish, and the area that I eventually fished was only about three feet in diameter and surrounded by solid weed at about forty yards' range.

Plumbing for clear areas in this situation can be a very hit or miss affair but a few pointers are worth mentioning that can make the job a lot easier and give a more accurate representation of what lies below the surface. Marker floats can be almost impossible to handle in extra weedy conditions as they never surface when you want them to and the added buoyancy makes the lead a lot less responsive to the bottom contours. If a marker is needed, though, due to the range being plumbed, I usually just let it surface where it lands and use it as a point of reference only. By casting a lead and rig all around the marker, a better idea of what weed is present and where, can be ascertained. I've noticed people in the past pulling a lead across the bottom and assuming it is clear only to find in the morning that they've been fishing in a solid weedbed. If you stop at the end of a pull back and lower the tip back down to the surface the line should fall slack immediately, if not then the lead is obviously not on the bottom and the most common cause is pulling vertically up through solid weed. A gentle pull back after casting will reveal a slight tap on the rod tip as the lead snags momentarily in the top strands of weed and every foot of line that can be paid back out before the lead hits the bottom relates to the depth or length of the weed. It all sounds like common sense but time and time again I've seen anglers fishing these false clear areas. Also the length or width of the area can be found by measuring the distance that the lead can be dragged without it lifting from the bottom. As an example, I fished in the Dead Tree one day when the weed was at its worst and, using a marker float, I thought that I'd found a clear strip across the top of the bar. It felt the same on every cast and it was only when putting on a set of Polaroids that I could make out the marker float skimming across the top of solid weed! The first pull had lifted the lead and float vertically and after a slight tap as it pulled out of the weed it then slid easily over the solid carpet of Canadian pondweed.

By the beginning of October, the aforementioned weed had started to lose its hold and drifted around in large floating rafts frequently wiping out both lines at some time during the night. I started combatting this with the use of back leads placed just off the rod tips. The first few times that I tried it I started suffering from strange little bites. The bobbin would jerk up to the rod before dropping back to its original position or on other occasions it would hold tight under the rod, trembling on a taut line. Striking at these plucks and short takes never produced a fish and the lack of sleep was worse than the drifting weed problem. Desperate to find out if they were definitely line bites as I suspected, I reeled both rods in and removed the baits, one rod I recast and fitted a back lead and the other I cast out and set up with a tight line. Within moments the bobbin on the back lead rod smacked into the butt, and held there. Line bites were obviously the problem, but the swim would have to be crawling with carp to produce so many. The rod without a back lead never even twitched in the short time it took to register three or four occurrences on the other rod. Eventually, I tracked down the source of the problem as being the large head of tench that lived in Horton. As they were feeding along the margins, they were trapping the line across their heads and dragging it along as they chugged up and down in a vertical position. Every time they righted themselves to move spots, the line would ping back again. They seemed totally undisturbed by the pressure of the line and I decided to suffer the floating weed instead.

The warm nights of summer had disappeared suddenly and, as the high pressure brought cold winds sweeping in, I resorted to using the dome and fishing a slightly more static approach, generally only moving once a day. Fat Sam was also starting to feel the cold and a scratching on the side of my sleeping bag woke me up early on one particularly chilly October morning. As I pulled the bag open a crack, she leapt in and worked her way down to the bottom where she curled up on my feet and drifted off to sleep. I'd just managed to drop off again myself when a drop back on my closest rod occurred. I peered out of the door and was greeted by the early winter sight of tufted ducks and seagulls squabbling over the consumption of my carefully placed baits. I was tempted to just leave them to it, but I knew that mornings provided the best chance of a take. So, leaving the dog to keep the bag warm, I wound in and unceremoniously hurled a single bottom bait as far away from the menagerie as possible, landing eighty yards out to my right, before crawling back into bed.

I couldn't have been in the bag ten minutes before the same rod absolutely melted off. The single tone of the alarm being almost drowned out by the noise of the clutch, and the yelping of Sam, as I trampled her at the bottom of the sleeping bag in the rush to get to the rod. It's not often that a fish hooked at range can strip line from you at will and against a tight clutch, but this one was re-writing the rules as he almost made the opposite side of the lake on his first attempt. By the time I'd got him anywhere near ready for the net, my arm was hanging off and I was so glad when Chrissie scooped him out at the first attempt. As he did so he recognised him instantly as the one big fish that had managed to avoid capture since his stocking into Horton. It was the biggest fish from the Road Lake at Longfield and went by the name of Lumpy. He had been stocked at thirty one pounds but looked way over that mark as he dwarfed my unhooking mat. The scales were zeroed and up he went, we cheered as the needle spun past thirty five, and then forty pounds, settling eventually on forty one pounds and twelve ounces. For once, I was totally speechless.

Shortly after we'd returned Lumpy, Chrissie managed to sneak yet another fish out of the Salt Circle, a swim that was gaining popularity at an alarming rate now. It was the same long mirror that I'd had off the plateau in the summer and weighed in at twenty six pounds.

I decided to go home the next morning but not without a detour to the developers on the way home to put the Lumpy films in and, as soon as they opened the next morning I was there to collect. The photos came out brilliantly and although I could not possibly have seen the fish before, I couldn't help thinking that somehow I recognised him. It was only when I walked into Keith's living room the next afternoon that the full picture became clear. There on the wall was a ten by eight framed photograph of the twenty five pounder that Keith had caught on our second ever visit. This was the fish that everyone had said looked so much bigger than twenty five and the reason now was obvious, it was. The two fish were one and the same, and on further investigation we found that my old set of Avons that we'd weighed the fish on back then, when pulled to their absolute limit, offered four choices of weight at different points along the needle. Reading from the wrong line a weight of exactly twenty five pounds and ten ounces could be reached, even the highest reading of thirty three and a half would have been inaccurate as the scales needed to be totally bottomed out to give the reading that they had at the time. How the bloody hell we'd ever made a cock-up of this magnitude I'll never know.

I blame Chris Eubanks myself, if he'd been knocked out in the first round as I'd predicted we'd never have had to drink all that Guinness!

The season sort of fizzled out after the capture of Lumpy, although I did manage one more twenty pound common at the beginning of November. The winter was once again spent blanking in good company, although a brief feeding spell in February gave Chrissie a recapture of the big mirror that had been his first thirty, now at an even heavier weight of thirty seven pounds, and another mirror of twenty four pounds. Quite why we suffered this second winter on a water that we knew would be absolutely rock-hard I don't know. Maybe we were just a bunch of sad blokes with sad dogs, with nowhere else to go. On the other hand, I bet we had a lot more fun than most people who were stuck in a nice centrally heated, and incredibly boring house all winter. Beside which, Sam would never have let me stay at home for a whole week as she had a new hobby of her own and she's bringing out a book about it soon called 'An Obsession with Food'. Little Robbie had an old and extremely bad tempered Jack Russell dog that went by the name of Gypsy. She steadfastly refused to let Sam into her bivvy and would growl and snarl as soon as the Fat Dog came anywhere near. Now, Gypsy had good reason for this anti-social behaviour as Sam's hobby was to outsmart both Robbie and Gypsy's best attempts at bivvy security, and at some stage of the weekend steal all of Gypsy's food. This little stunt she managed to pull every single week, due mainly to the fact that Sam never misses an opportunity as, in her eyes, the

. . . taking into account Keith's fish.

consumption of food is the main reason for her very existence. Also the broken zip on Robbie's dome tent was, to Sam, like an open invitation.

One Saturday night in January Robbie and Gypsy turned up in my swim on the causeway after first having secured his dome tent on the bank opposite.

"She'll never get in there tonight, boy," he stated with confidence. "I've used about twenty pegs to hold the door in place and I've hidden Gypsy's bowl inside a folded up low chair underneath a jacket and hidden that under the bedchair. I'd like to see her get through that little lot."

Ten minutes later and without either of us noticing her leave, Sam had suddenly disappeared. In fact, the first we realised of it was when a dog that looked just like her appeared on the opposite bank making a bee-line for Robbie's swim.

"Look at that crafty cow," Robbie said. "She'll be in for a disappointment tonight."

We watched as she sniffed around the sealed-up doorway before turning and plodding away. After about fifteen feet she turned and, with an impressive burst of speed, she ran and threw herself at the middle of the door bringing the whole lot crashing down around her! Ten minutes later, she came wandering back home as if nothing had happened. I'm sure she was so convinced that we hadn't seen her perform, that she never even considered looking guilty. The next day I found out from a very pissed-off Robbie that, not only had she eaten all the dog's dinner, but she'd also polished off a double pack of Bourbon biscuits as well!

When the time came to tally the books at the end of the season our Mainline account was looking very impressive indeed. I'd taken the most fish of the year with sixteen specimens, including four over the thirty pound mark. Phil had the next biggest account with ten fish and adding Keith and Chrissie's combined total of nine carp meant, that of the sixty three fish landed that year, our little team had clocked up thirty five of them. I suppose you could say the pre-baiting had paid off !

Apart from the fish that we had captured, some of the others were caught at incredibly high weights, like my own personal quest Shoulders for example. He fell to the rods of Decibel during the summer at an all time high of forty one pounds and ten ounces, and with Lumpy, Jack, and The Parrot this made four possible forty plus carp with plenty of fast growing thirties on the way up. The fish that C.P. had bagged, had stuck on an incredible sixteen pounds in only thirty months. Horton was fast turning into the premier water in the country and a lot of the anglers who had at first dismissed it as Micky Mouse now sat patiently on the waiting list.

An end of season party was held in the lodge that year and everybody was set the task throughout the day of writing a poem or ode about another angler. All done in very bad taste, of course. At the height of the evening's festivities, each person had to stand up on the coffee table and, in front of a video camera and the whole syndicate, read out the poem that had been written about themselves. Big John Buckley however, after putting his head through the ceiling, was made to stand on a copy of the yellow pages instead.

Massive amounts of food and drink were laid on and a fitting end to a wonderful season was had by one and all. I awoke at twelve o'clock the next day in the grass, a good twenty feet away from my bivvy, and slowly and painfully packed my kit away for the big three month lay off, and at that moment in time I really felt as if I could do with it.

A fitting end.

Chapter 7

Horton
The Third Season

As we prepared ourselves for our third season on Horton one thing became instantly apparent. Obviously, other people were not blind to our results over the previous season, but unfortunately there seemed to be a feeling that throwing tons of bait in throughout the close season would guarantee similar results to ours throughout the coming year. I think that some. even thought that by putting even more bait. in they could somehow negate the advantage that they thought we had gained. Now, obviously the bait had gone a long way to helping with our results but so had bloody hard work and a willingness to create the time, at the sacrifice of all other pursuits, to be at the lake as often as possible in an attempt to keep in contact with the fish and their movements. There is a distinct difference between chucking in twenty kilos of bait and sitting there expecting miracles, to being prepared to pack up all your tackle and move it around the lake four or five times a day to stay on feeding fish. The thing that worried us most was the amount of uneaten bait that would get left on the bottom to rot by the combined effort of all the newly formed bait teams throughout the close season.

There was no way that we were going to allow ourselves to be dragged into some kind of bait war, and we decided eventually to put a much smaller amount of the same bait in during the spring and only ever put it to fish that we could see to be feeding, this would at least ensure that we were not contributing to any bait mountain that may have been stacking up out of sight in the middle of the lake. There were no shortages of offers for new recruits either, but in the end we increased our number by only one. Little Robbie had wanted to be in on the bait from the start, but finances had not allowed it and although he was still a bit strapped for cash, as indeed so was I, we desperately wanted him to catch a Horton whacker so he was in. Robbie had provided a constant source of entertainment with his unique style of humour throughout the first season and had also endured the long and fruitless winter along with the small band of stalwarts who were mad enough to sit it out throughout one of the coldest winters for years.

Due to the underwater springs that feed Horton it very rarely freezes over and at times we were still fishing when even the mighty Wraysbury over the road was frozen solid. On one particular night, as I sat huddled in my dome, the temperature hit a recorded low of minus ten degrees, even Sam's dog food froze solid in the can! The close season could not pass quickly enough and by the time we assembled once again for the draw, we were all champing at the bit to get back on and do the business. With the barbecue and other formalities over with, the draw for swims began. We held our collective breath hoping for a repeat of the previous year when we had all fared so well in the allotment of swims. There had been a certain amount

10 degrees below!

of confusion at last year's departure as to exactly where some anglers were headed as they left the lodge, and the fact that some swims went by more than one name only further compounded the problem. So, in an effort to alleviate this, I had taken it upon myself to draw up a large map of the lake on a six foot by four foot piece of paper. All the swims were marked and named and each angler, on drawing his ticket out of the hat simply wrote his name next to his choice of swim. The weed this year had been severely held back due to a slight algae bloom in the spring. As a result I was absolutely convinced that, with no other sanctuary, the fish would seek refuge in the centre section of the lake once the early season barrage of leads began again. On the North Bank section of the map, I'd marked all the swim names accordingly, the middle one being The Blank Swim. Keith and I had named it thus due to our total lack of action over the last two years, but the mere inference of a dodgy swim had a beneficial effect as events transpired. The Blank wouldn't have been my ideal choice of swim, but the easy access that it offered to the centre section of the lake made it a fair shout at least. I stood and watched and waited as the other twenty one anglers before me chose their prospective plots. A lot of them were new members and I noticed that for some strange reason they all avoided the one with the word BLANK emblazoned across it. A short while later I was brewing up my first cup of tea in there!

We had all had terrible draws that year. Keith had pulled twenty four and Chrissie had fared no better, Robbie had the best draw out of our little band with number thirteen. After sitting in my swim watching the goings on around the pond for a while, I decided to refrain from putting out any bait as the lake was already getting a hammering with boilies flying in from all directions and manic plumbing going on in most swims. I thought the best attack was to leave my swim undisturbed and await the start of the season by keeping well back from the water's edge, at the other side of the potato field, where, by a strange coincidence somebody had built a pub!

When the season finally kicked off expectations were high, but the first day ended without a single bite for anyone. The fish had shown occasionally all over the lake, but as the second night fell there was a noticeable build up of action in the middle in front of myself and my two immediate neighbours. The plan was coming together. By midnight I could take it no longer, I had only the two hookbaits out there and although I knew the theory was sound, I was getting an itchy baiting hand. Fish had been crashing out steadily all evening and I couldn't help thinking that they would respond to a bit of bait. Even though the idea had been to have two single hookbaits presented in the only bait-free area of the lake, I knew they loved the stuff that I had to offer them. So, using the distant tree as a marker in the moonlight, I put two hundred baits out with the throwing stick, landing them on the hard strip of ground that ran up the centre of this area. I also brought in one of the rods and changed the rig over to a pop-up bait fished ten inches straight up off the lead, reasoning that maybe the lack of action was due to some sort of algae or dead weed putrefying on the bottom. As the night inevitably turned into a new day, the first bite alarm hadn't yet shattered the still and heavily expectant air, but events were about to change and halfway through my second tea of the morning the pop-up rod screamed the lake's first battle cry.

It was obvious from the start that the fish was no monster, but it managed all the same to gain the safety of a snag that sits in the middle to the right of the swim. I'd just managed to get a bit of movement again when the other rod tore off as well! Grabbing it with my left hand, I found myself standing there attached to both the first and second fish of the season at the same time and I felt like that proverbial dog with two dicks! The first fish managed to re-gain the snag so I landed the second one first, that turned out to be a scattered scale mirror of about mid-twenties who was known as Starburst, and eventually I persuaded his partner in arms (or fins) to join him as well. The first job was to put on two fresh baits and re-cast as soon as possible before preparing one mirror and one common, of twenty-four and seventeen pounds respectively, for the cameras.

The photographers were duly summoned and, after laying out the wet unhooking mat, and pot of water etc, on the higher bank behind the swim, I went back down for the fish. The sack cords were looped over the front banksticks and, as I started to lift the first one, the rod butt flew up in the air beside me. At first I thought I'd snagged the rod on my jumper, but when the spool became a blur before my eyes, I got the message and struck into a much more powerful-feeling fish. The problem with The Blank swim is that, due to a large bush at the front, the space to cast or play a fish from is severely reduced, but then if you stuff ten anglers into every available space it all becomes a bit ridiculous. I had to rely on the running commentary from the 'front row' to know what was going on as I could hardly even see the lake let alone the fish. Eventually a big cheer went up and I knew that I must have landed something so I stopped pulling and fought my way to the front.

"It's my fish," C.P. announced as if he owned it.

"What fish is it?" somebody at the back shouted and somebody else replied "It's C.P.'s!"

The poor beast inherited Chrissie's initials as his moniker for the rest of his days. It looked a fair bit bigger than when Chris had had him last winter at thirty seven pounds, but the weighing went on without me, I was desperately trying to get another bait out there to the remaining fish that were still showing over my baited area. I heard a whoop and a holler as the scales spun past forty pounds, and I

Three in 45 minutes!

arrived up at the back of the swim to a weight of forty pounds and six ounces. For some reason, we decided to take a more definite reading using a tripod and were mystified to find that the fish was now only thirty nine pounds and six ounces! Later on, when we tested the scales and the method used, we found that the scales had been held by their sides which increases the weight dramatically, as most dial scales are designed to be hung from the hook or metal loop at the top only. Later that day we filled water bottles up to various weights and ran a few tests and found that at twenty pounds the Rueben Heaton scales we were using added half a pound when held incorrectly and one pound extra when weighing forty pounds.

While the fish was out and the cameras were already assembled, I decided to photograph this one straight away and besides I'd run out of sacks! We held him in the water for a while, first in the landing net and then, just as we reached the top bank I was away again on the rod that had been moved ten times during the fight with C.P.'s. Unfortunately, the baitrunner had been switched off at some stage during this fiasco and the rod shot forward like an arrow until the reel caught on the buzzer! Moments before I could reach the rod, the line snapped with a loud crack!

Four takes in forty five minutes would be an incredible occurrence on any water but on somewhere like Horton it was nothing short of miraculous! It also seemed to throw the switch into feeding position for the rest of the lake. Shortly after my result the angler fishing opposite, who was aptly named Decibel had, after a very ambitious cast, a fast take and a spirited battle that provided him with The Koi at a new all time high of forty one pounds. A few other fish came out over the next two days, and I managed to bag one more myself on my last morning, also from the middle section of the lake on a popped-up bait. I caught a new personal best common of thirty two pounds.

Decibel nicks The Koi.

A film crew were present at the lake at the time making a video with Alan Taylor and it wasn't until after we'd returned the common that we realised I'd missed my chance to slide in and make a guest appearance. On my next trip a few days later, though, I played my cards a bit more shrewdly and after managing to coincidentally set-up right next door to the 'luvvies' (as they had quickly become known) I was soon posing for their movie camera with a dumpy mid-twenty mirror.

Throughout the next month, I was blessed with mixed fortunes, for although I was still managing to receive far more runs than anybody else on the lake, it seemed that I could only land commons. They came in all shapes and sizes, but every time a mirror picked up the bait it would be a prelude to some disaster or another. I had two drop off under the boat in one day, and as soon as a better fish was felt on the end a wand would be waved somewhere and off it would fall. The most crippling of these disasters happened in the Church Bay at the end of July. The bay had grown progressively weedier throughout the season until now, where from up the tree it looked like the hanging gardens of Babylon. Every conceivable variation of subterranean plant sprouted and flourished at various levels and clear spots were at a premium. I'd spent a fair amount of time in the swim on the west side of the bay and knew one small spot that had remained clear. This was in part due to the bait that had steadily been trickled in there including a fair quantity of hemp which draws in the tench, who in turn strip everything in their path to get at those black grains. I had this spot firmly marked against a single baby poplar on the bottom bank, and could drop a bait on it even in the middle of the darkest night. The other rod however, was becoming a little more difficult to deploy and on this particular day I sat at the top of the overhanging tree to the right of the swim watching two carp drifting slowly into the bay and waiting to see where, if anywhere, they sank down to feed.

The problem with this swim was the water depth. Only a few yards out, it was eighteen feet deep, so holes in the weed near the surface could not be guaranteed to go all the way to the bottom as the visibility was only about ten feet. As I watched, one of the two fish swam right under the branches below me and I could clearly see the large scales adorning his flanks and his gill covers rising and falling as he circled a small hole just off the outermost branches. His mate, a mid-twenty common, had been separated from him behind a wall of weed that extended within inches of the top, and he was just hanging below the surface looking in my general direction. The mirror, once satisfied that all was as it should be, upended and sank down out of view into the hole and after a few moments some tiny bubbles appeared struggling for the surface. This indicated that he'd made the bottom and I marked this down as a definite spot for the other rod. While this had been going on, the common had been getting steadily more and more agitated and patrolled up and down the back of the wall of weed until eventually he rose up and gently popped his head out of the water. I was unsure as to quite what he was up to, so I watched with interest as he circled around once before rising again and this time sticking half of his length out of the pond before falling backwards with a splash and I got the impression that he may somehow be calling for his mate.

The bubbles continued to rise from the close spot and eventually, in what seemed to me to be desperation, the common came around once more and hurled himself clear of the water, thrashing his tail as he did so and creating a hell of a row in the process. Instantly, the mirror surfaced from his little hole and practically bolted up and over the weed wall, breaking the surface in order to do so, and came to a brief halt next to the common who turned and led him out of the bay and away across the lake. If I could have heard what the common was saying as they swam off it probably would have been, "Where were you, didn't you hear me calling? There was a bloke up that willow you know, you should be more careful!"

Later that afternoon, and with one bait on each spot, the fish that I desired more than any other appeared halfway across the bay. I was back up the tree and I could clearly see the unmistakable bulk of Shoulders making his way diligently across the weed, and he had four friends in tow as well. None of the others could hold a candle to the imposing magnificence of this fish and, as they passed under the branches below me, the entourage stopped at the new right hand hole allowing His Majesty the pick of the prime feeding spot to the left, to peruse at his leisure.

I couldn't believe my luck, a choreographer could not have planned the moves any better. There at the bottom of each tiny feeding area was a perfectly presented hookbait and a couple of pouchfuls of hemp. I was almost tempted to reel in the right hand rod so as not to hook the wrong fish! I was that confident of a take and worried that one of the lesser beasts would charge in and ruin my chances, but in the end I decided to leave everything as it was and just watch. Watch I did. All afternoon I spent up that tree until finally the circulation had totally left my legs and I had to clamber down to see if I could still walk or not. During this time Shoulders had repeatedly dipped down into the left hand hole sending a sheet of pinprick bubbles up to the surface. Every time I'd been convinced that I was about to catch him. The other fish were showing some interest in the right hand area but in the main they were content to lay in a stack within the confines of the hole all at different depths and angles. The fish were still present as it eventually grew dark and a large grey cloud formation gathered to the south, eventually breaking overhead and sending penny-sized raindrops hurtling down into the lake.

My bite alarms were turned up to quite a sensitive setting and the rain bouncing off the line was playing a highly annoying tune on them so, risking a soaking, I ran down to the rods and turned off the alarms before adjusting the sensitivity right down low. Seeing no forthcoming break in the conditions, I turned in for the night convinced that at some stage I would be summoned back out to do battle with Shoulders. As if to further endorse the fact, a massive crash from the left hand spot occurred shortly before I drifted off into a carp-filled dream.

On opening my eyes and seeing that it was morning my first thoughts were of incredulity, there was just no way that both baits could have survived the night uneaten. I stared accusingly at the rods and saw that the left hand one was bent double! Cursing, I leapt out of bed and ran to the rods. I'd forgotten to turn the bloody alarms back on! I couldn't believe that I could have been that stupid but all the evidence spoke to the contrary. I wound as fast as I could but everything soon became solid in weed, and unsure if there was a fish still on, I ran to the lodge for

Just as well I didn't fish the other bank!

the boat. After half an hour of carefully freeing my line from the hideous weed, I found the hooklink on the other side of the bay, tangled in a clump of Canadian that had been forced together into a solid mass!

I slowly rowed the boat back to the lodge, convinced in my own mind that I had just hooked and lost my greatest obsession, and although I knew that any of the other fish may have sneaked into that hole, and made a mistake, I was sure in my heart of hearts that Shoulders was currently swimming around nursing a sore lip.

It was to be late August before the voodoo doll finally lost its hold over me and a big old mirror carp once again graced the bottom of my landing net.

My plan of attack this year had changed dramatically, especially as far as baiting-up was concerned. I was safe in the knowledge that the carp loved our bait and would have no hesitation in picking up a single offering without the added attraction of a bed of freebies. As far as I could ascertain, most people were still of the opinion that the more bait they put in the higher the chances of a take and this obviously led to a large amount of bait lying uneaten on the lake bed. I had also witnessed, while watching from up trees, the fishes reaction to large beds of boilies and noticed how drastically they had changed from the piggery that they had once showed. It seemed to me that the sight of a bed of baits spooked the fish more often than it invited them to feed. By fishing single hookbaits only I was still experiencing takes on a regular basis while others struggled. Also, apart from in the weedier bays, the coloured water that was a result of the algae bloom present this year had held back the growth of weed in the main body of the lake and the fish were more willing to feed at range than in the exposed margins. Fishing in this manner suited my mobile approach perfectly, as there was no need to bait or plumb swims. It was just move in and cast out two hookbaits to areas that I knew from previous experience were capable of producing fish. As a result, I felt less tied to any particular swim than usual, which was not much at the best of times. I was on about my fifth move of the day as evening approached and I was currently ensconced in the reeds on the North Bank. I'd grudgingly set up my brolly and bedchair ready for the night, although I was unsure of my final choice of swim. Time was running out and I had yet to eat anything. The bulk of my tackle was still packed away and Little Robbie and I sat sipping tea and chatting about the lake and its latest moods as the shadows lengthened into evening. He could tell I wasn't happy with my choice of swim for the night and suddenly announced, "Come on then, pack up and and I'll help you move." Within ten minutes I was casting out in the Heart Tail swim and Robbie was making yet another cup of tea. I've never known anybody, with the possible exception of Chrissie, to put away so much tea per day. I thought I was a bit of a tea-head but those Slough boys must run tannin for blood!

Over the previous two weeks I had seen a few fish show in this area, situated just outside the mouth of the Church Bay, and knew exactly where I wanted the baits to go. A small overgrown jetty, long lost to the encroaching bramble and hawthorn, lay along the margins to my left and by a simple defiance of gravity, I could just lean out over the lake far enough to be able to flick a bait a couple of feet off the end of it. The Church Bay weed had spilled out as far as here but a small channel of clear water ran the length of the extreme margin. The other rod I cast twenty yards out, against the weed barrier that marked the start of the bay. After Robbie had left for home, I sat alone and watched as the sky faded into night punctuated only by the lights and incessant roar of the planes as the evening's procession of holiday makers returned from far and wide. Given the choice, I knew where I'd want to spend my vacation, and I was already there.

Six a.m., and I suddenly came into full consciousness standing on the end of the jetty bending into a fish on the margin rod, I gave it the big heave-ho and he shot out from the edge and straight past my jetty on his way into the long sub-surface reed bed to my right. Once firmly buried in there, he stubbornly refused to be budged, leaving me no alternative but to swim to the other jetty further along to my right and try and remove him from a different angle. If it wasn't for the presence of one solitary tall tree between the two jetties then the whole affair would have been that much easier. Risking the dawn swarm of gnats that had already started to mass above my swim, I stripped off and started to lower myself into the pond. It was bloody freezing and no sooner had I got my feet in than I realised I'd be left stranded without a net on the other jetty, so laying the rod on the deck I ran the net around there in readiness. On picking up the rod in preparation for my dip, I found that the fish had come free and was on the move again. The problem now was that I'd just taken my net ten yards up the bank and left it there. I was gaining line now and knew that at any minute, he may surface and I'd be faced with jumping in and wrestling him up onto the bank. So, making an executive decision, I slackened off the clutch and placed the rod back into the rests while I ran back for the net. I had only taken about fifteen seconds but in that time the carp had re-snagged me in the original spot and everything had returned to the way it was in the first instance. This was quickly becoming a farce and, deciding that enough was enough, I lent back as hard as I dared, feeling the tearing of reeds as the fish was dragged protestingly towards my side of the jetty. Just then Chris Haswell appeared in the swim and, admirably suppressing a grin at the sight of me standing there in just my underpants while struggling with, and swearing at, a large mirror carp, he grabbed the net and at the first time of asking scooped up my prize.

After all those commons it was a massive relief to gaze upon the mirror clad bulk of The Koi, lying on the mat in the early morning sunshine, and at thirty nine pounds and six ounces he looked very well indeed, especially as he was showing signs of having spawned to some extent already. This constituted my fifth member of the six strong, original Longfield 'A Team', on which I had set my sights, although obviously fish like Lumpy and C.P.'s had since changed the line up into a new and improved Horton 'A Team'. Ironically enough, the one I still had to catch was the very one that I had wanted the most, the all singing, all dancing Shoulders. I wouldn't rest until he was mine. The Koi was my tenth fish of the season and, as I packed away my tackle to avoid the oncoming Friday afternoon rush of anglers, I couldn't have guessed that my next carp would come before I even reached the car park!

As I dragged the trolley past the Dog Bay, I noticed three or four backs cruising along the outskirts of the bay, close to The Shoulders swim that Keith loved so much. I shinned up a tree for a quick look before I left and there, circling behind the weed, were five carp. Three of them were commons including the famous Split Tail and the bigger of the two mirrors was a fish called the Grey One which had only been caught once in his time at Horton, by Chrissie at twenty nine pounds, two years earlier. I really did want a photo of this beautiful near leather carp in my album, so I broke one of the rods back out and re-baited the rig.

As I watched from up the tree, waiting for an opportunity, I noticed that they all visited a small sand area next to the marginal reeds and so I started off there. As I said earlier, I had been using hookbaits only, but for some reason I decided to break up half a dozen baits and scatter them on the sand before carefully placing the rig on top and hiding the line through the reeds. Watching from up the tree, I saw the five fish, led by the Grey One, approach the spot, but, on seeing the bits of bait littering their feeding spot, they froze momentarily before darting for the cover of the very tree that I was hanging out of at the time.

It was obvious that I was not getting a pick-up from that spot today, so a new plan was needed. Time was definitely not on my side either, as I'd heard the gate start its relentless Friday afternoon squeaking as the weekenders arrived. I knew that all the bankside disturbance would soon spook these jittery fish from under the tree. Waiting until they had left on another circuit of the weed, I flicked my single bait under the branches of the tree, trying to land it in as shallow water as possible. The fish milled about behind the weed for a while before returning to their safe haven under the tree. Ten minutes later I was rewarded for my efforts when a fast take and a spirited tussle in the edge gave me the Grey One at thirty pounds and eight ounces, just as the first wave of anglers arrived in time to take the photo's.

Robbie arrived in the car park just as I was leaving and he was well chuffed to know that our last minute move had paid off with The Koi. Full of confidence as ever, he told me in glorious detail how he was going to provide the undoing of a Horton whacker. Robbie had been soldiering on for nearly three years now and,

Above: Moonscale at an incredible 38lb 12oz from Horton.
Right: Dave with Heart Tail at 35lb.

Shoulders, the final piece of the jigsaw from Horton at 40lb 12oz.

Above: The Parrot at 43lb and below: Admiration all round, Dave's final Horton capture.

Just as the first wave arrived. . .

barring a couple of small commons, he had yet to get to grips with the lake, although if confidence was a measure of success he should have emptied the place by now. His unfaltering determination and plethora of new, all conquering ideas spurred him on from one session to the next and this week's gambit revolved around bait.

The bait we were all using arrived from Mainline in ten kilo tubes of rolled baits, and in every tube there were one or two massive boilies that someone had rolled by hand from the scrag ends - as much for a joke as anything. Some of these gob stoppers were up to 50mm in diameter! Robbie however, had decided that these were the lucky ones and he'd been saving them up especially. Today was the day to unleash his super weapon. I listened in amazement to his plan and proposed bait and rig, eventually bidding him good luck. I drove off down the motorway, musing all the way home about Robbie's unwavering resolve and hoping that one day it may be rewarded in full, although I couldn't quite see it happening on the 'golf balls' he was using this week. I suppose it just goes to show how little you really know about feeding habits even when you think that you've got it all sussed out nicely. On Sunday, I received the phone call on which I'd been waiting for two years, Robbie had at last bagged a whacker! At some time on Sunday morning C.P.'s had been swimming along in front of the Reeds Swim and thought, "Oh look, a bloody great big boilie, I'll eat that then!"

The end result was little Robbie holding a thirty nine pound carp for the cameras and, as you can see from the photo, he was more than a little pleased about it, as indeed were the rest of the syndicate.

Keith and Phil were both struggling this year and both had still to catch their first fish, although Chrissie was keeping the side going and had notched up a few

The smile says it all. Robbie holding a thirty nine pounder.

fish culminating in the capture of a cracking personal best common of thirty four pounds. Chrissie also fished mainly midweeks and, like I, did everything in his power to keep his finger on Horton's 'pulse'. As a result of this, a game of cat and mouse, bluff and double bluff, had developed between us. We were more than willing to pool information about recent sightings and possible 'hot' areas, but there was always just a little snippet held back in the hope of a slight advantage. Likewise, the estimated time of arrival each week tended to be a slight distortion of the truth. Keith would arrive home on Sunday and report to me all the happenings over the weekend and at sometime during the evening I would ring Chris and the game would begin.

"Hello mate, I hear there's a few showing down in the Dog Bay."

"There was mate, but I think they've moved off now though," would come the dubious reply.

"When are you getting over there this week then?" I'd ask, barely able to suppress a giggle.

"Oh, not until at least Tuesday afternoon," he'd reply.

Now, I knew that this meant Monday morning at the latest, and knowing that I could get down there as soon as I liked I'd add, "I don't think I'll make it much before Tuesday evening, so I'll see you down there. Good luck."

Forty five minutes later, we'd be racing each other down the causeway for the best swim! On one occasion, so I found out later, his missus called him back from the car as he loaded his tackle and he stood in the front garden with the phone poked through the window and still had the bare-faced cheek to tell me he wouldn't be there for two days!

Keith, Phil and Robbie all fished mainly at the weekends and were quick to point out that midweeks, due to the lack of pressure, had to be that much easier than competing with anglers as well as fish. I tried explaining that it got busy in the week as well, but they wouldn't have it. There was practically a challenge being offered here, so I decided to have a little go over the next couple of weekends. Besides, I missed the company of the three of them as well as all my other friends who held down Monday to Friday jobs, and I knew from past experience that all the better socials happened on a weekend as well.

The next Thursday afternoon, I packed up all my kit at home and set out for the lake. If I was going to have to fish the weekend the least I could do was get there a bit early and secure myself a half-decent swim. As it happened, though, on my arrival I found the lake very busy already. Phil was down early and firmly ensconced in the bottom of the Church Bay, and on the mouth of the bay Richard Skidmore held court along with his missus and their mad springer spaniel, whose food Fat Sam instantly devoured, the second she trotted into their swim. After a long walk around, I finally settled for the Dog Bay as I'd seen three or four fish cruising around in the corner. During the evening one fish in particular repeatedly threw itself out of the water a mere twenty feet from the end of my rod tips. All my best efforts seemed in vain as I tried and tried to persuade this considerable sized fish to take one of my meagre offerings. Over the course of the evening he must have showed at least thirty times and appeared to be a dead cert, but the reality was something entirely different and by the time darkness fell I was sick to death of watching him perform. Reeling in both rods, I made my way over to Phil's for a cup of tea and a chat. Phil's swim was little more than an indentation in the bank at the extreme bottom corner of the bay and only just big enough to house the pair of us. Phil listened to my tale of the Dog Bay Dolphin before telling me of the shedful of fish that had been showing in and around his bay since darkness had fallen. Over the next couple of hours, we sat and watched as massive fish launched themselves out of the pond. Silhouetted against the moonlight, they appeared as big black dishes before sliding almost silently back into the water. By midnight, I was chomping at the bit for a move as there were two swims to the right of Phil that sat unoccupied. I would have moved instantly, but I was being polite by not crowding in on a mate who was obviously in with a terrific chance of a fish. Just when I could take no more he turned and started the sentence, "Are you going to move or what?"

By the time he finished it, I was half way around the bay and in with the chance of an Olympic sprinting medal! As I threw the last of my belongings on the trolley the Dog Bay Dolphin crashed out of the water one last time, as if to say, "Oi! don't forget about me!" So I hurled a rock at him and hurried on back to the mouth of the Church Bay.

I settled for the Heart Tail swim as it wasn't too close to Phil, but was still in the right area. Casting out was purely academic, as I knew the spots like the back of my hand although the weed had grown up with a vengeance. Small areas were still fishable and fish were rolling all over them as if to highlight the fact. At one stage two fish left the water simultaneously, surely I couldn't fail? Expecting to be woken up at any moment, I crawled into the sleeping bag for some much needed sleep and was amazed to wake up around seven and find both rods still unmolested. Even more unbelievable was the fact that Phil had also received no action down in the bay. Around ten, I went off for a walk and stopped off at Skiddy's swim to feed Sam and have a chat. Skid was chuckling about my midnight move, stating categorically, that from his angle he could clearly see that all the fish jumping had been tench! All I could assume was that thirty pound tench must be a lot more common up north than down here, and told him that if they were indeed tench he'd better phone the Angling Times as I was just about to break the record. It all seemed a bit strange that afternoon as the gate started to squeak and squeal its Friday afternoon arietta, usually this fanfare heralded my departure rather than practically the start of my session!

By four o'clock that afternoon, the whole crew had arrived, Keith was there, dressed as usual in head to toe fluorescence. He looked like a jazzed-up '70's peacock! Little Robbie, Tony Badham, Reg and Sticky, it was looking like it could turn into an incredibly social weekend, especially as they were currently all crowded at the back of my swim as I gingerly played out my first ever weekend carp!

Shortly after the last few stragglers had turned up and joined in the mad scramble for swims, something had picked up my margin fished single boilie and charged off into the weed that now covered most of the swim. After an awful lot of advice from the Rogue's Gallery that sat along the high bank behind me, including I might add, a lot of awful advice, I somehow managed to get the fish clear and back on the move. No sooner had I gained the upper hand, than he made a very determined dash for the sanctuary of the bay and succeeded admirably. Once safe in the jungle, there was no way that I could persuade him to leave and offers of the boat were coming thick and fast. Somehow, the thought of this lot in a punt parked in the middle of my swim full of carp, all yelling, shouting and getting generally 'carp excited' did not fire me with enthusiasm! Whipping off the trousers, I took to the water. Phil had managed to smash his way through the brambles and reach the old and overgrown jetty that I had been casting next to and, from here, he could assist with the netting. I, however, had to swim around the brambles and try to clamber up to join him. Once the angle of attack had been changed everything

"Weekends are easy!" Dave with a gorgeous linear.

went swimmingly (if you'll excuse the pathetic pun) and I guided a big old mirror carp into the waiting net. I couldn't see, from my precarious position behind Phil, exactly which one I'd caught but I was left in no doubt as Phil roared, "Moonscale," across the lake to the band of onlookers on the other side of the bay. As he passed me the net I looked in disbelief, as this former upper twenty that had been on the missing list for nearly two years, looked to be nearer forty pounds than twenty! The scales agreed with me and settled on a weight of thirty eight pounds and twelve ounces, and the serious piss-taking began in earnest. After all, it wasn't me who said it was rock-hard at weekends, in fact at that exact moment nobody could quite remember who had said it. Nobody except for me of course!

Just to add insult to injury, I managed another one at midnight as well! This second fish, although not one of the real monsters, was one of the nicest looking fish in the lake, a perfect linear carp that had been painted in a beautiful dark mahogany and turned the scales to nearly twenty five pounds. The next morning I walked down to the lodge, to where the log book was kept. I took great pleasure in entering my two fish and, in the comments section, I wrote (naturally), "Weekends are easy!" Under the confident exterior I couldn't believe how fortunate I had been, not only to have caught so many, but to be catching the fish that I wanted, as if working through an invisible list. The one burning question was, when would my path cross with that one fish that I desired more than all others? I was sure that I'd hooked and lost him at least once and I'd netted him three times for other people, surely sooner or later my time must come and Shoulders would be mine?

I decided that this weekend angling was a lot more enjoyable than I'd originally thought and, although the hangovers were a bit more severe, I figured that I could live with that. The next Friday I set up in the Waiting Swim along the North Bank as the fish had visibly moved out from the bays and could be heard throughout the night, crashing and rolling on the back of the weeds which petered out at about sixty yards range. The bottom in this area was covered in decaying black silkweed, which normally would signify an area to avoid like the plague. However, at certain times of the year the fish seem to tolerate it in favour of the bumper food crop that wriggles inside. One handful of this weed would contain anything up to five or six different varieties of pond life including bloodworm and various larvae, also present were large numbers of tubifex worms which I am led to believe the carp find particularly palatable. In fact so much life resided in each bunch, that I was almost afraid to pull it from the lead in case it bit me!

Pop-ups were the obvious choice in these conditions as, although the weed and its attendant buffet was an attraction, the actual silt that lay below had rotted into a noxious black ooze that would render a bottom bait inedible within minutes. Unfortunately for me, I had no pop-ups with me, but after a quick trip up to the kitchen in the lodge I microwaved a couple of dozen baits and I was back in business. The fist night produced an old friend in the form of C.P.'s at a slightly lower weight of thirty eight pounds and was one of the few 'double ups' that I suffered at Horton. On Saturday night I had a slow take at around eleven p.m. that weeded me up to such an extent that there were only two options. One was the boat, which I really didn't fancy at all, and the other was to go back to bed and hope that it swam out of its own accord, which seemed a far more sensible idea. So, setting the rod on an alarm in the bivvy doorway with the rod butt under the bedchair for easy access, I climbed back into bed. Obviously it is hard to relax with a fish on the end and every hour or so I'd wake up and, still lying in bed, heave on the rod in the vain hope that the fish had miraculously freed itself. At some time in the wee small hours I relented and walked round to the lodge for the boat, but after a near impossible single-handed row against the wind I found that I still could not shift him, even with extreme pressure from above. I retired again, vowing to sort it out at first light. Eventually at six a.m., the weed gave up the struggle and I started to gain line and before long an immaculate common of twenty seven pounds rolled into the net a mere seven hours after first hooking him! This weekend lark was starting to prove well worthwhile, although I refrained from gloating too much about it as, for some reason, a few hackles had started to rise a bit!

All this took place at the beginning of September, a month that has been very kind to me over the years. It has provided me with numerous personal bests and multiple catches but I could not have envisaged the incredible result that lay in wait for me on my next session.

The wind on the previous weekend had been pushing strongly into the lodge end of the lake from where I had taken C.P.'s and the common. The fish had obviously been there in numbers although the current trend towards showing only at night had made it hard to ascertain exactly how many had been present. On my arrival the next week everything had changed dramatically, the wind had switched to a near gale force north easterly and large waves charged relentlessly along the pit coming to an abrupt halt as they crashed into the bank at the bottom of the Dog Bay. The car park was inordinately busy for a Thursday, although from the lodge steps not a bivvy could be seen, so dressing in waterproofs against the torrential rain I set off to try and find some signs of life. All the anglers present had elected to fish in or around the two bays at the far end of the lake and, given the conditions, I think I might well have had the same idea. Nothing had been caught, though, and very little seen, so I decided to stick with the lodge end of the lake and sploshed my way back up to the car park. The lake narrows off a lot around the area of the previous week's captures and I figured that I could fish the same basic area from the Salt Circle on the South Bank, and in a lot more comfort as well. Due to the weather, I had brought the dome tent for this session and in the back of the van were numerous pieces of old carpet, so after launching the rods out into the storm, I set about making myself as comfortable as possible. Out from the Circle at about sixty or seventy yards range is a small piece of ground that sits a few feet proud of the surrounding area, being approximately three feet shallower. This patch of hard ground is usually clear of weed and made a convenient spot to start off, considering the terrible conditions for plumbing.

By the time everything was set I was drenched and, after a change of clothes, I zipped down the apparently clear door on the dome and spent the evening monged out in bed. No visitors were forthcoming that evening and I probably wouldn't have let them in anyway as the rain and consequent mud were turning the outside world into Noah's back garden. I, on the other hand, was nice and dry and warm within the confines of my little green cell.

That is, until one of the rods decided to register a typical breamy-type bite. I was half way through struggling with a waterproof jacket when all thoughts of bream vanished! The rod in question had launched into a full blooded battle cry as a very impatient carp screamed for my immediate attention. The rain was still lashing down and before I had got the fish half way in, I was soaked to the skin. Water was running down the back of my neck and disappearing into the waistband of my trousers only to emerge from the leg holes slightly warmer for its journey. There had been no time for boots either, and socks did not really offer much protection against the muddy puddle that I was currently standing in. I was never under the impression that it was a particularly big fish on the end so, not wanting to hang about out in the elements all night, I doubled the pressure and hauled as hard as I dared. Everything went fairly painlessly until the fish reached the margins, where a notorious snag nestled on the bottom to the right of the swim waiting to pounce on the unwary angler. A piece of old and frayed steel cable had been left behind, half embedded in the bottom, presumably when the pit had been dug, and I knew from bitter experience that it was more than a match for eleven pound line. If a fish reaches the cable on a tight line it is instantly lost, the only possible chance an angler has is to slacken off immediately and boat around to the other side of it and resume the fight from there. I, for one, was buggered if I was getting the boat out again single-handedly after last week's fiasco, and I knew there would be slim chances of gathering much help in these conditions in the middle of the night, so I took the other option. Clamping down the clutch, I walked backwards, putting more pressure on the fish than I would ever do under normal conditions. Luckily, all held firm and from deep down in the margins I felt victory as my opponent rolled over in defeat. Once away from danger I led him like the proverbial dog on a lead up through the margins towards the net. The fish although already beaten was still reluctant to wave that final white flag and swirled angrily just out of netting range. Finally, with the net at full stretch, I inched him over the cord and kept the pressure on until the large silver swirls were right next to the spreader block. Dropping the rod, I struggled to regain my balance and pulled the net back into the edge. I left the fish in the net while I fumbled around in the bivvy for a torch which, once found, I instantly dropped on the floor and little pieces of spring and bulb flew in all directions as it exploded on impact. Staring hard into the net I could make out a large grey lump with big bulbous eyes staring back at me, and on feeling my way down the line to remove the hook I knew straight away to whom they belonged. Where a top lip should have been only a large protrusion of hard bone existed and, once again, The Parrot, had fallen foul of the bait. He was still as pig-ugly as the first time we had met, only now (unlike me) he was considerably fatter as well. I secured him in a sack until the morning and, after adding all my clothes to the steaming pile already festering in the corner of my bivvy, I leapt back into bed for the remainder of the night. Tetley was the first person up and around in the morning and between us we weighed the ugly old warrior in at forty three pounds and twelve ounces, a new personal best and my third forty pounder. Hanging outside the lodge was a small inflatable parrot that somebody had left there months before so, after securing it to my shoulder with a set of forceps, we set about taking the photo's during a much needed break in the rain.

The capture of this fish coincided with a couple of other notable events, the first of which followed a few hours later in the Church Bay. Tony Badham, who had been a syndicate member since the beginning, had yet to capture his first Horton carp and eventually we took pity on him and furbished him with a small quantity of the bait, this coupled with the new found confidence that it obviously inspired led to his first capture of a Horton mirror. While all this was occurring, over the road at Taplow, Gary Bond who was a regular visitor at Horton and a bailiff at the adjacent Kingsmead Pit, banked his first forty pound plus carp. It would have been an act close to gross negligence not to celebrate this triangulation of success, so gathering as much moral support as we could muster we all trouped across the field to the Five Bells for a liquid lunch. By the time that we all tottered off back to our respective plots, we were in severe danger of becoming skittles in the still formidable wind but for the first time since my arrival I was warm and dry. Even the fat dog had managed to dry out in front of the fire, in fact she was the most reluctant of all to leave the pub, and she certainly beat off some stiff competition.

Being a Friday, Keith was due down shortly and he was obviously well fired up after receiving my phone call from the pub. I decided to grab a little siesta before his arrival. Just as I was sorting out my rods before retiring though, Steve Morgan from Mainline came wandering down the bank for a social. As we sat chatting, one of the recently cast rods ripped off and after an embarrassingly protracted fight a small common of around nineteen pounds made a brief appearance. The topic of conversation turned to where was I going to angle after Horton? I'd already caught all the known big fish, with the exception of Shoulders, of course. I tried not to think about it too hard, as for all I knew, it may still take forever to finish my quest on here, and finish it I would. One day that Shoulders fella would lay in the bottom of my landing net. Realistically, though, Wraysbury offered me the best choice of venue and I decided that before the season was over I'd pop over and have a look around. Just the mere mention of Wraysbury conjured up a picture of hallowed ground on which only the fully accomplished or terminally insane angler would dare tread. After Steve's departure, there was little point in trying to grab any kip as the Friday afternoon deluge had begun and before long Keith appeared clanking his way along the bank, his barrow laden with lager topped off with a smattering of fishing tackle and, I hoped, a substantial amount of food.

We celebrated grandly that evening and the weather even allowed us to sit out under the stars and swap tall stories until, eventually, I had to crawl off to my bed exhausted. At some unearthly hour the next morning, I was wrenched from a wonderful sleep by the incessant drone of a bite alarm, and eventually realising that it must be mine, I stumbled, bleary-eyed, out into the real world to deal with it. For some strange reason that I had no explanation for, I had no trousers on and stood there freezing my nuts off in the wind as I played the fish in toward the bank. Eventually, when I was shaking too much to hold the rod steady, I tried to dress myself with one hand while keeping some carp control with the other and, as a result, the fish managed to gain the refuge of the Weedy Bay to my immediate left. The weed in the bay was of the totally and utterly solid as a bloody jungle variety, and it resisted my entire repertoire of ruses and dodges for extracting snagged-up carp for at least an hour. It didn't help that for some reason my bottle seemed to have well and truly gone and I was shaking uncontrollably. Eventually Del and Keith arrived in the boat to lend a hand, and Chris Haswell also wandered along to help. After yet another hour had passed, we were no nearer a conclusion so, putting in to shore again, I made some tea and toast while we figured out a new plan of attack.

The thing with weeded fish is, no matter how long it has been since any movement has been felt they are nearly always still on the end, and I for one refuse to give up until a broken line or empty hook give me no other alternative. After all, the hardest part has already been accomplished by getting him on the end in the first place. So who cares how long it takes to land him? It may be weeks or even months before another chance comes along. After a total of three hours had elapsed, Del remembered an old rake that lay behind the fish huts attached to a piece of metal conduit fully twenty feet in length. Armed with this new found

Good times - the crew at Horton.

equaliser, we set sail once again. Tony Badham and Del steered the boat, while I fished around in the weed next to the line with the rake. After a few minutes a large clump of weed floated to the surface and to my absolute horror the rake tugged in my hands before starting to pull slowly through my fingers. Obviously, I had snagged the line and now the fish had decided to make a move. With only precious inches of pole remaining, I managed to disentangle it and grab the rod again, but the fish was still heavily weeded, although I could now clearly feel some degree of movement. Turning the rake upside down, I pushed the handle deep into the silt under the weed and and by levering off the boat I lifted an entire weedbed up to the surface. The lead was in full view on the top but the line snaked down through the weed and away in another direction so, after freeing the line, we set off in pursuit again. We eventually discovered the fish close to the bank in the thickest weed at the bottom of the bay and, by mooring a few yards away, I was able to gently coax him to the top. The second that he broke the surface we all knew what I'd hooked. If my bottle had gone earlier then it shattered into a thousand pieces as I saw first the hump and then the unmistakable shoulders of my ultimate carp, waddling across the bay toward the net! Painfully slowly he came, inch by inch, my obsession grew nearer and nearer, and as he allowed himself to be enfolded into the mesh it was like an injection of pure adrenalin coursing through my veins. The rush of relief and ecstacy was overwhelming and I roared my delight across the lake. Oblivious to the fact that we were still in the boat I leaped about like a wild thing, as Tony slapped me on the back and almost shook my hand off in congratulations.

I had done it at last, whatever that first lost monster three seasons past had been I'd definitely got my own back in full. Shoulders had been the one fish that I'd wanted from the very start and it had taken forty three captures to get him, but now after all that he was mine. I phoned Phil, as he was about the only one not already present, and he turned up in time for the photo's clutching a bottle of champagne. For the record, Shoulders weighed in at forty pounds and twelve ounces and made me the happiest man alive.

It looked now like a visit to that hallowed ground of Wraysbury may well become a reality, but I was content to fish the rest of the season out on Horton albeit from a very laid-back position. A couple of weeks later, I even managed to sneak out one last fish for luck, when I recaptured Starburst at twenty seven pounds.

It had been my first and last fish of an incredible season in which I banked twenty one carp and he made a fitting end to my time at Horton.

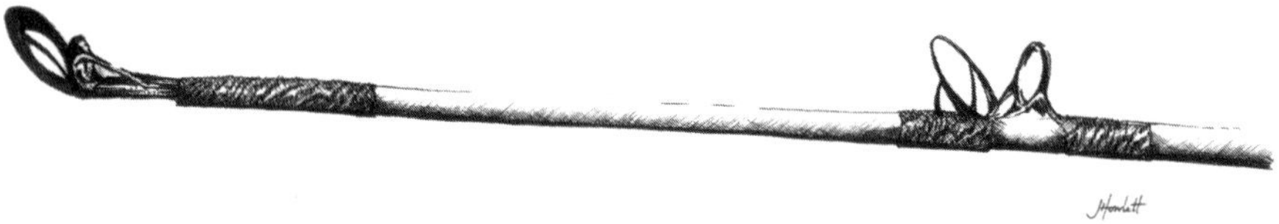

Chapter 8

Wraysbury

My first look at Wraysbury came in March 1994 on my way home from a session at Horton. I knew that realistically, this had to be my last season on Horton as I had finally realised my ambition in the September of that year with the capture of Shoulders. I had enjoyed my time at Horton immensely, but it was time to move on. The big question was where? I wanted somewhere that I would have a chance of catching fish comparable to the stamp of those that I had become used to in Horton. Also, the lure of an unknown carp had started to draw me. Somewhere a little bigger and quieter would be nice, and Wraysbury fitted all of these requirements perfectly, at least, in my mind's eye it did.

My first look at the place was little short of frightening. I had parked my latest edition to the ever lengthening list of old bangers outside the Wraysbury Sailing Club gates on Welly Road. It was a tatty old Datsun van that eventually cost me two cylinder head transplants before following his predecessors up to the scrap dealers. Now, according to the Leisure Sport guidebook that I clutched hopefully, these gates should lead on to a small peninsula that split the lake into 'North' and 'South' lakes on either side. I walked through the small pedestrian gate and wandered up the track with Fatty in tow. Immediately, I thought that I'd got the wrong place. If this was a peninsula, where was the other side? Surely it couldn't be a hundred yards wide, could it? I checked my three inch square map again, for all the use it was, but it seemed to suggest that I was in the right place. I tried to put it all into some form of perspective. If this vast area of land in front of me was represented by that little squiggle there, and the forty acre piece of water on my left was the little puddle marked down here, then somewhere over to my right must be a chunk of water big enough to constitute an inland sea! I followed the track further down to see what horrors awaited me.

Although I had never set eyes on the Dredger Bay before, it was instantly apparent that I had arrived there. After all, no matter how big the lake was, there could only be one swim that housed a twenty five foot long, half submerged, rusting hulk of an old gravel dredger. I had seen some horrendous snags in my time but this one really took

SUNNYMEADS CORNER
BUS STOP
CIGAR ISLAND
THE LAWN
DOG WALKERS PATH
NORTH LAKE
SPRINGATES POINT
GRASSY POINT
TURFS
ROCKY BARGE
THE GAP
SAILING CLUB
STILE
SECRET REEDY
DIVING BOARD
OFF LICENCE
GIANTS FOOTSTEPS
HOOLIGAN SWIM
WRAYSBURY

RAILWAY TRACK
DOCTORS
RAILWAY LAKE
THE POINT
PLATEAU
WHITE FENCE
ROOT NIGHTMARE
CAR PARK
DOUGLAS LANE
BONSAI TREE
SOUTH LAKE
MAD DOGS
HUT ISLAND
BRYANTS BAY
BRYANTS POINT
SAILING CLUB
THE BAR
ANT HILL ISLAND
THE REEDS
CARP BAY
FOOTBALL PITCH
TO THE PUB and THE CHINESE
MARYS POINT
SWIMMING POOL
CESS PIT

One hell of a snag! The Dredger Bay.

the biscuit! Behind this, through the gaps in the islands, I could see glimpses of the larger South Lake. Some of these 'glimpses' seemed to go on in one direction for a frightening distance. Once again I consulted the map. Had I really only got to there? Walking off to the right of the Dredger Bay I came up against the fence that housed the sailing club's grounds. From this vantage point I could see a vast area of water dotted with islands. Far out in the middle of it two large blue boats of the inboard engine type were being tossed about like toys in the swell. Proper North Sea-style waves complete with white froth were testing their dubious moorings to the limit. Surely you were more likely to drag in a cod or turbot from water like this, not a serene old mirror carp? The far bank seemed miles away and massive bays cut even further into the shoreline. Following the perimeter fence, I emerged into No Carp Bay. A bay at Wraysbury is a fair sized lake at most other venues! Climbing up onto the root structure of an old fallen tree I could see down through the amazingly clear water. Dotted along the bottom of the marginal shelf I could clearly make out the shape of an old Vespa scooter and a bit further out, the obligatory shopping trolley. Further down into the bay was no better either, four oil drums, a pair of tights and an old boot adorned the bank side, I had made up my mind, I was going home!

I thought about Wraysbury an awful lot over the next week or two, it was the obvious choice of venue for me to fish, but that first look had been enough to shake any man's resolve. I remembered back to the first time that Keith and I had set eyes on Harefield, and how intimidated we'd been then, but how we eventually came to love the place after a time. I knew that this too could be true of Wraysbury. I had to return, I couldn't be beaten with just one look. So, after another unsuccessful Horton

January on the Causeway. Inset: funny looking carp! Dave catches a 32lb pike from The Lodge steps at Horton

It's not just about catching fish, it's about being there.

trip, I once again stopped off at Wraysbury on my way home. This time I'd decided to try the South Lake instead, but unfortunately the weather was even worse than before and the gigantic north-westerly gale that lashed its surface did nothing to satiate my original assessments of the place.

During the close season, and as the weather improved, I decided once more to attempt to come to terms with Wraysbury. Phil Thompson had expressed a desire to join me if I was seriously 'up for it' and this obviously softened the blow. I do very much enjoy fishing alone, but a companion and an ally on a pit of this magnitude would be a blessing. The day I picked to return could not have been nicer. The sun shone down and the wind held off. I met up with Phil on the banks of what seemed like a totally different pit to the inhospitable monster that I remembered. We decided to take a stroll around the entire pit, I don't think either of us realised at first quite what this entailed. Most of the paths were overgrown with brambles and fallen trees blocking your way at regular intervals, it was obvious that a set of secateurs and a saw would be of benefit in the coming weeks! Even if the paths had been clear it would still have taken us somewhere in the region of three hours! About halfway round we spotted a couple of carp. They were only backs breaking the surface at distance, but that was all the encouragement we needed. Our little strolls around Wraysbury became more and more regular and when I went on my own, I would often pick an area and explore it in more detail. We read all the available literature about the lake, which amounted to very little, and bent poor old Pete Springate's ears until they bled, extracting from him every last grain of information.

Oil drums adorned the bankside.

The problem when writing about Wraysbury, knowing it as intimately as I now do, is that it is all too easy to fall into the trap of assuming that the reader can visualise the scene the way I can myself. The reality, however, is that unless you have walked the banks and can summon up a picture of certain areas at will, the mind's eye picture that you paint for yourself will bear little resemblance to the original. Therefore, in this chapter I'll attempt to set the scene for the rest of the book by taking the reader on a walk around this vast and historic pit, pointing out as we go areas of interest, past and present, and hopefully add to the enjoyment of the chapters to come.

Imagine, if you will, that we have just turned off the M25 motorway at junction 13, a few miles shy of Heathrow airport. This would instantly become apparent due to the incessant roar of the planes overhead. We are making our way through the village of Wraysbury, driving past The Perseverance pub (a more aptly named retreat for anglers I'd be hard pressed to imagine). Eventually we come to Douglas Lane, a residential street of somewhat dubious notoriety, which leads into the Wraysbury complex. I say 'complex' as, although Wraysbury One is technically one piece of water, it has been split 'metaphorically' into two parts, the North and South Lakes totalling one hundred and thirty acres in area. Heavily wooded around most of its banks, it twists and turns through numerous bays and thirteen islands. The fish, all twenty or so of them, have no barriers and can come and go at will, switching from North to South Lakes as and when the fancy takes them. The Douglas Lane is situated on the southern most part of the South Lake, a large grass car park provides ample parking for anglers. The first swim we come to is actually in the car park and is known affectionately as the Root Nightmare due to the hideous tree roots poking up through the ground which make setting up here a very uncomfortable affair indeed. The view of the South Lake that it provides, however, makes it a favourite first stop for many anglers. The water here is deep, dropping off to eighteen feet or more in places. At the far side of the swim, some one hundred and fifty yards distant, are the chain of

The enormity of Wraysbury from The Root.

three islands that separate the Dredger Bay from the rest of the South Lake. As we look out to the left, we get an impression of the real enormity of Wraysbury. The huge middle section of the lake stretches out for hundreds of yards before us. Only three swims can fish into this area, and some of the better spots are one hundred and fifty yards in any direction from the nearest one. Turning on our heels and walking back down to our left we circumnavigate Bryants Bay. This twenty acre bay is backed on two sides by the gardens of the houses in Douglas Lane. As a result of this, the trees in this bay have been decimated by the residents, in order to give them a more scenic view from their kitchen windows. None more so than by Dutch Bloke who lives in a small bungalow halfway down the bay. Although, technically, the residents are not even allowed access on to the lake, this man has made it his mission in life to raze to the ground any tree, bush or shrub that dares to stand between him and his vista.

The water in Bryants Bay is probably the deepest of any of the bays, although not as deep as local legend would have you believe. The stories of a sixty foot trench running the length of the bay, bear no more relation to the truth, than the myth surrounding a certain six foot long pike, said to patrol the bay in search of hapless swimmers or lone geese.

The bottom of the lake is broken up by a liberal scattering of large lumps of concrete or 'ironstone'. These boulders, some as large as twenty feet long by ten feet high, can give the impression, whilst plumbing, of an ideal gravel bar for placing a bait on. In reality, they are absolutely useless for angling purposes, being far too sharp and unforgiving for carp to feed on. The third side of the bay is formed by Bryants Point which is a long peninsula jutting out into the centre section of the lake. The main swim is situated on the extreme end of it and is the obvious spot for fishing the middle of the South Lake. With the aid of a boat, some of the otherwise unfishable bars can be covered from here, and in strong winds and low pressure the carp can often be found out there in the wilderness. It's also only a short walk across the football pitch behind, to the pub and the Chinese take-away which is obviously a bonus. Returning to the base of the peninsula, we set off away from the bay, past the football pitch to a small secluded swim jutting out on a small point opposite a large island. This swim also offers you a shot at the middle, albeit at very long range. This coupled with the overgrown island, which at its closest point is a mere thirty yard chuck, should in theory make it one of the top swims. However, theory is an unreliable beast at the best of times, and as far as I know, there has never been a carp caught from this swim.

Following the contours of the lake we find ourselves once again doubling back around a large bay, not as impressive as Bryant's however, this one is a mere six acres in size and is well known as the Swimming Pool. In my humble opinion this area is, (contrary to popular belief) one of the poorest areas in which to angle. In my time on the pit, only one twenty pound common was landed from here. Apparently, in days gone by, it had considerable form, but nowadays you're far more likely to find it populated by the local kids than carp. In the summer they are present in large numbers, chucking each other in the water by day and holding the battle of the car stereos by night, around a blazing fire, as often as not constructed using the tyres of the loser's car.

We make our way via a treacherous path around the bay (don't forget to hold your nose as we pass the cess pit!) Ignoring the small point that only looks back into the Swimming Pool area, we hasten on along a hundred yards of bank hidden to us by thick trees and bushes, until we reach the infamous Mary's Point. Ducking through a small opening in the bushes brings us out on a bivvy-sized spit of land. If the water level was up another foot we'd be paddling! We are now situated at the eastern end of the South Lake. To our right we look through the gap in the islands one hundred yards away at the distant form of the car, parked in the Douglas Lane four hundred yards or more in the distance, from here we can see the lake stretching on past the car park down into the Railway Lake, although from here a bivvy would appear as a tiny green dot. Directly in front of us at twenty yards is a small island. When the water is low you can wade out to it, and beyond that at just over one hundred yards away on the far bank is the the Wraysbury sailing club. Many a line has been cut whilst fishing on this point by over enthusiastic and under qualified yachtsmen and I'm sure abuse isn't the only thing that's been hurled as a result. The general depth is twelve feet but there are a couple of shallower marks that stay reasonably clear of weed, in the summer months. When the weed is at its worst there are only three fishable spots in the entire three acres or so available to you. Off the right hand edge of the close island are two marks that can produce takes. One is a small clear area under the tree branches, and it is better known as Mary's Table. I think she has been caught twice from there and the legend was formed! One

Mary's Table.

of these captures has been well documented, being half of 'Sir' Pete Springate's famous brace.

A police diver searches No Carp Bay. . .

To the left and forming the end of the South Lake is an area known as No Carp Bay. This fifteen acre bay is directly left as you stand on Mary's Point. In fact the swim and the island lie across the mouth of the bay. Legend has it that the carp rarely, if ever, visit this area but we were to find out that this, like so many other Wraysbury legends, bore little resemblance to reality. A small round point is situated at the extreme bottom of the bay, from this swim you can look straight up the middle of the South Lake through the gaps in the islands to the Railway Lake. This is an awesome sight with approximately three quarters of a mile of lake in front of you! Now that is a long cast! The ground here shows little or no signs of attention from anglers. The bottom of the lake here is like an egg box with little humps and bumps rising up at assorted depths all over the place. It also has the disadvantage of being the swimmers' second most favourite spot in the summer. If the Swimming Pool is full they all crowd around to here! They swim out to the sailing club to steal boats and then jump up and down in them until they sink, only to swim back out there and steal another one!

Around to our left is another little point that bears testament to the regularity of non-carp angling visitors during the summer. The ground is permanently littered with beer cans, various articles of clothing (none of it worth keeping) and bits of old boat half burnt on a big fire. A tree swing sends screaming kids at the rate of one every five minutes plunging into the margins. And one fine evening I had all my tyres slashed here as well so all in all it's an interesting place to angle! This is the first swim on the peninsula that forms the divide between North and South Lakes. It is probably in the region of two hundred

. . . and bags himself a new jeep!

yards wide in places and a dirt track leads from the entrance gates at one end to the sailing club at the other and then ultimately to the Dredger Bay. A large percentage of the lake can be viewed from this peninsula. Apart from No Carp Bay and the Dredger Bay we get to look along the length of the Finger Bays and behind us lies the North Lake most of which can also be seen from here. I have already described this area so we'll cut straight across the base of the peninsula and on to the North Lake.

The corner nearest the gates is well littered with the cast-offs from neighbouring civilisation, old washing machines and tyres pepper the bottom. The large bay here, is formed by the two large islands one hundred yards out into the lake, and are known as The Giant's Footsteps. This is due to the series of gravel humps that stagger their way around the margins, as if left by the tread of some mythical monster. This, like a lot of the names given to the different areas were created by Phil or myself in order that we would have a 'point of reference' when discussing the pit. The bank here is very close to the road and not angled in much as a result, but as the road and lake part company we come across two very popular spots. The first of these is The Bend or Behind The Off Licence, and in the past some good catches have been made from here. I believe that Mary among others has fallen to baits fished tight under the larger island. The second is The Style and home to Dave Cumpstone's historic winter brace. Walking across the lawn of the Nat West sailing club we pass The Turfs and make our way down toward Sunnymeads Corner. This is essentially the shallows of Wraysbury and the area where Phil and I had seen most of the fish so far. Along the Railway Bank at the bottom (The North Bank) the water is only a few feet deep and it is here that the fish come, under the safety of the close season, to bask in the sunlight and warm water. No significant catches (that we knew of) had occurred in this area, but as I've said we knew very little at this stage. Past the Bus Stop and behind the Cigar Island we arrive on an open area of lawn.

The Gap.

The Lawn.

It looks for all the world as if it's been regularly mowed, but the droppings of rabbits and geese that liberally cover the area, give the game away. In the height of summer, and with no shade, a man can fry in no time out on this area. The last swim on the shallows is The Point, and a large plateau extends from the end of it before the bottom plummets away into twenty feet of water in front of the Rocky Barge. An old gravel carrying barge that used to drift at will, has finally come to rest in the bushes to the right of the swim. The area of bank beyond this is totally overgrown with only one other swim on the end of this large spit of land that separates the North from the Finger Bays. The resulting channel of water, known as The Gap, is the fish's route from North to South and being only twenty yards wide offers a very handy short cut in a dinghy when heading for this section of the lake. The bays actually start out as one strip of water fifty yards in width and split at the end into two small pools. It can be like walking onto a different lake as you come into the bays, the weather always seems that much warmer due to the shelter of the surrounding trees. Fat Sam always becomes decidedly frisky at this point and rolls around on her back on the short grass. It can be very hard not to linger for a while in this comparatively tranquil spot, and take in its own peculiar atmosphere. At the bottom of the smaller bay lies the Tench Tree and, when sat within its branches, large tench and the occasional carp can be seen to glide happily through its root structure. Back around the bays and through a small wood we emerge onto The Party Point. We are now back in the 'South' and at the very bottom of a large semi-sheltered area we call the Railway Lake. Half a dozen swims intersperse the heavily wooded bank that stretches all the way down to the

Douglas Lane Bay. Although not a renowned area for captures, the sheer aesthetic beauty of this bay in summer makes it a noteworthy section of Wraysbury. As we come to the end of this, the Railway Bank, only one large point stands between us and our place of origin, this is the Douglas Lane Point. An incredibly popular spot to angle from, it gives access to two of the main islands and a large shallow plateau, and has a track record of producing good catches of carp over the years gone by. A large tree that sprouts from the end affords the climber an excellent view of the plateau and any fish that may be present. Leaving this point behind us we pass the few remaining car park swims and return to where we set off from a mere three hours previously!

Looking back from Douglas Lane Point.

Chapter 9

The Start of the Campaign

As often as not, as part of the normal daily close season routine, even when we found fish in Sunnymeads or the Finger Bays, we would finish the day with a quick tour. By the end of the close season we knew an awful lot more about the fish and their habitat.

Certain characters kept appearing within the crystal clear waters especially around the Sunnymeads area. One group of three fish were spotted regularly, two of these appeared to hold no place in the Wraysbury legends and even Sir Pete was unsure of their existence. Two of the fish were comparable in size and we put their weights at around mid-thirties. The known one was a linear mirror, short and dumpy in appearance, its last capture was an incredible eleven years previously. The other thirty, also a heavily-set fish, we christened The Pug and we could find no record of any previous captures. Both of these Wraysbury monsters, however, palled into insignificance when joined by the third and mightiest of the trio. This enormous carp whose smooth sides gave the impression of a leather carp, was a clear ten pounds bigger than his two amigos. Surely a fish of these stupendous proportions would be well documented even in a pit as large and daunting as this? But no record of his ever having been caught could we find. The only possibility lay in a capture twelve years previously of an upper twenty pounder that Chris Ball had taken, on a bottom bait for a change. This was only a maybe, and the fish we were seeing this close season, was considerably larger now. We often saw the big known fish such as Mary and Mary's Mate along with three or four more, well publicised mirrors. Steve Allcott informed us they were known as Mary's Gang and they had constituted ninety percent of all captures at Wraysbury over the years. We watched and fed these impressive beasts all close season and eventually, after what seemed like an eternity, the new season was upon us.

We were under no illusions about the carp sticking to their close season areas for long, and our strategy for the season was based on mobility. We planned to be doing an awful lot of walking, but for now I was determined to secure one of the areas where we had spotted and fed the fish during the close season. Phil couldn't get down until the first day of the season, but I arrived about twenty four hours before the 'off' and carted my tackle around the North Lake to the Lawn Swim. A couple of other anglers were drifting about and there seemed to be some confusion as to exactly when you could set-up camp, I decided the best plan was just to set-up and worry about the finer details later.

The weather was ideal for the shallows and a couple of fish could be seen cruising around the area in front of me. To say I was confident would have been the understatement of the century. Shortly after setting up camp Pete Springate arrived. Apart from being a friend from Horton he was also the head bailiff. He had no qualms about my early arrival and that was good enough for me, in fact, he had enough tackle with him to secure a swim for himself. We sat on the edge of the lawn with our feet dangling above the water and chatted for a while. Well, I chatted in a very thinly veiled interrogative-style whilst he tried not to give too much away in the true 'cat and mouse' style of anglers throughout the ages. One thing that I did want to clear up, was if there were any major no no's in the rule department at Wraysbury and was told, to my delight, that only two rules applied. One was always wear a life jacket, (unless of course you didn't happen to be in a boat) the other was that there was no fishing from any of the islands. Anything else it seemed was alright as long as common sense prevailed.

This suited me down to the ground as rules had never exactly been my strong point. More times than I care to remember I have fallen foul of the jobsworth bailiff. Every lake seems to own one, the sort of bloke who dreams of becoming a traffic warden or car park attendant. "You can't park there mate, that's reserved that is." You know the sort.

As we sat there a fish made its way slowly along the margins to our right, disappearing for a while only to reappear directly under our feet. It was no more than a foot from the bank and paraded tantalisingly in front of us for a few minutes. It was the Short Fat Linear, and we set about guestimating its weight. Pete was convinced it was near forty pounds, but I still couldn't give it more than thirty six or seven pounds. I assured him that we'd know the truth soon enough, even though it had eluded capture for the past eleven years! I had fed him all close season and set up right on top of him today. Surely my name had to be firmly emblazoned across his armour plated flanks? What of his two friends The Pug and the massive Leather? I'd lay money that they were not very far away either. Pete set up next to me on The Point, and throughout the day more and more anglers appeared from out of the woodwork. By the time the season was ready to begin the North Lake was packed!

I had mixed emotions that first morning when I awoke, although I'd heard a fish crash out of the water in front of me during the night. The sight of all those brollies put me off a bit. I'd seen next to no one all close season and really hadn't expected it to be this busy. The more I looked out at the scene, the more I began to feel 'trapped' in my little corner, cut off by all the other lines stretching out across the pit. Phil had started the season according to our main game plan of mobility, and by the time he arrived in my swim around mid-morning, had covered a high percentage of the lake. He, like myself, was appalled at the number of anglers present and despite Pete's constant assurances that by the third week, "They'll all have buggered off, never to return," we were still sceptical. Phil's tour had not been totally without event, he'd spotted a couple of fish at the very bottom of Bryants Bay in the South Lake. Apparently there was nobody fishing anywhere near them, Phil was game and asked if I wanted to join him and, after a bit of deliberation, I packed away my gear and thereby initiate the first and biggest cock-up that I was ever to make at Wraysbury!

In retrospect, I was just too eager to instigate our plans of total mobility. I'd seen a fish crash out and I'd fed carp here throughout the close season and that should have been enough to make me stay put, but it wasn't, and I was soon set-up at the bottom of Bryants Bay with Phil. We had no action in the bay, and the next day one of the other anglers wandered round for a chat and took great pleasure in breaking the bad news to me. After I had left the Lawn Swim, Del Porter had moved in and caught his first Wraysbury carp, it weighed thirty six pounds and was none other than The Pug. A few days later, he took his second fish from this swim as well The Short Fat

Tall thin Del with the Short Fat Linear.

Linear, also at thirty six pounds! At least I knew my guestimations of weights were accurate, even if my location was a bit off! After having fed these two fish, among others, in these swims all close season and then having fished and moved from there only days earlier, it felt a bit strange to be photographing somebody else holding them! It was nice to see them on the bank anyhow. Del was obviously over the moon having tried for two years to bank a Wraysbury carp and well deserved his result.

After a brief visit home later in the week I returned on the Friday evening all set for another crack at it. As I pulled up in the Douglas Lane car park, I came across Phil on his way back from the chip shop. He told me that he was already set-up on the point at Bryants Bay. He was all excited and told me about the fish that he'd been stalking earlier in the day at the bottom of the bay. Mary had been there along with several of her friends and showed some interest in Chum Mixers. After a bit of 'thrashing' with a floater rod they had eventually moved away and Phil had set up here, on the end of The Point, hoping to intercept them on their way back into the bay. I decided to set-up nearby on the side of The Point and start the session off on a social note. After helping to alleviate Phil's blatant excess in the canned lager department, I eventually tottered off to bed. The night passed without event and in the morning I wandered back down to Phil to relieve him of any other surplus provisions that he might be carrying about with him, such as tea, biscuits, bacon

Mary - it emptied Phil's spool.

sandwiches etc.. It must have been his lucky day though, as before I could make any serious inroads into his supplies, we were distracted by our first Wraysbury occurrence.

When faced with a piece of water in front of you which is approximately the size of Wales, most people would be tempted to cast, at least a reasonable distance, out into the pit. Phil in his own inimitable style had decided to 'cast' one rod about six inches from the bank and the other a good two feet. It was this 'long range' rod that had burst into life! Due to its close proximity, I thought at first that a tench or even a water vole may have picked up his single Grange boilie, but it became apparent very quickly that Phil was in fact attached to a monstrous great big carp. Phil's tackle is, quite simply, a bloody joke and in no time at all practically all the line on his old Mitchell 410 had been dragged out into the lake. Luckily, the fish went to ground a few yards short of a total disaster and then steadfastly refused to be budged. After a while, I was dispatched back to the car park to fetch the inflatable dinghy. Apparently during my absence the fish had started moving again, and had indeed emptied Phil's spool, to the extent whereby he had to grab the line above the knot and hold on for dear life! By the time I arrived back with one inflated boat and two seriously deflated lungs, Phil had managed to get the fish quite close in but a large clump of weed was preventing him gaining any more line so I shot out in the boat quickly and removed

Spawny git!

this latest obstacle. The fish, realising that he was almost beaten, tried the age-old trick with the overhanging bushes and came damn close to succeeding! But we were made of more determined stuff and loading Phil into the boat, I waded out up to my neck pushing the boat in front of me. With Phil in a better position (and me up to my nostrils in muddy pond water) the rest of the battle continued and despite Phil apparently trying everything he could to lose it, the fish was finally beaten, and rolled into the net. As Phil clambered out onto dry land he passed me the net to hold and on looking inside I could instantly see which fish he'd landed. We'd both seen and caught a fair few very big carp in our time but nothing can ever prepare you for your first glimpse of Mary. The largest carp in the lake and indeed the whole land, lay there, crammed into the bottom of Phil's manky old 36" landing net. This was without doubt a pretty impressive way to open our account at Wraysbury, and at an incredible forty nine and a quarter pounds it was going to take a fair bit of celebrating. I was just glad that Phil was paying!

The very next week, as if to prove that he wasn't just a 'spawny git', Phil caught the highly impressive Mary's Mate from a tiny swim at the totally opposite end of the lake near to Sunnymeads Corner. Thirty eight pounds of pure muscle, heavily laden with huge golden scales along its copper coloured flanks. Was I jealous? Bloody right I was! Things were starting to look good for us at Wraysbury or at least, they were for Phil. I had fished long and hard from the start of the season and six weeks in, had only been absent for about three days in total. We had been putting in a lot of work walking around the pit looking for signs of fish, quite often twice a day, and Fat Sam was starting to look a little less statuesque as a result. It was all a long way from the frying pans and free biscuits of Horton. The area where Phil had caught Mary's Mate from was along the Railway Bank of the North Lake and true to Pete's prediction had been practically devoid of anglers after the first couple of weeks of the season had passed. In fact the whole lake had started to settle into a routine, whereby the same few week-enders would appear on a Friday afternoon and, come Sunday evening peace would descend over Wraysbury once again.

The Railway Bank constitutes the shallows of Wraysbury on both the North and South lakes and during the early part of the summer the fish were often to be found along this bank. As a result, we ended up spending a fair amount of time along this stretch. Although the train line runs along a mere twenty yards behind you, it's only a branch line to Windsor and apart from commuter rush hours, it remains nice and quiet for most of the time.

I don't envy those commuters on the Windsor line one little bit. Not just because of the fact that they are trudging to and from the same old job every day, although that must be bad enough. No, the worst part of their working day must be the hideous sights they are forced to endure through the train windows on the journey. The

Windsor line runs along the banks of many of the lakes in the lower Colne Valley. As a result, the hapless train traveller gets an early morning glimpse into the lives of any number of dirty, smelly carp anglers, none more so than the occupants of the 8.32am at Sunnymeads station one sunny July morning. I'd been struck down with the need to visit the bushes at very short notice and was, let's just say, at a very delicate stage of the operation. I heard the train slowly approach, and, thinking I was concealed within the copse of trees, I just sort of crouched a bit lower. I risked a quick glance as the train crawled past, and to my absolute horror, I found myself staring straight into the eyes of one very perplexed-looking commuter. The train was only travelling at a brisk walking pace and it was packed! It was too late to run for it, so I just stared at the floor, praying for the ground to split open and suck me into the chasm, all the while I could feel the eyes on the train burning into the back of my neck. . .

On another occasion, a red hot afternoon later in the summer, I had carried all my tackle almost a mile from the South Lake, and by the time I arrived at the Railway Bank on the North Lake, I was drenched in sweat. The sun was beating down relentlessly and my clothes were soaked. I stripped off down to my pants in an attempt to cool down, but as soon as I did so, a marauding band of insects charged in for the kill. I tried beating them off but there were far too many of them. Like kamakazi pilots, wave upon wave of mozzies tried to systematically drain me of blood. I rummaged through the rucksack, dragging out an old net curtain that I usually hung from the brolly ribs as a mosquito net at night. Still dressed in only my underpants, I draped the net curtain over my head and by stooping slightly it almost reached the ground. I was gasping for a drink, so in this strange position I shuffled up along the bank to where I'd left the water. Half way there, and in the most exposed part of the bank, along came the homeward bound office train. I had to snigger as I saw the totally bemused, and with some, almost petrified looks on the faces of the commuters as they trundled past. I wonder how many reports of a ghost on the Windsor line, that little caper started?

Although I put in maximum effort throughout this time, the fish always managed to stay one step ahead of me, but Phil did manage to wheedle out another one from the Railway Lake on the South side. We'd been for a walk around the pit in the morning and found nothing but I was determined to find the fish before setting up. So, after a brief rest, I set off for another tour. As luck would have it I didn't have to walk overly far, just around to a small swim on the left of the Rocky Barge area of the North Lake. We were about a month or so into the season and, neither Phil or myself had seen a fish actually leap out of the water as yet. Cruising fish and the odd roll had made up the bulk of our sightings up until now. Standing there squinting against the sun looking over towards the island, a great mirror carp rose from the depths about fifty yards away. It appeared in silhouette form against the dazzling backdrop of the sunlight reflecting surface. I stared in mute disbelief for a moment at the spreading ripples, before setting off at a flat out run back to the car park to collect my tackle. Phil was still standing in the car park chatting to another couple of anglers, and as everybody seemed to be looking for a place to fish from I thought it wise not to say to much. So, trying my hardest to hide my excitement, I gave Phil the nod and told him to meet me near the Finger Bays. I figured that once he got there he'd be able to work out my exact location. Throwing everything into the barrow and dragging Sam out from under the van where she'd curled up and gone to sleep, we set off again.

I'd noticed over the previous few weeks that most of the old hands at Wraysbury tended to rely heavily on the boat to place their baits, and up until now I'd thought this to be a bit of a strange move, especially when a lot of the time they were fishing well within casting range. In retrospect, if I'd been equipped with a boat that day I'd have probably stood a very good chance of hooking my first Wraysbury carp. As it was, I spent the next three quarters of an hour maniacally whipping the water up with a marker float in a futile effort to find a clear spot on which to present a bait. It was the first time that I'd ever really come across the milfoil type of weed. I'd thought I'd seen it all at Horton when fishing in beds of Canadian pondweed that reached the surface in sixteen feet of water, but that was mere child's play when compared to a forest of milfoil. When casting out a new marker float into this sub-surface jungle that the North Lake became, there was no guarantee that you'd ever see it again and even if a spot was found, any stray cast with a rig could end up in a total re-tackle. Apart from being a complete wind-up, it could end up being bloody expensive as well.

Just as I'd reached the stage where I knew that I'd well and truly blown my chances with all the disturbance that I'd caused, Phil popped his head through the bushes at the back of the swim.

"Can you give me hand?" he asked "I've got one on and it's stuck in the weed, I think we're going to need the boat."

I was totally flabbergasted at this piece of news. As far as I knew he wasn't even angling! I'd wondered what had been keeping him as I'd expected him ages ago. As we ran around to the Railway Lake he told me how, while looking for me, a carp had very obligingly leapt out practically at his feet and, even more obligingly, it had instantly taken the bait that he had dropped in - no more than two yards from the bank. On feeling the hook, the fish had apparently shot out into the middle and become solid in weed. Nothing had changed on our return, so whilst Phil took charge of the rod, I ran around to the car park for the boat. By the time I reached the car park I was totally shagged-out. So far that day I'd walked one and a half circuits of the lake and then ran back another half for my gear before pushing a fully laden barrow half a mile. I'd fly fished for an hour only to end up running all the way back to the car park again. The worst unfortunately, was still to come.

I pulled the dinghy out of the van and attached the electric pump to the battery. "At least this will be easy," I stupidly thought as I pressed the 'on' switch. Ten seconds later, a tortured squeal and a puff of blue smoke marked the demise of the pump.There was unfortunately, only one option left and that was to blow the damn thing up by mouth using what little remained of my lung power. By the time that I'd finished, I felt like Jim Carey in that film 'The Mask' when his eyes and his heart simultaneously pop out from their moorings as if on elastic. Once again, I found myself rowing across Wraysbury on a mission of mercy. What a mission it turned out to be! The milfoil out in the middle in front of Phil was equally as thick as it had been in my swim, and a total of another hour was spent chasing the fish from one weedbed to another. Defeat of course, was never an option, and eventually the carp conceded to this irrefutable fact and waved the white flag as he slid into the waiting net. The sun, seemingly disinterested in the result of our titanic battle, had knocked off for the day shortly beforehand, and we rowed back to shore under the long shadows of evening. Of course, I made Phil row back as it seemed only fair. On the bank, in the company of Tench Bloke and a couple of dubious-looking territorial army types wielding rifles, I helped Phil weigh and photograph a pristine mirror carp of thirty seven pounds and ten ounces, before collapsing in total exhaustion into a catatonic heap of uselessness on the ground.

The next morning, I decided it was about time that I visited my home, as for all that I knew I could have been evicted weeks earlier. I'd also reached a stage where I

A pristine 37lb 10oz mirror for Phil.

needed to recharge my batteries, as it were, and create a new strategy for the rest of the summer. I wanted to remain mobile, but carry with me, at all times, anything that I may need which had to include an inflatable boat and a diving mask, to overcome the horrific weed problems that were increasing by the day.

I was gone for a mere twenty four hours, but during my absence Leisure Sport in their infinite wisdom, decided to stock some small mirrors into Wraysbury. About twenty fish around the two pound mark were introduced via the Douglas Lane car park, two commons of ten and fifteen pounds had also joined them on their journey to this, their new home. The commons were easily identified through scale damage that had apparently occurred when they jumped out of the holding tanks at Horton onto the gravel! Twenty four hours after the introduction of the fish and at the opposite and windward end of the lake, the first fatality was found. The dead mirror washed up in Sunnymeads and, to everyone's amazement, was totally encased in fungus. Now, unless it had contracted a super fast acting, Martian wasting disease, which is unlikely, serious questions had to be asked about the condition of these fish when they were stocked. As we stood there discussing the matter, King Harold as he is affectionately known, and his troupe of four Dobermans came bowling along the bank and, without the slightest hesitation the larger of the four jumped into the margins. It picked out the rotting fish, and swallowed it whole! Over the next few weeks at least eight or nine more 'stockie's' were found, all in a similar condition and as such the remaining few were christened 'The Fungus Mirrors'.

The Army type and his mate made regular appearances, and, as it turned out, they were a lot less intimidating than at first they appeared. The Shootist, as he soon became known, lived in the Douglas Lane, his garden backing onto the lake, and every Sunday he, and any one of an assortment of like-minded, camouflage-clad nutters, would disappear into the jungles of Wraysbury for a frenzy of lager soaked genocide.

Chapter 10

Mallin's

The fish that Phil had caught from the Railway Lake had turned out to be the same one that I had been drooling over during the close season, having found a picture of Dave Mallin holding it in Big Carp publication at the Horton lodge. In fact, until I'd set eyes on the Leather, I'd nominated it as the one fish that I'd most wanted to bag out of Wraysbury. I was sure, though, that one day our paths would cross and I had all the time in the world to make sure that they did.

We were experiencing a few problems with the Fungus Mirrors, mistaking them at range for bigger, 'proper' carp. At times, when they were bow-waving it was almost impossible to differentiate. It always amazes me when people can apparently size fish in the water, especially at any sort of range as I seem to regularly come a cropper in this department. I firmly believe that to make a fair estimate of a fish you must first observe it at very close quarters and for a considerable length of time. It also helps considerably if a fish of a known weight can provide a point of reference to compare it with.

Shortly after Phil's capture, I was installed in a swim known as The Doctors on the Railway Lake. It was a scorching hot day and a few fish could be seen cruising about on the surface about fifty yards out. Twenty yards out in front of me a large weedbed peppered the surface with small yellow flower heads, and damsel flies darted to and fro across its green facade. Just on the back of the weed, a foot or two below the algae mottled surface, I could make out a large humped back and dorsal fin patrolling back and forth, reluctant to break from the cover of the weed. After firing a few Chum Mixers beyond the weedbed, I scrambled up a spindly little tree that adorned the bank to watch and wait in anticipation. Every time the baits would drift within range of the fish, he would casually reposition himself into a different location, never spooking from the Mixers but never showing any particular interest. As the day grew hotter, he rose steadily into the more oxygenated upper layers until his back occasionally flashed in the sunlight as it broke the surface. The hotter the day grew the more I suffered as a result. There was precious little shade available, and so engrossed was I in our game of cat and mouse, that I neglected to see the skin on my shoulders turning a bright crimson, I even grew oblivious to the constant worryings of midges and gnats. Eventually, after three or four hours of artfully stalking my prey, he left the sanctuary of the back of the weed and risked a passage along the margins in search of some shade. As he passed within a few feet of where I stood, I could clearly make out the form of a bream of about eight or nine pounds in weight. A bream! I'd spent all day stalking a bloody bream! I laughed until it hurt, before packing up and walking slowly off in the general direction of the Perseverance.

My next session commenced in early August and, after a good look around, Phil and myself decided that the Finger Bay area would be as good a starting point as anywhere. Phil had been baiting up a small bar in Poet's Corner over the last few weeks so he started in there. I preferred a swim at the other end of the bays by the gap that leads through to the North Lake. From here the bays lie in front of you and just a few yards behind is a small swim that we'd named The Rockets, that looks out into the North Lake. As there is very little to see in the bay, whenever I fished there I'd usually end up spending most of the time staring out from The Rockets hoping for a rare sighting to inspire me.

Having just acquired a new boat, I decided to row all my gear, and the fat dog, across the gap from the van, thus cutting out half a mile of walking. The boat was a collapsible affair made of aluminium tubing and oiled canvas roughly held together with flexible garden hose. Apparently the army had once used them and this one definitely looked as if it could have been through a war. Probably the First World War. Oars were, as always, in short supply, so I had to be content with anything flat that I could lay my hands on. In this instance a bait bucket lid and a frying pan, but the main problem turned out to be that the boat leaked like a sieve. It was never in danger of sinking due to a large polystyrene buoyancy chamber in the centre that doubled as a seat, but it had a permanent pond in the bottom of it soaking everything that it carried. Even after a small journey like this I had to lay everything out across the grass to dry out and Sam's soaking wet fur was plastered all over her formidable bum. Once across the gap and with everything dried out, I set up camp and strolled, like the lord of the manor, around my little peninsula.

The Finger Bays are a truly beautiful place to spend time in, especially when the trees are in full bloom and the hawthorn bushes are flowering. With such a secluded piece of water in front of you it's very easy to forget that you are fishing in one small part of one hundred and thirty acres of water. As is often the way, though, when I fish in here, by the time the morning came creeping around I'd had enough of seclusion and the limited view so, taking my tea making kit and low chair, I settled in to the small swim behind to watch and wait. Sam contented

Mallin's and Fat Sam gets in on the act.

herself with half heartedly chasing rabbits for a while, before creeping off under a bush to curl up for her mid-morning nap. I was just beginning to nod off in the morning sun myself, when suddenly through half closed lids, I saw a fish roll over in the Diving Board swim half way along the far bank to my left. I couldn't be sure that it was a carp, but a few minutes later, I was left in no doubt, as a large mirror carp launched itself skywards in the same spot. In two shakes of the fat dog's tail, I was all packed up and ready to go. As I loaded the kit into The Sieve, I noticed somebody else also packing up their tackle from the Little Stile on the far side of the North Lake, and I prayed that he wasn't heading for the same spot as me. I popped round to Phil's swim to tell him what was happening and while I was there the angler from the Little Stile turned up and informed us that he'd just caught Mary at over fifty pounds! For some strange reason he was now going home, having achieved what he came to Wraysbury for in the first place. A lot of people seem to approach Wraysbury with this bounty hunter approach, almost as if there was only one carp worth catching in the whole pit but, from the fish that I'd seen so far in my short time here, I knew that this was far from the truth. Some of the more elusive smaller fish already held a far greater allure as far as I was concerned. Don't get me wrong. I'm not saying that I did not want to catch Mary - I did - and passionately at that. I also wanted to catch all the others as well, especially the ones that had not graced the banks with their presence for ten years or more! It was with this in mind that I found myself rowing across the North Lake to the Diving Board swim with all my tackle, and Sam, bobbing about in the deepening puddle in the bottom of The Sieve.

After the fiasco with the weed a few weeks earlier, I had already planned my strategy should I be fortunate enough to see another fish jump in the North Lake and, after dumping off all my gear in the swim, I set my plan into action. I tied up a couple of fixed markers and, digging the face mask and some baits out of the van, I set off to find a gap in the forest of milfoil that I knew covered most of this area. After rowing half way out to the large island that dominated the swim, I triangulated my position using the Rocket Swim and Diving Board as markers and when I was fairly sure I was around the area that the fish had showed I put on the mask and stuck my head over the side into the water. The sight that I saw beneath the boat will be etched onto my retinas for the rest of my days. Six bloody great big mirror carp were circling around no more than ten feet below me! I could see every scale and marking on their gargantuan bodies and I almost capsized the boat at the sight of them. I didn't have a clue what to do now as the bottom below them was absolutely solid with weed, but I thought that if I searched around for ages in search of a clear spot to fish I'd probably end up spooking them off. As luck would have it, as I reversed quietly out of the area keeping my face under the pond, a gravel hump with a large sandy area on the top loomed up out of the weed below me. It was only a short way from the fish so I quickly dropped a marker and tipped a saucepan full of hemp and tigers over the top before sneaking off back to the shore. Positioning the baits went surprisingly smoothly and within an hour of moving, I was all set-up and, for the first time that season, fishing bang on 'the money'. Phil had also moved around to join me and was set-up on a small point down to my left and, throughout the next few hours we counted, incredibly enough, at least seven more fish showing in the general area that I was fishing. As is always the way in these situations, I tortured myself with all the usual doubts and fears about tangled rigs and the wrong bait or should I be popped-up, or do I put more bait in and countless other apprehensions. Eventually it grew dark and, as we sat in my swim eating curry, we could still hear the occasional splash resounding from out in the lake. By the time the next morning arrived, and the fish were still showing, I'd practically worn a trench into the bankside from pacing up and down in frustration, I knew that I wouldn't get a better chance than this and I could see it all slowly slipping away from me. Finally, when I could take no more torture, I decided to re-cast all the rods putting long pop-ups straight off the lead and to drop them into the weed in the vain hope that they might be presented just above the top of it. The problem was that I knew the weed to be in the region of ten feet thick over most of the swim! Turning off the alarms, I picked up the first rod and pulled it off the clear bar but, after only a few yards it became solid in weed. It was so solid that it took a quarter of an hour just to drag it all in to the bank where a huge forest of milfoil surfaced like the creature from the Black Lagoon. As I stood in the margins trying to rip it all away from the line, the spool on the middle rod clicked twice against the clutch. I could see that I hadn't tangled the line and, reminiscent of the old Jaws movie, the clutch clicked twice more before bursting into life as the spool spun furiously. Screaming to Phil that I was in, I swept the rod high over my shoulder and the fight began. Phil arrived in no time and before long it was apparent that The Sieve would have to be launched. After all, it had taken fifteen minutes just to land a two ounce lead let alone a very angry and unobliging carp! I took up position at the front of the boat and handed Phil the oars, explaining that the plate worked better on the right and the frying pan on the left! Resigned to the fact that I was never going to be properly equipped for anything, he took the proffered kitchen utensils and paddled us out to the weedbed. I was desperate to land this, my first Wraysbury carp, and although Phil kept assuring me that there was indeed no other option, it still took us the best part of an hour to coax it out of one weedbed after another. At times, a big grey mirror would roll on the surface tantalisingly close but always just out of reach. But, true to his word, Phil eventually scooped up my prize as I steered it alongside the boat and I screamed my victory cry across the pond. At last the ultimate trophy was mine! I'd dreamed of catching a Wraysbury carp for years and now, at last, the dream had become reality, and to make it even more special it was Mallin's! The one fish that I'd wanted the most! I'd vowed that our paths would cross one day, but I hadn't thought that it would be so soon after Phil's capture. We were soon to realise that this was the way at Wraysbury. As Steve had said, twenty percent of the carp made up ninety percent of the captures. The scales read thirty six and a half pounds, but even if they had said sixty six I couldn't have been happier. I drove straight over to Horton to fetch all my old mates, even little Robbie deserted his gear and came over for the spectacle, and there was much slapping of backs and shaking of hands, ring pulls popped all around me and at last I really felt that I'd arrived. There was certainly no shortage of budding David Baileys as I laid out the foam matting for the photo's. Fat Sam took her cue and curled up right in the middle of it, so we took a few brace shots before I waded out and gently released my first Wraysbury carp back to its watery home.

I stayed on in the Diving Board for a few more days, but the fish had obviously done the off after all the commotion with the boat. I packed up and set off for home brimming with confidence for my next session. Unfortunately, the journey home was just the first in a catalogue of disasters that seemed determined to keep me from angling. It was almost as if Wraysbury operated some form of pay back system. For everything good that it may allow to happen, you were forced to endure ten times that amount of pure and unadulterated crap in return. Aside from the head gasket blowing apart on the return journey, and then me crashing Keith's car on the way back from towing mine home, I found out that, due to a technicality, I wasn't even insured to drive it in the first place. This left Keith with one very badly bent motor and me with no bloody motor at all! It took a week to rebuild the top end of mine using an old cornflake packet, and a strategically placed one ounce lead hammered into a little hole that I could have sworn wasn't there when I took it apart. As if that lot wasn't pay back enough, over the next month at Wraysbury I had my new bite alarms swiped from my swim in the Rocky Barge. Then I had all my tackle stolen out of the motor, having only left it unattended for ten minutes while I shared a cup of tea with Phil! My boat, The Sieve, was stolen from its hiding place in the bushes. Just to add insult to injury, my replacement boat sprung a leak in the middle of the South Lake one evening, thus marooning me and Sam on an island for twelve hours! All the while I kept reminding myself that I had managed to bag one Wraysbury carp and if I could put up with all this rigmarole then eventually I was bound to get another one.

The insurance company eventually, after much hassling, replaced my fishing tackle (but not Keith's car) and yet another inflatable boat was purchased. I also invested in yet another cheap old banger from Honest John's Second Hand Motors, as the one ounce lead had unexpectedly melted on the old van, letting out all the oil and consequently blowing up the whole cylinder head!

So, by the time that I was once again fully equipped for angling, the summer had drifted away and the rain that had been absent for so long returned with a vengeance, only this time it had brought all its mates with it.

Chapter 11

Cluster's last stand

It had been raining cats, dogs, and various other domestic pets for days and I sat there staring at the teletext 'weather guess' page hoping for a break in the conditions. Tomorrow, they said, would be changeable, only they were not overly explicit about what it would change into. Figuring anything must be an improvement, I set about boiling up some hemp and packing loads of dry clothes for a few days angling.

Early the next morning, I loaded up the new motor and set off. Stopping off at Keith's house on the way, I dug two bags of The Grange bait out of the freezer and hightailed it up the M25 through the changeable weather! The windscreen wiper was going like the clappers - the other one had dropped off the day before. I made quite good time really, considering this latest mode of transport. It was a dilapidated Volvo 245, a fifteen year old, sold as scrap, estate car or was it 'a state' - probably the latter. An array of multicolored warning lights flashed relentlessly on and off - oil warning, brake fluid, automatic transmission fluid, blown bulb warning - they all vied for my immediate attention. What it really needed was a carbon monoxide poisoning warning light as the exhaust was in a terrible state. The whole thing sounded like a tractor and looked like one. Hand painted very badly in farmyard green, it sported the very latest in spiders web-effect windscreen, the most badly cracked part being held together with an out of date tax disk, and a small ivy garden adorned the back window sills. I must have made at least 20 miles that day before my first breakdown. I was getting used to all this by now, so I calmly pulled over to the hard shoulder and set about the ritual kicking and twiddling of anything under the bonnet that looked vaguely familiar. Eventually I coaxed it back to life and finally arrived at the Douglas Lane car park, in a cloud of steam, about midday.

The weather was still changeable (pissing down), so on went the waterproofs and off I set towards The Point swim, this gave a good view of the Railway Lake without actually having to go round there and get drenched in the process. By the time we reached The Point the poor old carp dog was soaked to the skin and, even in waterproofs, I wasn't far behind. The bushes were doing a good impression of a car wash and it didn't take long to make up my mind that a drive in swim would be favourite for the first night, and I'd save the walking around for the morning if it eased off a bit. Opposite the Douglas Lane is the Dredger Bay, which I considered to be worth a try. I could see the dredger from here but not the swim so back to the Volvo it was and off we set. To get there from Douglas Lane involves leaving the lake altogether and driving back through the village, out the other side and up Welley Road to the sailing club, then it is just a matter of getting out in the rain, unlocking the big double gates, driving in, getting back out in the rain to lock up and driving down past the sailing club to the bay at the end of the peninsula. The whole affair covers about a mile and a half and takes in the region of a quarter of an hour, only to end up 250 yards, as the fish swims, from where you started! There are two swims in the bay, the left hand one is set on solid concrete ten feet above water level and offers the shallower water, being only two or three feet deep by the left hand ten acre island, and generally six or seven feet deep over the rest. The rusting old hulk of the dredger marks the middle of the two swims and the bottom slopes away from it into fifteen feet at the deepest point under the right hand island. The large round central island forms the back of the bay at 100 yards and is fishable from both swims. It was the deeper side I was heading for and luckily nobody was in there. In fact, thinking about it, I realised I hadn't seen a soul during the whole journey. The swim itself is a spur of hard ground about four feet higher than the water and just big enough for a car and a bivvy to tuck out of sight on. Reversing in around the adjacent bushes could be a bit tricky in the wet, as the sides of the swim slope away quite quickly into the pond. Today seemed to be exceptionally dodgy, and, as I backed in, I felt the wheels start to glide away towards the edge. Sticking it into drive, I pulled forwards for another go. At least that was the intention, the reality however was that the back end spun round and, with a sickening lurch, the green demon's left hand wheels dropped straight off the edge. It was like the closing scene in that film The Italian Job, where the coach full of gold bullion teeters on the edge of the mountain road. I didn't mind too much if the motor ended up in the drink as long as me, Sam and the fishing tackle stayed up here in the comparative dry of the pouring rain, so I gingerly climbed out and assessed the damage. It wasn't too bad, one wheel was in mid-air and the other one was up to its axle in mud and brambles, but it wasn't in any danger of an immediate departure into the lake. In fact, it didn't look as if it was in any danger of departing anywhere at all for a while so, dragging out my gear, I set about making camp in the Dredger Bay for the night.

By the time I'd got everything set-up and ready to cast out, I was starving. I'd got no food with me as I had been planning on driving up to the Chinese later for dinner but that didn't seem a very realistic option at the moment. Still no one had turned up so, eventually, I settled for a walk in the still unchanged weather, up to the off licence.

By the time I got back I was soaked to the skin, and clutching a dinner of peanuts, chocolate and lager, then after chucking the rods out I climbed into bed to polish it all off. My sleeping bag was about the only dry thing left so, cursing the weatherman one last time, I drank myself to sleep.

The first thing I noticed in the morning was the weather. At last, the 'changeable' had arrived, and the sky was blue for the first time in an eternity. The second thing that struck me was the sound of laughter. I stuck my head out of the bivvy and found Tench Bloke admiring my parking skills. Between us we spent the best part of the morning with car jacks and bits of wood, bricks and rope but only managed to bury the two remaining wheels further into the mire. Towing it out wasn't an option as T.B's 650cc Nissan van couldn't even pull the cork out of a bottle of wine, so we drove over to Horton and enlisted the help of Keith and Reg. After suffering the ritual of piss-taking and manic belly laughter, I soon had an Escort van and a V.W estate firmly lashed to the front with ropes. An old sign bearing the legend 'Wraysbury sailing regatta and open day' was broken up and rammed under the wheels to provide a bit of grip, and on the count of three and the waving of an old tee shirt Reg and Keith revved up and shot forward. Onlookers scattered in all directions, as pieces of plywood spun through the air threatening to decapitate the less nimble. Great plumes of liquid mud sprayed around the clearing, covering the windscreen of the Volvo as I sat inside, knuckles white on the steering wheel, waiting to be jettisoned to freedom. Nothing moved. I stuck my head out of the window to see what was going on only to receive a face full of mud for my trouble! It soon became clear that more serious measures were needed. The ground around the vehicles looked like the aftermath of the battle of the Somme. You could barely stand upright on it let alone tow a car through it, so it was a quick trip to the nearest farm to wave a tenner under the nose of the tractor driver. I even got a ride back in the tractor! The farmer turned out to be a mate of Phil's from way back and was most obliging. He had the good grace not to laugh as well, although I could tell he was dying to. He made it look so easy, one heave and the Green Demon was back on dry land. I thanked him again and off he went along with Keith and Reg and the assorted onlookers. Eventually just Tench Bloke and myself were left, I decided to pretend that the last 24 hours hadn't really happened, so we started off on a walk to find a couple of nice dry mud-free swims to set-up in. We left the gear locked up in the cars, under the watchful eye of a fellow angler further back along the peninsula, and set off around No Carp Bay sloshing through the mud as we went. In the same way that a group of carp sometimes act as if possessed of a single mind, veering off in tight formation to feed under a certain bush, so Tench Bloke and myself veered off in unspoken agreement across the football pitch and straight into the public bar of the Perseverance.

After the rain and the mud of the last twenty four hours, not to mention the

The Angler's Retreat.

disasters with the car, the warmth of the log fire and still settling Guinness told me that we'd definitely made the best choice of swim. As Fat Sam curled up next to the fire, I decided this was the perfect opportunity to speak to Tench Bloke about my radical plans for the coming week. Although, throughout most of my time on Wraysbury, any thoughts of work had been put firmly aside in favour of the unhampered pursuit of my obsession, on occasions, as the year wears on and the bills mount up there comes a time when some form of gainful employment becomes unavoidable. It was this harsh reality that had led to me agreeing to undertake a few days work, sticking up coving on a housing project in Chelsea. The hardest part was going to be convincing Tench Bloke into labouring for me. I waited until the third pint had taken effect and popped the question. After the initial shock had worn off and the shaking and dribbling had subsided, he eventually agreed. But, just because we'd got a bit of work to do didn't mean that we couldn't still fish the nights, so we set about finding a couple of swims off the beaten track where it would be comparatively safe to leave the bivvies during the day time. After a lot of deliberation we opted for the far bank of the North Lake. T.B set up in the Rocky Barge and I cut myself a new swim a bit further along the bank. At the time there was no path to my chosen area, just dense bushes and old fallen trees, so the first day was spent hacking a path and chopping out the swim. There was a strong easterly wind blowing into our faces the whole time, keeping the temperatures well down on the normal October conditions. In fact, a good welder could have taken a fortune off the brass monkey population. Cutting the swim didn't present too many problems, the main hurdle was a large tree trunk complete with top branches that had fallen into the margins. It was far too heavy for just Tench Bloke and myself to drag out, but far too dodgy to leave it in there. Wading in to remove it definitely was not an option either but, then, just as we were wondering how the bloody hell we were going to shift it, into the swim strolled a big strapping German chap.

"I am coming all zee vay from Germany to be seeing Wraysbury," he announced. "Vot are you doing viz dat tree?"

I instantly translated that as, "I've flown twelve hundred miles to help you drag that tree out of the margins."

So it was that, an hour and a half later, the offending tree was neatly sawn and placed across the front of the swim. While off through the bushes staggered one German chappie, soaking wet, covered in mud, slime, and Wraysbury weed! It goes without saying that we never saw him again! That night we put the stockpile of fallen dead trees and cleared undergrowth to good use by building a massive bonfire in the shelter of the Finger Bays, situated just behind us. Spuds were wrapped in silver foil and poked into the embers. We even tried cooking garlic bread but it came out so cremated that even Fat Sam rejected it. There was so much spare wood in need of disposal that before long we were seated a good twenty feet back from the flames just to avoid scorching.

The next morning (Sunday) the fire was still glowing cherry-red as we set about adding the finishing touches to the swim. By lunchtime we'd built a lovely little spot fairly well hidden in the bushes and just big enough for one bivvy. The water came almost to the door, making getting in and out a bit tricky, but we were soon both set up in our respective swims and ready for work the next day. The plan was to get up at six in the morning and stash the rods and alarms in the bushes before driving off to London to work. This meant leaving before light and returning after dark, which was a bit of a grind, but at least we were still angling. The first couple of days went pretty much according to plan apart from the traffic which was an absolute nightmare. Fat Sam wasn't too keen on spending most of the day in the car either, but I promised her a big slap up feast come pay day. By Wednesday, we'd both had more than enough of queuing for miles just to get into work, so we devised a master plan. As we were living on the lake anyway, it didn't really matter what the actual time was so, by moving our clocks forward an hour or so, we could beat the traffic in the mornings and get back before dark to cast out. The security guard on site thought we'd lost the plot when we turned up at quarter to six in the morning to start work, but by three thirty that afternoon we were whipping the water to a foam back at the lake trying to get the baits positioned before dark. The swim that I'd made had an island lying across in front of it at about ninety yards, so I put one rod out on each side of this with single hookbaits.

The third was fished on a small bar thirty yards out over a scattering of free offerings. The Easterly wind was still blowing hard so, after dinner, it was off early to bed and into the comparative warmth of the sleeping bag.

Now, an alarm clock is not a normal part of my fishing kit. In fact, I don't usually even have a watch, but I'd managed to borrow a travelling alarm clock especially for this week. It was all still a bit of a shock though, when, at some unearthly hour of the morning, its relentless bleeping dragged me reluctantly from the land of dreams and into the real world. I scrabbled about with one hand under the bed until I found the offending article and shook it into submission. I still hadn't figured out exactly how to turn it off properly. It had one of those snooze button things that just allows you time to drop back into a blissful sleep before waking you up all over again. I lay there freezing in the wind that was piling through the broken doorway, and the last thing I wanted to do was to get up and go to bloody work. I'd just covered my head with the sleeping bag against the wind when off went the clock again, bleeping incessantly. I snatched it up and shook it furiously but it was more determined this time, even bashing it on the ground wouldn't shut it up. Pulling wide the door with one hand I was just about to launch it out into the darkness, when I saw the LED glowing on my left hand rod. It was one of the two rods that I'd cast up against the side of the island a hundred yards away. Even then it took a few seconds to sink in to my sleep-addled brain. I looked accusingly at the clock and then back at the rod which was bleeping away merrily as something out there in the darkness pulled tentatively at my string. Hurling the offending clock into the back of the bivvy, I launched myself out of bed. I wound down and swept the rod back over my shoulder but met with only a pathetic resistance from the other end and I decided straight away that a tench was the culprit. My feet were absolutely freezing and I realised that in my haste, I'd overshot the mark and was standing up to my ankles in the icy cold margins wearing only my socks, and all for a tench! This was only the second bite that I'd had since catching the thirty six pounder two months previously, and the other one had also turned out to be one of the red-eyed demons. Unceremoniously, I winched the fish in towards the net, but as I got him within thirty yards of the bank he started to struggle a bit, sending up small swirls to the surface and I wondered if maybe a small common might not be responsible after all. A few slightly larger swirls later and he was in the net. You could have knocked me down with a feather when I peered in and saw a considerable expanse of mirror carp laying there in the mesh peering back at me. I couldn't believe the size of it after such a nondescript fight, I knew it was well over thirty pounds as I hoisted him ashore and laid him on the mat. I searched around in vain for my torch which I must have lost the night before somewhere. Looking at the fish in the half light, I thought at first that I'd re-bagged Mallin's fish, which would have been a bit of a blow to double up on only my second capture. However, on closer inspection, it turned out to be a fish known as Cluster and he was obviously thirty five pounds plus. Waking Tench Bloke up turned out to be more of a struggle than landing the fish but, eventually, after promising him the day off work, he staggered from his pit and put the kettle on before wandering down to view my prize. Even the wind had started to ease, and on the horizon clear patches streaked the dawn sky. Later that morning, the sun broke free from its cloudy confines so we carefully carried the fish out through the back of the swim and into the Finger Bays to do the photo's and weighing. At thirty six and a half pounds he looked absolutely magnificent, and in the little bursts of sunshine in the shelter of the bays it was almost like a spring morning. We knew deep in our hearts that working for a living was going to be a very short lived affair and somehow throughout the course of the day, we managed to convince ourselves that we'd finally stumbled across a few fish in feeding mode, and that a big catch was on the cards.

The lake however, held a different view and, as autumn drifted into winter, I sat expectantly behind motionless indicators. It wasn't all doom and gloom though, as Phil managed to bag a brace of Wraysbury mirrors out of the otherwise unproductive Finger Bays in November. After sitting in the same swim blanking for two nights something possessed him to stay for a third during which he managed to extract The Hoover and Mary's Mate at thirty five and forty pounds respectively. An incredible result for Phil and, if you ever get to see the tiny little swim that he extracted them from, I think you'd agree that it was no mean feat landing them both either. As I said, the next few months passed by without event for me, from a catching point at least, and it was February before I once again bent a Wraysbury rod in anger.

Cluster waddles off.

Mallin's goes back to the depths.

The sun goes down at Wraysbury. Inset: Cluster.

Diving Board island at Wraysbury.

Chapter 12

Mary

Winter fishing seems to have become progressively harder over the last few years. Just why this should be so I'm not sure but it definitely seems to be the case. As a direct result of this, every winter for the last few seasons, my friends and I have embarked on 'The Winter Tour'. Making full use of all the invitations that we've received throughout the summer, we trot off to various waters all over the country in pursuit of that rarest of creatures, a winter carp.

This year, as indeed every year before, we were singularly unsuccessful on every water we fished. All excepting, that is, Jacko who, in an unprecedented display of fine angling, managed to extract not one but two winter carp from two different venues on The Tour. Thereby he elevated himself to the status of Winter Specialist practically overnight. As is usually the case with The Tour, the enthusiasm started to dwindle by about February and, one by one, we drifted back to our main waters.

So it was, then, that the first week of February found Phil and myself back down at Wraysbury for a brief session on the North Lake. We saw nothing of note, and decided on a move into the South Lake for our next visit, next weekend, which started on Friday the 10th February. By coincidence, it also happened to be the leaving date of one of Phil's work colleagues, so it came as no surprise when he eventually staggered along four hours late! I'd decided, after some deliberation, to fish on the end of Bryants Point as, from here, I'd be able to get at the middle section of Wraysbury. Although, technically, Wraysbury has quite a few different 'middle' areas, the piece of water in front of Bryant's Point is the largest single expanse and the area in which I'd convinced myself, the fish were hiding.

Jacko - the winter specialist.

Unfortunately, during our winter's absence, the level of the lake had risen a good three feet, which had effectively turned the swim that I fancied into a small lagoon! Apart from the floods, conditions were perfect with heavy overcast skies and rising temperatures. Not a breath of wind rippled the surface in front of The Point and I was determined to fish at least one rod out from there even if I had to wade out to do so. There is a small swim to the right of the swim, only a few yards away but on higher ground, so I set up camp in there and fished my other two rods back into the bay. The rod on the end of The Point was cast out about forty yards to an area that I'd fished earlier in the year. This was not a bar as such, but more a strip of hard bottom amongst silt. It took a few casts to get it on target. The first couple landed 'soft' and I retrieved them covered in decaying weed. The third, though, went down with a satisfying thump. I fired out twenty or so baits around the spot and then paddled out into the flooded swim to push the banksticks in and set the alarm. The reel that I was currently using on this rod was one of my trusted old Cardinal 55's, but, due to an earlier accident, the handle had snapped off. I'd 'fixed' it by pushing a long 4mm diameter bolt through the hole and, by loading this up with nuts and masking tape, created a new handle. It looked a bit 'iffy', but it did the job.

I was still using The Grange bait, having been assured by Steve at Mainline that it would perform as well in the colder water as it had in the warmer months. A 1oz running lead with a long nylon hooklink completed the set up. After getting the rods and bivvy sorted out, I set about preparing a dinner for myself and Phil, who was due along at about half past five. Or so I thought!

By ten o'clock that evening, I'd just about given up hope of Phil turning up, and Fat Sam could sense another dinner looming. I was sat in my dome tent, wondering where the hell he'd got to, when a pair of legs appeared in the bivvy doorway. As I watched, they swayed briefly before suddenly disappearing sideways in a perfect parody of a drunken hermit crab. I clambered out of the bivvy in time to see a rather inebriated Phil picking himself out of the bushes. Grinning inanely, he apologised for being late and proceeded to wolf down the stone cold dinner that I'd prepared for him hours earlier. Sam was less than pleased as she'd been praying to it non-stop the whole time. After a cup of tea and a smoke, Phil decided that he'd got it together enough to set up his house in the swim directly behind me and off he staggered like a new born giraffe. I sat and watched him struggle for a while, giggling to myself, before wandering over to help.

We'd just pushed in the final peg when a short burst of bleeps rang out from my swim. I looked over and saw the LED on the lone rod, on the end of The Point, glowing happily to itself. It was obviously a bird picking up the bait, wasn't it? After all this was Wraysbury and it was the middle of February! The short burst was replaced by a single tone, an absolute screaming run from hell. All thoughts of birds flew out of the window! I legged it over to the rod, splashing through the mire as I went, and struck into what was obviously, but nevertheless still unbelievably, a fish. The rod wrenched over and, as line was torn from the reel against a protesting clutch, all I could do was hang on and shout repeatedly at Phil.

"I've got a bloody carp on the end. It's February, we're at Wraysbury, and I've got a bloody carp on the end."

The fish, I think, must have been as surprised as I was, as it seemed determined to put as much distance between himself and me as possible. On its first run it must have taken at least fifty yards off me before I managed to slow it to an eventual stop. The next trick up his slimy sleeve was to kite around into the bay to my right. The swim was totally flooded and, as a result, the bushes that would normally form the side of the swim were twenty feet further out into the lake than I was. As he charged into the bay, I could see the line cutting through the surface, getting closer and closer to the outermost branches. Seeing no other option, I paddled out further into the freezing cold flood water in an attempt to keep it clear, but to no avail. A horrible grating feeling transmitted up the line as the unseen monster pulled my line deeper into the bushes and, although it was only snagged a few feet from the rod tip, no amount of persuasion would free it. The fish was still eighty yards of line in credit, and I was now not even sure exactly where? A bit of a stalemate situation had occurred, as the fish no longer seemed to be moving and neither did the branches. The only option left was the big heave. I was confident of the line as I'd dragged it through worst snags than this before, so I piled on the pressure and, with a crack, the branch gave and the rod sprung back over my shoulder. There was slack line everywhere and at first I was convinced the fish had gone but, winding frantically and cursing as I did so, I eventually came back into contact with him forty or fifty yards straight out in front of me. He must have kited back out of the bay while the line had been

Nuts and bolts and masking tape.

snagged and was now in a much better position for me to land him from. I think the fish must have known that the game was up as well. His efforts became less and less determined and, without further ado, I had him swirling under the rod tip. Phil paddled out to hold the net as I coaxed him up and over the cord. We hadn't seen the fish at all yet but when Phil struggled out of the water and passed me the net we knew straight away what we'd bagged. There could only be one fish that enormous and, sure enough, as we shone the torch in the net, there lay Mary. Even though I had seen her on the bank before I was totally blown away by the sheer bulk of her. It was hard to believe that it still classified as a carp.

Now, at the time there had been a lot of talk about the possibility of Mary breaking the record of fifty one pounds if anyone was lucky enough to drag her out in the winter. We knew Pete Springate was fishing on the North Lake and thought that we'd better get him round to witness the weighing (just in case) and, anyway, regardless of the weight I knew he'd like to see her on the bank again. So, after Phil had shot off on a brief sortie and returned with Pete in tow, eventually everything was set. I'd lashed the scales to the bough of a tree making double sure of my knots. In fact, I even swung on them first to be on the safe side! Out of the sack and into the sling it went, a truly massive and incredibly impressive fish, the needle raced around the dial settling, after a brief shudder, on forty nine pounds and fifteen ounces. It was hard to take it all in, at this time of year the last thing you expect is to suddenly be holding a fish of this magnitude, but here we were nevertheless. Mary and me at Wraysbury in the middle of winter! I sacked her up carefully for the night and stuck the kettle on. It was going to be a long night. As soon as it became light enough to see my way, I floated on a cushion of air over to Horton to break the news. Trying (unsuccessfully) to conceal a smile the size of Wembley stadium I sauntered up to my old mate Jenkins and said, "Wind your rods in, fella, I've had a little bit of a result." Robbie was there as well and between the two of them they almost patted and shook me to death.

Thinking back on it now, I can't remember who gathered the other photographers and, to be perfectly honest, I can't really even remember who they were. From the moment that I unzipped the sack that morning I was oblivious to everything other than that carp. Blinded by the aura that seemed to exude from every pore of this majestic yet formidable beast, I was aware of nothing else, not returning her to her home, nor watching her glide back into the depths. I was totally numbed by the whole experience. A few days later, it finally all sank in. I felt like running out into the street and yelling at total strangers, "I've caught Mary you know, and in bloody February!"

After the pub, I probably did!

Even without the capture of Mary I'd had an exceptional first season on Wraysbury, but obviously the biggest fish in the lake in the middle of winter really was the icing on the cake, and a perfect end to a perfect season. Just before the season was due to come to a close, news came through that this year due to a change of legislation, there would be no close season after all. I can't say that I was exactly in favour of a total open season for angling, as I firmly believe that the carp and their surroundings need time to recover from the abuse that we as anglers, put them through during the course of our pursuits. Nevertheless, I was certainly not about to stage a one man protest in opposition to the nationwide abolishment of the close season and, if everybody else was going to be angling this spring, then you bet your last quid that I'd be there beside them!

I was aware of nothing else - Mary on the mat.

Chapter 13

The Shootist Helps Out

Throughout the winter, I'd been unwilling to go out afloat on the lake. I reasoned that an inflatable dinghy was no match for the vast expanse of freezing cold wind lashed water that Wraysbury in winter offered.

However, on one cold dark evening in March, as I was sitting around a fire in the Finger Bays chatting to The Shootist, it came up in conversation that he owned a solid fibre glass rowing boat. Now, not being backward at coming forward it wasn't long before I'd procured the use of it for the coming year as, apparently, he only used it for rowing out to the islands on the occasional Sunday evening. Once there, he'd hide up a tree and shoot anything stupid enough to come within range of his laser-sighted air rifle. It seemed like a pretty strange pastime to me. Although I suppose, sitting by a lake for months, hoping to catch a fish and then chucking it back seemed, like a pretty strange pastime to him too. By the time he left, he'd given me a spare key to the back gate of his house, and permission to use the boat as often as I wanted.

His garden backed on to Bryants Bay, making it a piece of cake to drive up to the Douglas Lane car park, unload the van straight into the boat and row to anywhere I chose. This new found method of transport could, realistically, cut out all of the walking and humping of tackle and have the added bonus of being stable enough to stand up in. This meant that, by drifting around with Polaroids on, I could explore the weed beds and bars that were out of normal viewing range and I was looking forward to learning a lot more about Wraysbury in the very near future. Hopefully, though, I wouldn't need it throughout the spring as I was planning on some close up stalking work before the weed got bad enough to warrant using the boat. It was nice to know that the days of faffing about with inflatables were behind me now, although I didn't realise at the time quite how useful the solid boat would be over the next two seasons.

Chapter 14

Encounters and Captures in Sunnymeads Corner

Fishing throughout the old close season took some getting used to, and the first thing that we noticed was that it wasn't as much of a walkover as we'd first thought it would be.

Reports from other waters seemed to confirm the fact that, after the feeding spell that most lakes go through at the end of the old season, there was a noted close down of activity. It was always assumed that the short burst of action throughout the first two weeks of March was only brought to an end by the untimely cessation of the open fishing season, but it now seemed as if the fish, rather than coming out of 'hibernation', were just having a much needed scoff up before disappearing again to wait for the onset of warmer weather.

By mid-April the only action so far had been one small stockie common from Bryant's Bay that I'd taken a few weeks earlier and, although the weather had been fairly mild over the previous couple of weeks, we were still waiting on the first real hot spell of spring. The telling temperature usually seems to be around twenty degrees, this is often the first real showing of fish as they gather in the shallower waters, enjoying the sunlight and rapidly rising water temperatures. One of the top areas on Wraysbury for this early 'show up' was the extreme northerly most point of the lake, this area is known as Sunnymeads Corner, due to its close proximity to Sunnymeads train station, and was the area where we had seen, and fed, a lot of big old mirror carp last close season. The big difference this year though was, due to the abolishment of the close season, we were to be allowed to angle for them.

The weather forecast assured me that by lunchtime the temperature would hit twenty or twenty one degrees, so I spent the morning charging about like a lunatic, trying to get everything done in time to get down to the lake before anybody else thought of climbing the tree overlooking Sunnymeads Corner where, I had totally convinced myself, the fish would be. The problem was that, although I knew there were only two anglers on the pit at the moment, I also knew that they both knew the score. Visions of Tench Bloke, or Phil, sat in Sunnymeads surrounded by big fat mirror carp haunted my every moment until, finally, I could take it no longer. The list of chores I'd been working on all morning was screwed up into a tiny ball and launched across the room. I grabbed the rods, bait and dog, and legged it before the bloody phone rang again with yet another hurdle in the race for a carp. Along the motorway I drove like a man possessed, which is exactly what I was. The closer I got the hotter the day was getting, and the more paranoid I grew about someone's butt being parked in Sunnymeads. When I'd left the lake a few days earlier Phil was just getting settled in for a week's fishing, the area he had chosen to start was only a few hundred yards from Sunnymeads and, given the weather, I was sure that he would wander up for a look.

I pulled up by the Nat West sailing club and only Phil and T.B.'s cars were there so, loading up my tackle on my back, I half walked and half ran along the narrow dog walkers' path down to the corner. Due to a single skin of trees separating the path from the lake I couldn't see the actual swim until the last moment. The sweat was pouring off me, stinging my eyes, whilst I was desperately trying to convince myself that it wasn't the end of the world if one of the other two were already in there but, in truth, I knew it might as well be. The feeling of relief as I dropped my gear in the empty swim was incredible, a bit like being first past the post at the London marathon. My body certainly felt like I'd just ran one, that was for sure. Summoning up some reserve adrenalin, I hoisted myself up into the branches of the long spindly tree that hangs over the water, giving me an excellent view of the swim. I'd only made it half way up and a quick glance confirmed everything I'd hoped and prayed would be - three bloody great big mirror carp were circling under the tree and a couple of other shapes loomed in the background - I was down the tree in seconds. At last, the moment I'd been dreaming about all winter was upon me and I frantically started dragging tackle and rods out all over the swim.

Sunnymeads Corner

I was trying hard to remember exactly what to do in a situation like this when I came across a big bag of bait that I'd promised to bring down for Phil. Given my present condition of shaking like a leaf, whilst running around like a headless chicken, I decided to calm down with a brisk jog up to Phil's swim to announce my arrival and deliver the bait. At least then I could settle down and seriously try to extract one of these denizens of the deep from his watery abode. I arrived in Phil's swim two minutes later, wheezing and panting. Tench Bloke was also there, visiting. Throwing the bait down at their feet, I quickly abused them for missing out on the opportunity of a lifetime before showing them a clean pair of heels. As I departed I heard Phil moaning, "I told you we should have looked in Sunnymeads. I said so didn't I?"

But it was too late, I was on the case. As I turned the corner, my toe stubbed on something in the long grass, I scrabbled about and uncovered a small black rubber torch. It was vaguely familiar and when I noticed the electrical tape holding it together I recognised it as one I'd lost way back last year in October, the day before I'd caught Cluster. On pressing the button, I was absolutely amazed to find that it worked perfectly so I slipped it in my pocket and hurried on.

Back at the swim things were looking good. It's often all too easy to rush into things only to be left, after the fish have bolted, thinking, "If only I'd done this, that or the other." So, stuffing my pockets full of Grange boilies, I clambered back up the tree to try to assess the best angle of attack, while Sam the fat carp dog curled up at the base of the tree to catch up on some serious dog napping.

The three main targets, as far as I was concerned, were all mirrors in the thirty five pound range and all three were milling about, only twenty feet from the bank. The bottom of the lake looked much as it had done this time last year, when Phil and myself had watched them feeding confidently on our bait. That year they had spent most of their time on two clean areas amongst the short Canadian pond weed, the water was only four feet deep here, with the clear spots being about a foot higher. The tree, which was a skinny affair (more one bough really), curved out over the lake and afforded the careful climber an unrivalled view of the lake bed. After some careful manoeuvring I put myself in a precarious position directly over and between the two spots which were about fifteen feet apart and slowly, one by one, I started dropping baits onto the spots. Some landed perfectly on the clean sand and exposed gravel, while others nestled in the short weed, but still visible from my lofty perch and, as I watched, one of three mirrors cruised closer. Ambling up to the left hand spot he dipped down and readily took half a dozen baits. Through the glare I could just make out the scale pattern on his flanks and the acute slope of his head. His dark bluey-grey back, and his definitive split into the pale grey lower sides and belly, told me that he was The Pug, a mid thirty pound mirror and highly desirable Wraysbury whacker. All I had to do now was get a bait to him! From last close season's observations coupled with the way this fella was behaving I knew my best chance of a pick up was bang on top of the clearest part of the hump. However, from ground level I couldn't make out

A perilous journey!

the spot at all. I could only see the outline of the fish and tantalising little patches of bubbles rising as he brushed across the weed. The other two fish stood sentinel behind him, unwilling to make the commitment. There was only one thing for it so, slipping a single bottom bait onto a hair rig and taking the rod butt between my teeth, I started the perilous journey back up the tree with twelve feet of carbon swinging like a pendulum from my gnashers. After what seemed like an eternity I was in position and, after waiting until The Pug looked the other way, I gently lowered the rig until it swayed inches above the surface. Swinging it to and fro until I'd got the right momentum, I flicked it the last few feet, trapping it as it hit the surface and swinging it back to land smack bang on target. I let a few yards of slack out and unceremoniously hurled the rod down into the bushes at the side of the swim. Most of the bait had gone and I could see the fish lining up for another visit so, hurriedly, I flicked twenty baits on and around the clearly visible hookbait before making my way back down the tree. Dragging the rod out of the bush, I set it up on an alarm, fully expecting it to be torn from my grasp at any moment.

As I sat on the ground behind the rod, watching tiny pinpricks of bubbles rising around the area, I knew I was just about to get a take - no if's, but's or maybe's. Only how soon and how big! My heart was trying its damnedest to batter its way out through my rib cage, the tension was killing me, he must be on the baits by now! But the slack line didn't twitch, it all seemed to be taking a lifetime. Then all of a sudden I could take it no longer. I was a bloody nervous wreck, I had to have a look. I crawled over to the tree and, putting the trunk firmly between me and the lake, I slowly hoisted myself up to the first foothold. Six feet higher I could see the spot clearly, so clearly, I could see my hook a mere twelve inches and three baits away from success and, as I watched, two more baits disappeared down that cavernous throat. Scrambling down the tree, I just made it back to the rod in time to watch the line twitch and tighten slowly to the tip. Taking the rod firmly, I bent into the fish, the tip wrenched over and pulled smoothly down towards the surface, and then flew back over my shoulder. Suddenly, attached only to thin air, my own momentum sent me flying backwards dumping me soundly down on my butt in the nettles!

As I sat there looking past a flapping broken line at the bow-wave charging off across the pond, I could have cried. All that effort and planning for nothing! I grabbed the line and looked accusingly at the end of it. It had broken with pathetic ease and now I could see why, a small flat spot bore testament to the winter's usage that it had been subjected to. Why hadn't I checked it? Complacency had cost me my first fish of the year and as I sat there shaking quietly for a while, I didn't know if I was more annoyed or embarrassed. Eventually I re-spooled and tackled the offending rod and set up a second, totally renewing every component part of both, two more trips up the tree saw both rigs on clear spots but the swim was devoid of carp, for the time being at least, so I put the kettle on, telling myself they'd be back.

Phil and Tench Bloke came along for a chat and after recounting my tale of woe, Phil did the decent thing and wandered up to the off licence, returning with a carrier bag full of ice cold lagers and we drowned my sorrows. By the time they left a few fish had been spotted on the outskirts of my swim, which was an encouraging sight. The fish always seemed to approach this corner along the same route, picking their way carefully along, tight to the bushes and fallen trees that line the dog walkers' path to my right, almost as if they themselves were making their way back from the off licence. By early evening things were looking good again, Tench Bloke returned about nine that evening and after a few cups of tea, just as I'd started to tell him for the twenty fifth time how gutted I was over this morning's mishap, the rod cast to the other spot just off the branches of the climbing tree burst into life. I was too line-paranoid to strike, so I gingerly tightened into one very

The final flick.

surprised and angry carp, but after the initial mad charge for freedom was dealt with, most of the fight was conducted under the rod tip.

Although the water here was only two feet deep, he hugged the bottom, hardly sending up even the smallest of swirls, and steadfastly refused to be coaxed up to the top. Eventually, though, the constant pressure had him beaten and as he rose, gasping for air in the moonlight, T.B. made no mistake with the net. Laying him on the mat, in the light of my reclaimed torch, we could see the unmistakable form of The Hoover and, after placing him in a wet sack, we carefully carried him up to the deeper margins along to my left where we lowered him into the water under a big old willow. I crawled out along an overhanging bough and the torch between my teeth shone down through seven feet of water to where he lay in recuperation. Just as I finished tying the sack cord off to the tree branch that I was balanced on, the torch slipped from my mouth and followed the fish down to its watery resting place, the beam darting this way and that as it tumbled over and away, coming to rest two feet away from the sack, the still shining beam illuminating the scene. Easy come, easy go, I thought, and made my way off to bed a far happier man than a couple of hours earlier.

There is a dog walker at Wraysbury known as The Schoolteacher, for obvious reasons, and he usually wanders around about six in the morning with his two golden retrievers, one of which is a beautiful and friendly hound. The other, however, takes his job far too seriously and seems totally unable to pass by a bivvy without retrieving something. One day it could be a marker float or an empty beer can, the next it might be a bag of bait or box of tea bags. So it was, then, that the next morning at ten past six I was chasing my toilet roll down the Railway Bank and, as I was halfway back to my swim, still coiling soggy tissue paper around a chewed up piece of cardboard tube, I heard an almighty splash. I ran full pelt the last few yards and got there in time to see the ring of ripples spreading out from the bush to my right, a large patch of frothy bubbles marking the spot where an unseen carp had obviously left the pond. I pulled out the low chair, put the kettle on and sat there determined to see the next one jump. There was a light mist lifting off the surface of the lake and the clear skies and lack of wind held the promise of another hot day ahead All things taken into consideration I couldn't think of anywhere I'd rather be, especially as I had a thirty pound plus mirror carp waiting patiently in the wings for photographing - he was going to look good in the morning sun. I was torn from my reverie by the clatter of the kettle lid as the water boiled for tea and just as I turned my back to switch off the cooker,....spadoosshh! I almost rocketed out of the chair with shock. Not twenty feet from where I sat, a fish had cleared the water sending a massive wash to lap the bank at my feet. It could only be about a rod length from my bait and once again the patch of froth marked the spot. I'd only missed seeing the fish by a split second. Sitting there glued to the spot with tea in hand, my heart started up the quickstep again, my stomach however danced to a different tune. As I rummaged through the rucksack for some biscuits,....spadoosshh!

This time it was right over my bait. I never got a chance to drink that tea as moments later the rod was almost dragged in and although it was plainly a good fish, the fight was very one-sided in my favour. He just plodded about for a couple of minutes and then rolled on the surface waving the white flag and once in the net I recognised him instantly as the Short Fat Linear that we'd seen so often with The Pug last close season. This fish also looked about mid-thirty but a totally different shape to The Hoover. I popped him in a sack and took him up to join his mate under the willow. Unbelievably, the torch was still shining away on the bottom! I checked The Hoover and lowered the other fish down next to him before wandering up to find Tench Bloke to do the photo's, Phil having had to return to work the previous evening.

The fish weighed thirty three and a half pounds each, and both behaved admirably for the camera. We photographed them separately, not wanting to risk a brace shot with two lively fish of this size. The Hoover is one of the better known Wraysbury characters, a long lean fish with a few scales along the lateral line, whereas the Fat Linear was exactly that, a short fat fish with a perfect linear scaling pattern and this was only its second visit to the bank in the last eleven years! After photographing each one, we slipped them back and watched as they slowly swam away. I was still annoyed at losing The Pug but the blow had been softened somewhat by the capture of a brace of Wraysbury thirty's so I figured I could survive, at least until the off licence opened, after all there was serious need for celebration today.

There were a lot of people waiting in the wings that first spring season on Wraysbury, people who would openly admit to be waiting for something to happen before starting to fish themselves. I'm not usually the secretive type but after a chat between the three of us we decided that we had nothing to gain and everything to lose by shouting about my recent captures in Sunnymeads. If I had gone ahead and told all and sundry that the Wraysbury carp were on the move and feeding well, then I'm sure there would have been more than just the one extra car there to greet me a few days later when I returned for my next assault.

The promise of another hot dry day ahead.

As it was, only The Doctor's and

The Short Fat Linear!

Tench Bloke's motors were parked up against the sailing club fence, slowly frying in the ever strengthening spring sunlight. Twenty four degrees today, according to Michael (definitely no gales tonight, madam) Fish. I started to unload my gear as the Doctor appeared from nowhere, like he does, and collecting his bed roll and bait bucket, made off in the direction of Sunnymeads Corner. I followed behind at a safe distance, praying that he hadn't chosen the corner to take root in, but Lady Luck smiled her sweet smile at me once more and he marched straight past the swim, off on a mission somewhere at the back of beyond. As soon as he was out of sight, I dumped my gear and shot up the tree and a vision of four carp greeted me. I couldn't believe my luck! The closer two were once again the better fish and from what I could make out these were an entirely different group of fish to the ones a few days earlier. One of them was by far the largest I'd seen so far this year and was somewhere in excess of forty pounds. They were behaving a bit differently as well, higher in the water and tilted slightly upwards, not nosing the surface or anything as blatant as that, but definitely looking as if they may consider a floater or two drifted down past them. There was a slight breeze pushing in to the corner, bringing the odd leaf or piece of flotsam into the swim so I sat up the tree for a while, watching and trying to suss the fish out. They hadn't so much as sniffed at the bottom over the little clear humps, although one fish, a short dumpy mid-twenty, had upended in the extreme margins right under my feet grubbing about momentarily before joining the others near the surface. As I gazed in awe at the biggest of the bunch trying to figure out if it was the elusive and much sought after Olive, (a fish that had not graced the banks for about three years or more) she slowly turned and lifted effortlessly up to swirl at a small leaf, blew a small patch of bubbles out, as if in disgust, and settled back down practically below my feet. I could make out a distinct two-tone effect from the grey of her back changing suddenly at the lateral line into a much more orange hue, From the photo's that I'd studied, more times than a teenager with his first dog-eared copy of Playboy, I was fairly sure this was her. The size would be about right as most people were guestimating that she'd be over forty pounds and this fish was definitely that.

This was more than enough encouragement for me, and I was down from the tree in a flash, dragging out Chum Mixers and a catapult from my rucksack. With the slight breeze it was all made so much easier. All I had to do was walk twenty yards along the path to my right to where there was a break in the bushes and fire mixers at different distances upwind of the fish. Fat Sam had woken up at the first rattle of the Mixer box and was trying desperately to catch any that fell out of the pouch before they hit the deck. I put out four batches and went back to set about tying up a floater rig, leaving Sam snuffling for missed titbits in the undergrowth. With shaking hands, I dug out a packet of size six Drennan Super Specialist hooks, and tied one direct to a length of nine pound mono, using the tail poked back through the eye as a hair, onto which went two Chum Mixers. I tend to leave some Mixers loose in the tackle box, or a pocket, to go soft. This saves the frustration of having them snap in two as you try to push a baiting needle through them. The controller I was using had been born out of winter boredom. It was constructed from a length of Wraysbury stick, about seven inches long and two inches in diameter. I took these home and drilled through them lengthwise, which sounds a lot easier than it actually was, I then glued a length of stiff tubing through the hole and on the second attempt I'd created a totally natural in-line controller. Unfortunately, the first batch sank!

By the time everything was ready, the fish were well and truly on the bait, making it a bit tricky to cast out without spooking them. So I stood and watched as they swirled at Mixers with merry abandon. The bigger fish - Olive - was easily recognisable from the others as, apart from the large hump on her back, she seemed to have a habit of gurgling as she ate, leaving little patches of bubbles in her wake. As the first drift of Mixers disappeared, the fish sank a bit lower again, giving me the opportunity to cast. The plan

She blew bubbles in disgust.

was to cast beyond the next drift and slowly ease it back into position to coincide with the Mixers reaching the feeding area. The first cast landed perfectly, without making a splash. Unfortunately, it landed perfectly up in the branches of the overhanging tree, but by some miracle, I managed to extract it again with the bait still intact and, by kneeling at the water's edge, I managed to send it sailing out into the pond on the next cast. Not being quite as aerodynamic as I'd hoped for, it sailed off a bit too far right, but considering the noise it made as it touched down, I decided the best plan was to leave it where it was.

I held the rod tip as far left as the bushes would allow and teased the rig a bit closer to the fish. It was only a few yards off target by the time it drifted into range of the back fish, a common of about twenty pounds which rose up and took two of the free offerings. He was soon joined by a mid-twenty mirror swirling happily at Fat Sam's dinner and, occasionally, a patch of bubbles would appear on the outskirts as Olive clumsily took the odd Mixer. She could clearly be seen due to the enormous hump of her shoulders as she pushed her weight around, trying to out-do her lesser brethren in the race for food. The problem was singling her out from the others but, as it happened, it was a problem that sorted itself out for, as soon as the hookbait complete with camouflage controller drifted into range she turned and pushed herself purposefully towards it. I gingerly picked the rod off the rests and waited, I could see her back rising as she lined up with the offering, her top lip just below the surface. I could hardly believe it, I was actually going to catch her, the determined way she rose for the bait and the perfect angle she approached from left me in no doubt, this was to be my finest hour. Her top lip broke the surface and the tell-tale bubbles started to spill from the corner of her voluminous mouth, straight past the bait she surged, still rising in the water on a direct line for my lump of Wraysbury stick!

I stood there, gob wide open in disbelief, as she took the stick controller square in the centre and pushed it a clear foot across the surface, creating a wake over its sides, before simply releasing it and sinking back down into the depths. As if possessed of a single mind the other fish, too, stopped feeding and slowly melted away. I'm still not sure to this day if that fish was incredibly stupid or a lot smarter than we give it credit for. I became even more baffled the next day when in the same swim, after an uneventful night, the same group of fish returned and in an almost repeat performance, this time in the presence of two visitors, the same fish, Olive lifted the same controller clear of the water on the top of her head!

I decided that maybe floater fishing wasn't exactly the way forward, so I set about laying a couple of traps on the bottom for them. I'd noticed that since my three runs in here the other day the fish had been unwilling to visit the main two marks again, so I sat aloft in my tree trying to decide on two fresh spots.The fish hadn't disappeared quite so convincingly today, and I could make out a group of three carp milling about just off the bushes fifty yards away, at the back of my swim. I was confident that they would visit this corner again this afternoon so I set one bait down on the small patch below my feet where the dumpy

"I've caught Mary, you know, and in bloody February!" 49lb 15oz.

The Hoover is returned on a cold spring day.

Above: Phil, Micky, and Del auditioning for Hairfield? Below: A cup of tea, Wraysbury style.

twenty pounder had rooted about the day before. Around this, I put six free offerings and a couple of handfuls of hemp. It was so close in that even from the bank I could make out the grains of hemp lying carpet-like over the spot and hanging in the three inch fronds of weed surrounding it. The other spot I chose was tight around to the right of the swim, just past the overhanging branches of a small bush. There, on the bottom, I could make out a very small area of clear lake bed where the sand had just started to peek through. It wasn't possible to reach this spot from up the tree due to some trailing branches from above, so I brought plan 'B' into action.

For this, using PVA thread, I tied a one inch cube of white marker foam to the hook next to a single boilie. Putting this back in the rests, I gathered up a handful of small sticks and climbed back up the tree. I flicked the sticks one by one at the spot until I got one on each side, then scrambling quickly down, I cast the PVA rig between the sticks. Putting the rod hastily down, I shot back up the tree in time to see the foam wavering over the clear spot and I watched as the PVA melted and the bait settled just on the edge of the sandy strip. There was a lot of monkey work involved, but as I set the rod in the rests, at least I was safe in the knowledge that I was fishing the best that I possibly could.

Everything was moved back onto the path away from the water's edge, and I spent the rest of the morning wandering up and down the dog walkers' path at the right of my swim, tracking the progress of the fish as they slowly made their way back to the corner. By early afternoon the dumpy mirror, an upper twenty common and Olive were holding court in Sunnymeads once again. Standing half hidden behind the tree trunk I watched through the Polaroids as their circuit brought them closer to the bait and at one stage all three of them passed over the bush rod to my right, so close that I could see every scale on them. The two smaller fish broke formation and veered off further out in front of me, but the big girl kept on coming, until grinding to a halt directly over the hemp and boilies at my feet. She was only yards from me, I could probably have jumped in and wrestled her to the bank, but I opted instead for more traditional methods!

As I watched, her fins stood erect from her body and her gills flared, I thought that I'd been sussed as I'd seen this reaction before, used in panic, but as I stared harder, I saw the short weed stand to attention below her mouth as a patch of hemp shot upwards from the lake bed caught in the vortex of her suck and into the waiting mouth at least twelve inches above. Within moments, using a couple more vacuum cleaner-type sucks, all the hemp had been removed from around the six boilies that hadn't so much as twitched the whole time. Satisfied that she'd well and truly stitched me up, she turned and plunged her head and shoulders into the spot and with one mighty flick of her tail she beat her side across the remaining baits sending up sheets of bubbles and bits of debris to the surface. I stood flabbergasted as the magnificent beast bow-waved out to about thirty yards and then threw herself out of the water, re-entering with an almighty crash before disappearing for good.

I never saw her again.

Chapter 15

The Pug Triumphs Again

Although we managed to keep the Sunnymeads affair under wraps for over a month, it didn't really do us any favours, as the weather deteriorated considerably and plunged us back into fishing blind, which on a pit the size of Wraysbury is not an easy task.

It was a full five weeks before the weather broke again but, when it did, all those long nights spent zipped up in a bivvy sheltering from torrential rain were soon forgotten. It was back out with the stalking gear and off on walkabouts in search of monsters - it didn't take long to find them, either. As I stood on the sailing club lawn on the west bank of the North Lake, whose surface was glimmering in the sunlight like the proverbial mill pond, I could clearly see a few backs just creasing the surface at long range out in the middle area of the pit. As I watched, they drifted slowly up to the south east corner where a large concrete block the size and shape of an old army pillar box sits on the water's edge, giving the angler a wonderful view of the corner and the exit from the North Lake through a narrow channel into the South. The fat Carp Dog and I were round there like a shot armed with only a rod, net and a box of Chum Mixers. The fish were about sixty yards away and closing fast. I fired out a few pouchfuls of Mixers, spreading them about a bit as I wasn't too sure exactly where the carp would end up.

Eventually as they drifted into full view I could see that the lead fish was The Pug, the same fish I'd lost at the other end of the pit a few weeks earlier. Maybe this would be my chance to even the score? They kept on coming on a direct line towards the corner where I stood, ignoring the first batch of bait as they swam underneath it - just a few inches from their snouts but not so much as a passing glance at it. They positively avoided the second batch which was at about twenty five yards range and then, swimming as if with a mission, they followed The Pug to the closest baits a mere ten yards from where I stood. Hardly even slowing in their approach they tilted up, drinking Mixers lazily off the surface with long gulps. For five minutes or so, they fed happily, and then as if with a single mind they turned and left, pushing great bow-waves over their backs as they accelerated away.

They slowed eventually to a more refined pace, as they plodded off around the middle island and away. I couldn't believe it. I hadn't even cast out yet and I'd blown it! I sat and watched for a while hoping to see where they were ultimately heading, but they seemed quite happy to mill about out of range. So, gathering up my bits and bobs, I was just about to leave when they reappeared on the other side of the island heading back in my direction. Firing out some more Mixers and hurriedly setting up the rod, I planned my strategy. Assuming that now they had tasted the bait, and were obviously coming back again, they would be on the lookout for more. I decided to intercept them so I cast out thirty yards, directly in their path, and waited. Slowly the gap closed, as sixty yards became fifty, then forty which was just on the outskirts of the free offerings. Then they were upon me, right next to the bait and I swear they ducked as they cruised straight under the first drift of Chum Mixers. Frantically, I wound in and repositioned the hookbait as near as I dared in their path and on the near side of the second batch.

Straight past they went again. Were they blind? They swam straight back to the same spot as before and started on the bait, taking half a dozen instantly and then searching for more. Although they were obviously willing to feed, for some reason known only to them, their willingness was limited to this one small area of water. I'd seen fish feed in this fastidious manner before, but usually only on the bottom. After all, what can be different in one small area of surface to another adjacent one? The problem that I had now was that they were already there, a cast onto the hot spot would surely spook them off. My dilemma was short lived, however as once again, as a single entity, they turned and made off towards the middle. I was beginning to get the hang of this now. Thirty minutes later and they were back, circuit complete, only this time my hookbait marked the exact centre of the spot. The lead fish, still The Pug, the one I really wanted, surged on ahead of the others making for the spot, its back rising out of the water cutting a path directly to the hookbait. I could see the greed in his eye and his lips part as he tilted up. I could already taste success as he tried for the bait, but in his haste he overshot. Only by an inch. One inch between victory and disaster! He stopped dead, hanging directly vertical, the Mixer was just behind his top lip and frantically he back-pedalled with his pectoral fins, desperate to take this morsel. My heart had long since stopped beating. Try as he might, he could not attain it and as gravity took over he rolled over and around, down through the clear waters. He turned four feet below the surface and came up at the bait again, but now from my side. A bad angle. The line seemed horribly visible now as he rose up for the kill. Then with only inches to go he spotted something amiss! The water erupted in fury, and a moment later all was still, with not a fish in sight. Devoid of carp, the spot was blown.

I packed up and left defeated, another chance at The Pug missed but one day I'd have him! When that day came I was going to lay him down on my unhooking mat and laugh at him.

One day!

I knew that the fish of Wraysbury were not entirely un-temptable on the surface though, and Phil managed to further endorse this theory the very next week, when in one afternoon he managed to bag two Wraysbury mirrors on chum mixers. One was a small but perfectly formed fish of eighteen pounds, but unfortunately the other one constituted his third capture of the 'Hoover' and although he was pleased at catching him, I know that deep down he was more than a little disappointed at not landing a 'new' fish. It was still an amazing result though, and it nicely opened Phil's account for the year.

The next session coincided with Phil's birthday and turned out to be memorable in the extreme. We had all decided to set up on the South Lake, and I'd chosen the end of Bryants Point while Tench Bloke had opted for the Bay. Phil had set up a bit further afield and we all arranged to meet up at seven o'clock in the car park before walking up to Wraysbury station. The train only has to travel two stops before reaching Windsor which, coincidentally, happens to be the town where Phil was originally 'spawned'. What more fitting place could there possibly be to celebrate his birthday than this?

For some reason we seemed unable to make up our minds on which pub to spend the night in, so in desperation we tried them all, which, in retrospect, was probably a bit of a mistake! By the time that we stumbled off the last train home I was glad that I'd brought along my 'guide dog for the blind drunk'! I followed that bushy little tail through the pitch black pathways and bushes until, thankfully, she led me back to my little green 'home'.

I think that I must have been asleep before my head touched the pillow, as the next thing I knew about, it was morning. I was laying there, nursing a sore head, and wincing as the memories of the night before came flooding back to remind me of just how bad I ought to feel. A familiar noise started vying with the pounding of my blood through swollen veins and eventually I recognised it as a bite alarm in full 'panic' mode. It certainly wasn't mine - that would have been too loud to even contemplate - so, falling out of bed I looked back down the bay in time to see Tench Bloke fight free of the sleeping bag, and strike. I waved down the lake at him and struggled into my boots, I really didn't feel too well at all, it must have been that last dodgy burger on the way home last night! When I turned up at T.B.'s and saw the state of him, though, I suddenly felt a lot better. He was desperately trying to hang on to an outraged carp that was, without a shadow of a doubt, getting the better of him. The fish had decided to leave the bay, via every snag on the houses side, which is a long way and a lot of snags. The locals have, over the years, dumped everything from washing machines to unwanted relations into these margins and some serious action was needed to sort it all out. One small tree prevented Tench Bloke from walking, the otherwise manicured bank of the bay, up to where the fish was currently snagged. In some strange moment of madness I somehow volunteered to swim the rod around this tree and pass it out so that T.B. could carry on the fight with a level pegging. I must have been temporarily insane, the water was absolutely freezing and I was doing the breaststroke in it, with a rod clamped between my teeth! It had the desired effect as, once he got over the fish, Tench Bloke steered him from his shelter inside an old milk float, and the battle was back on. The fish was a hell of a lot fitter that morning than either of us and managed to strip another seventy yards of line out before snagging up on the other side of the bay.

After a short while it was obvious that there was no way that fish was going to swim out of his own accord so we needed the boat. I'd left the boat in its usual hiding place on the North Lake, halfway up the peninsula in the secret reedy point, but that was miles away. Determined that we'd land this fish at any cost, I ran back to the motor and drove like a lunatic around the village to the Welly Lane peninsula gates. On getting there I realised that I'd left the gate key in my bivvy so I had to run the remaining four hundred yards to the swim. It was a long way to row from the secret reeds to Bryants Point so I decided, in my strange wisdom, that carrying the boat across the peninsula on my head to the sailing club, would somehow be easier! By the time that I reached the sailing club fence I was to all extents and purposes, clinically dead, it was only the adrenalin that was keeping me going.

Launching the boat from the Fence swim, I struck out across the lake, a mere five hundred yards of water stood between me and the distant speck that was Tench Bloke. I made it half way across the pond before collapsing over the oars, exhausted. I lay there for a while breathing heavily as my pulse raced in my eardrums, before picking up the mis-matched oars and continuing on, as fast as I was able. When I drew into earshot of Tench Bloke I shouted out and asked him what was happening, but all was still solid so I pulled up to the shore and held the boat steady while he clambered in. T.B. reeled us out to the other side of the bay, while I swallowed some much needed oxygen and tried not to pass out!

Before we reached the fish, T.B. managed to free the line and we opted to return to the shore to try and land it. Dutch Bloke had wandered out of his garden, to see what all the fuss was about, and he stood behind us, watching, as the fish slowly allowed itself to be brought to the shore. I stood at the front with the net and strained my eyes through the deep margins for a first glimpse, deep down in the murky water

I could just make out the silhouette of a carp, twisting and turning about as it rose through the layers. It kited off to the left and, as it made another pass in front of us, we could both clearly see the scaling of a large common carp. It looked to be in excess of thirty pounds and it was all very exciting. As he came up for the third time, however, it had transformed itself into an even larger mirror carp!

Most confused about the whole affair, I got the net ready and waited with anticipation for another look, who knows maybe it would be a grass carp this time! As T.B. brought it within range we could see exactly what was occurring, not one but two carp ducked and dived in a perfect parody of one another. So perfect, in fact,that it was only as the mirror came up to the net cord that we could be sure of which one was being played! Tench Bloke was over the moon, and when he looked in the net he practically went into orbit, for there in the bottom of the mesh lay his biggest carp by far.

We did not recognise him at first, which was strange, seeing as how I'd come so close to him in the past. Eventually though, we recognised him as that most elusive character The Pug. Neither of us had ever seen him out of the water before and he looked even more impressive than he had done in the water. On the scales he weighed thirty six pounds, and somehow all thoughts of hangovers and sheer exhaustion disappeared without a trace, for this truly was a session to remember.

Tench Bloke with The Pug.

Chapter 16

A Brace of 39's and a Cock-Up

Sometimes, when you're searching for fish, it's almost as if you can look too hard, not seeing what is under your nose. You get a picture in your mind of where the carp should be and you ignore the obvious. I think this is often why an angler who is new to a water may have an instant result, beginner's luck some say, but I think not. More likely, the effect of fishing without preconception of the hot swims or methods.

I think this was very much the case on one sunny morning in May, when Tench Bloke and myself set out on a tour of Wraysbury. It was, in fact, the day after the Carp Society's Wembley conference, where Phil and myself had presented a slide show about our previous year's antics on Wraysbury. After an awful lot of Guinness, I had announced to some other Wraysbury anglers, who were also propping up the bar alongside me, and anyone else who was stupid or drunk enough to listen, that I had three days ahead of me and I was definitely going to bag a Wraysbury carp!

In the true tradition of drunks the world over, this involved a lot of pointing, finger-wagging, and that strange attempt at a sincere stare that just makes you look like you've lost a set of contact lenses. But, in the sober light of the next morning, after dragging myself from the back of the van in the Douglas Lane car park, and with a head like a split melon, it all seemed a long way from reality. Myself and Tench Bloke, who had also been present and didn't look particularly healthy either, figured that a drop of fresh air would do us good so we set off on a tour of Wraysbury in search of carp. We'd opted, not for the whistle stop version, but the complete Tour De Force, determined to make the most of the time available. Starting out, as we often did, from the Douglas Lane car park, we headed off in an anti-clockwise direction, taking in all the many sights along the way. Climbing trees along the Railway Bank searching in the weed for the slightest sign, before cutting off through the Party Point towards the Fingers. All the favourite spots were checked. Under the Tench Tree in the Finger

Bays, the Rocky Barge, out on the plateau in the North Lake. I scaled the climbing tree by The Lawn, and the one in Sunnymeads Corner, but all to no avail.

After a brief rest on the sailing club lawn for ice creams and a smoke, it was on to the Diving Board swim, and then round into the Dredger Bay, but still no sign of a carp. It was a good day for spotting them as well. A clear sky let the sun shine down its uninhibited warmth all around, and a gentle easterly breeze kept the water fresh and oxygenated, but still the carp kept a low profile. After the Dredger Bay, we left the peninsula and marched purposefully on. This was always the worst part of the journey as, apart from Mary's Point, the next section held only No Carp Bay and The Swimming Pool. The former, by its own designation, inspired no confidence, after all it couldn't be called No Carp Bay for nothing, could it? The Swimming Pool had never inspired me at all. I couldn't help noticing as we walked past the bay though, that it did look quite nice with the easterly breeze pushing in to it, but we hurried on regardless.

After we had done Bryants Point and Bay, complete with climbing all the appropriate trees along the way, we returned once again to the car park in the Douglas Lane. We had been gone about three hours in all, and were sadly none the wiser for all our efforts. Still at a total loss as to where to fish, we decided on a different strategy, I would set off around the Railway Lake again on another circuit, while T.B. would go back the way we had just come, meeting me halfway around. This way, we could cover the same amount of ground in half the time, just in case we'd missed anything. So, armed as always, with a stalking rod and net, we set off in our respective directions.

Fat Sam didn't exactly look overawed at the prospect of another circuit, and by the time that I'd reached the North Lake I was beginning to have doubts myself. I settled down on the sailing club lawn and, pillowing my head on my little stalking bag, I lay back to await the arrival of Tench Bloke.

After a while, and with no sign of him on the horizon, I started to wonder if maybe he'd gone straight to the pub or something, so gathering up my possessions I carried on. As I reached the peninsula, I could see Tench Bloke from across the water sitting on the grass at the bottom of No Carp Bay and what was even more strange, was that he appeared to be fishing! I hurried round there.

"What's all this then, Tench Bloke? Angling in No Carp Bay?" I asked.

"It's not No Carp Bay today," he replied. "I've seen six jump already."

Now, six carp showing in a month at Wraysbury is good going, but six in an hour is nothing short of a bloody miracle! This warranted further investigation. "Have you been up that tree yet?" I asked, pointing to an absolutely massive specimen to his right.

"Up there? You must be joking! You know what I'm like with heights. Help yourself if you like."

I certainly did like, and a few minutes later I was forty feet above lake level and peering down over the bay. The view from here was amazing, and with the water being so clear, I could see the bottom in many parts, with the weedier areas standing out like big dark green stains. The tree was growing on the end of the Round Point, and as I looked down, Tench Bloke was in the only real swim as such, which was situated on the left of the tree and looked out from the side of the point. Also from my lofty perch I could see carp, about four or five big mirrors were milling about, no more than ten yards out, with a couple more further out into the bay. As I watched, a couple of the closer ones slowly made their way around in front of T.B. After a quick circuit of his swim they joined their mates back out in front.

"Can you see anything?" came the shout from below. "That all depends, Tench Bloke," I hollered back down, "on whether I can join you?"

"Be my guest, mate," came the reply.

I scrambled back down the tree to inform Tench

Up there? You must be joking!

Bloke that, if that was the case, we were sitting on a shedful, and then, after losing the toss, I ran off to fetch the van and all the tackle. Somehow, in my haste, I must have forgotten to mention that the fish weren't exactly in his swim but more in front of the swim that I was about to cut out - funny that, I can't think how I forgot! By the time I'd run the half a mile back to the car park, loaded T.B.'s gear into my motor, driven like a nutter around the village, through the gates and down the track into No Carp Bay, I was fit only to lay panting on the ground in a sweaty heap for ten minutes. That's exactly what I did. As soon as I could breathe, I was back up the tree armed with a pocketful of sticks and, after watching the fish parading up and down for a while, it became evident that one or two spots were definitely favoured over the rest of the lake bed.

This is something that I've noticed over and over again while watching fish feed, and a little time spent in observation before casting out can help to cross that fragile divide between a result and yet another blank. I could see the two different types of weed that covered the margins, one was a dark green blanket weed that the fish were noticeably avoiding, the other was a lighter green short weed that they seemed to like. I had come across this short crunchy-type of weed before and although I don't know its proper name, it has a smell like black pepper and the fish seem to love it. I bet it would be nice in a stir fry, I might even give it a try one day. After pinpointing the better spots, I flicked a stick out just behind the first one. I then raced down to the ground in time to cast a bait neatly underneath it, before it had a chance to drift off its target. Repeating the whole escapade for the second rod, I was soon angling perfectly. In order to cast, I'd pushed through the bushes to the right of the tree and stood in the margins, laying the rods in the edge as I finished with them. All that remained to do now, was to cut a narrow slot in the marginal bushes to poke the rods through and flatten the long grass and nettles just enough to take the brolly and bedchair. With this done, it was kettle on and wait, in the time honoured Wraysbury tradition.

Waiting patiently behind the rods has never been one of my strong points and, consequently, I was up and down that tree like a baboon on heat all afternoon. Every time that I got settled in the branches, a couple of fish would drift in and look like they were game, only to bugger off again as soon as I'd got back down behind the rods. We waited impatiently as day turned into night and night turned back into day once more. At about ten o'clock in the morning, we had the rare honour of Wraysbury visitors in the form of John Cross and The Hun. They were most intrigued as to what the hell we were doing in No Carp Bay. I was beginning to wonder myself! They all lounged around on the grass beside my camp, depleting my stocks of tea bags while we told our tale of monster mirrors. After a while, a distant call of nature that had been gently vying for my attention suddenly screamed at me in urgency so, leaving the others camped out in my swim, I tottered off into the small copse of trees thirty yards behind me. Hanging the Andrex on a conveniently protruding twig, I settled down to the task at hand. Now, there is an unwritten law regarding biting fish and otherwise occupied anglers. You can stare at a float all day and it will never twitch, but open a flask and pour steaming hot coffee into a cup balanced delicately between your knees and under it goes, resulting in a lap full of blisters. Stand up to stretch your legs for a second while stalking and bang goes your floater! Quite how the fish know is a mystery, but know they do. As a direct result of this extra sensory piscean perception, I ended up, a few moments later, charging across the clearing with my trousers around my ankles, spurred on by the relentless scream of my buzzer and the whoops and hollers of the crowd. The rod that I'd cast the closest in, just off the tree to my left, was being robbed of line at an alarming rate!

Battering my way through an absolute barrage of wise-cracks, I grabbed the rod and hung on for dear life. The fish had well and truly got its head and wasn't about to stop for anything. It was all I could do to eventually bring it to a halt about ninety yards out. The line was snagged in weed along the way, but the fish was free to do pretty much as he pleased. I was shaking like a leaf at the sheer power of that first mad charge for freedom. I wound down as tight as I could and lent back into him trying to cut the line up through the weed whilst out in the middle of the bay an enormous tail broke the surface and waved at us in defiance. The line thankfully pulled clear of the unseen tether, and I was suddenly in direct contact again. It was now just a matter of bullying him back to the bank. This was obviously easier said than done, but after much tugging and pulling, and an endless supply of helpful advice, I had him circling under the tree where I'd first hooked him. The water was clear enough for us to see a big dish-shaped mirror spinning over and over on the end, trying desperately to shake the hook free. Fortunately for me, the size six Super Specialist held firm, and as I drew him into the folds of the net, I let loose a victory yell that rattled windows in Windsor!

Once on the bank we all recognised him instantly as Mallin's but he looked a lot more impressive than the last time our paths had crossed. The scales were zeroed and up he went, the spinning dial came eventually to rest at thirty nine pounds fifteen ounces and a more impressive beast it would have been hard to imagine (see colour photo on page 258). Knowing that Keith was over the road at Horton, I sacked the fish and drove quickly over to fetch him. As it turned out, half the syndicate ended up driving back over for a look and to assist with the photo's. I'd never had so many cameras pointed at me! Thankfully, they all buggered off before totally finishing off my rations and I was left to reflect on the mornings events, and attend to some unfinished business!

By early afternoon, and after another dozen trips up the tree, it became obvious that the fish had done the off. The wind that had been blowing gently into our faces had swung more to the south east and was picking up nicely. It was time for a move, but where to? Any fish moving from this area on the wind, would have to travel through the Dredger Bay so this was the first port of call. I packed up my gear and drove it around to the Dredger Bay, but once I was actually there, it didn't look as good as I had imagined. The wind was pushing across from right to left, leaving the bay at a rate of knots through the channel and into the Finger Bays, but due to the channeling effect of the islands, the main flow pushed on through into the North Lake. Standing on the concrete block looking down towards Sunnymeads, I could see a dark swell racing down the entire length of the lake, it was almost breaking into white caps as it arrived, barging its way into the Railway Bank near Sunnymeads. Although it was over half a mile from where the fish had been only a couple of hours previously, I just knew that they were headed there now.

Bundling Sam back into the motor, I drove around to the Nat West sailing club and, after loading up with tackle, trudged the rest of the way down to a swim known as the Bus Stop on the bottom bank. As I passed The Hun, who was set-up in Sunnymeads, he was gobsmacked as to why I'd moved from a swim that I'd just caught a thirty nine pounder from, only to set up next to him when he'd caught bugger all for days! Half an hour later I had an answer for him. A bait that I'd dropped into the margins to my left on a light hair rig set up, ripped into action. Before long The Hun and Tench Bloke were beside me offering all the usual encouragements as I did battle!

In front of the Bus Stop, one hundred yards out into the lake, is a small round island and the fish had managed to reach this on his first run. The water beside the island is very shallow, only two feet deep in places, and as a result of the fish being high in the water, a long tight line stretched out sixty or more yards above the surface. If the fish had kited around to the left behind the closer cigar island, it would have been disastrous, as it was, my luck held and he started to swing to the right. Just then, from further up the pit, I could see disaster manifesting itself in another, more frightening form. A sailing boat that had been poncing about near the club house, chose this moment for a high speed charge down the lake. I knew that they used the round island as a turning post, and with this much line out of the water he would cut me off for sure, even sinking the tip would not clear the tiller that hangs down below the boat. Sinking the boat, however, would surely do the trick, but being a bit light in the guided missile department we had to rely on the old tried and tested method of screaming. I don't know quite what the poor git on his yacht must have thought, suddenly there were three scruffy looking Herberts hurling threats and abuse at him, whilst leaping up and down waving sticks. Whatever his thoughts were, the first one was obviously, "I'm getting the bloody hell out of here." He executed a perfect on a sixpence-type turn and fled. I eventually got the fish close enough into the bank so that we could see it rolling and flashing in the waves. The Hun had climbed a small sapling and yelled, "It's Mary's Mate!"

On hearing this, both angler and fish simultaneously crapped themselves, the former (unwilling now to put any pressure on the hookhold) backwound like a Catherine wheel, while the latter having seen The Hun hanging out of a tree, broke all speed records on his mad dash for Sunnymeads Corner. Before I realised what was happening he was a good sixty yards away and heading for the overhanging branches. With a bit of side-strain from me and a lot of brick throwing, jumping up and down and yelling at the top of their voices from the other two, we soon had him back out in front. At this stage I glanced over to the sailing club where the intrepid sailor was standing on the slipway shaking his head in utter disbelief at the whole episode. The rest was a mere formality and before long we were all gathered around, slack jawed, staring down at the phenomenal sight of Mary's Mate lying on my unhooking mat.

This carp is, without doubt, one of the most impressive fish around. (See colour photo on page 258). Its length is incredible and the scales stand so proud that they look as if they have been glued on at a later date, but its most striking feature is its face, it always looks so bloody angry!

It was a strange day for weights, I had to check my scales to make sure that someone hadn't glued a stopper on the dial just short of forty pounds. This one was an ounce lighter than the earlier leviathan, weighing in at a healthy thirty nine pounds and fourteen ounces. Strangely enough, the next day I moved again, into the Railway Lake this time, and bagged a big tench which weighed in at nine pounds fourteen. All in all, not a bad few days angling but you can't help thinking that, for

9lb 14oz of Wraysbury tench.

the sake of a handful of spare ounces, or a healthy bounce on the scales, I'd have bagged a brace of forties and a double figure tench. The question is would I have been any the happier for it? You wouldn't think so would you?

I decided, in my infinite wisdom, that the Rocky Barge could do with a serious tart up as the banks sloped treacherously down to a poxy little bit of gravel that could only just house a bedchair but not quite a bivvy. What I needed for my master plan, however, were some tools, materials, and a method of transportation to get them over to the back of beyond that constituted the Rocky Barge. The first two were not overly problematic as, at Horton, there were stock piles of railway sleepers and scaffold poles, there was also a fully equipped tool shed. The transport side of things needed a little more thought, but on driving in through the Horton gates the next day I spotted the very thing. One of the members was the proud owner of an American Big Foot pick-up truck, the sort with wheels about six feet high! He was also the not so proud owner of the obvious nickname of Big Foot. Now, Big Foot took surprisingly little convincing that it would be a good idea to load up his truck with at least eight full-sized railway sleepers and ten scaffold poles before driving the lot over to Wraysbury for us. Quite how we were going to then transport this lot to the far side of the North Lake was unclear at this point, although I had some ideas revolving around building a raft!

The ride over to Wraysbury was possibly the most uncomfortable of my life as I sat in the back of a metal box pick-up, with suspension that only a cliff top plunge could compress, perched on top of a pile of sleepers whilst clutching a bushel of scaffold poles. By the time we arrived, I'd decided that the easiest way to get them across the lake would be to simply lash the whole lot together and float it over on the convenient westerly wind. As is often the way with theories, they are fine until that old reality fella raises his ugly head. Having never had the need to build a boat before, I was blissfully unaware of the different buoyancy levels of various woods. Hardwood, so it would seem, would definitely not have been Noah's first choice! We strapped the whole lot together (complete with poles) and slowly manoeuvred them down the slipway and over the edge into the waiting pond where the cleverly constructed craft floated like the proverbial brick!

Now we were faced with half a ton of crap all lashed together sitting on the bottom in three feet of water. Big Foot then came up with what seemed, at the time, a fairly reasonable plan when he volunteered to back the truck down the slipway into the water and tow the whole bundle back out from the lake. Once again, reality waited patiently in the wings. My job was to hang off the back of the truck and attach the rope to the uppermost sleeper, to reach this we needed to back up until the rear wheels were perilously close to the edge of the drop off. Once in position, and with the exhaust pipe merrily blowing bubbles into the water that sat a mere two inches below it, I attached the rope and called the all clear. With much revving and rocking of the engine, Big Foot slammed the gearshift in and eased off the clutch. The resulting surge of power and lunge of the truck could have been very impressive but unfortunately Big Foot had accidentally stuck it into reverse! As we shot backwards, further into the lake, I made ready to abandon ship. The exhaust was totally submerged but, amazingly, the engine was still running as the massive tyres struggled to gain purchase on the very precipice of disaster and, by some small miracle born out of sheer panic, Big Foot managed to drag both the truck and the sleepers from the pond. On the safety of dry land, I laid on the grass and wept with laughter as I recalled Big Foot's face peering through the rear window as he had let out the clutch. For some reason he didn't find it all quite as amusing as everybody else had!

The contingency plan was put into action and we floated the sleepers one by one out into the lake, the timbers were so dense that they barely floated even without the added encumbrance of a dozen scaffold poles, which incidentally we had to carry all the way around the lake. Trying not to laugh, I thanked Big Foot for his help and bade him farewell. A few weeks later he sold his truck and bought a Porsche. I can't think why! We sat over in the Rocky Barge waiting for the arrival of the railway sleepers, Tench Bloke, Phil and myself all lined up on the high bank like the three wise monkeys. Only half of them ever arrived at our side of the pit, and even then they all managed to tangle in the outermost branches. By the time we had rescued them using long sticks and bits of rope we were all too knackered to even contemplate building a swim with them, so we hid the tools and put it off for a few days, which as it transpired turned into nearly two years!

Chapter 17

June Happenings

By June, the weed had grown to such an extent that I was making more and more use of The Shootist's boat. If I couldn't locate any fish by the traditional methods of walking a circuit of the lake and climbing trees etc, then I'd quite often take to the boat for a drift around some of the more inaccessible areas of the lake. The fish could often be found at range in the South Lake, sitting in weedbeds out of view from the bank. The only way to fish these spots was by using a boat as the weed could be up to ten feet thick all around a small bar or hump. A bait placed on one of these spots, at the right time, would produce a fish whereas one cast out from the bank into the weed would not.

Although I would never profess to being any form of an expert on the numerous

varieties of weed that populate our waters, I have built up over the years an understanding of which ones the fish find most favourable at any given time of the season. I could not, for instance, give the correct name to more than three or four types, but I know that the long stringy grass type that flourishes in early summer not only indicates hard shallower ground but provides an absolute haven for the discerning carp. Whether using a boat or plumbing around for suitable areas, the discovery of this 'grass' weed always warrants a more in depth investigation as usually, a shallow and possible clear area is close at hand.

At the mouth of Bryants Bay, and just prior to the old perimeter of Dutch Bloke's tree felling endeavours, is a swim that we had labelled The Mad Dog's, due to the rabid hound that resided in the garden directly behind the swim. I was stupid enough to attempt to stroke him one day and the little bastard nearly took my finger off!

A bar of sand and gravel runs through this area and down into the bay to the left, usually not a prolific area for runs, but come the end of June a crop of grass weed abounds along the entire length of the bar and the fish tend to use the back of this as a route in and out of the bay. All along the drop off of the bar, and tight to the weed, small tables of sand jut out and offer the perfect place to present a bait. The prime time only seems to last for a couple of weeks or so, in between the weed peaking and its sudden and untimely demise. During this short period I managed three pick ups from Mad Dog's, resulting in one small stockie, a lost fish, and my biggest Wraysbury common of twenty seven pounds, before the weed collapsed. Three or four other areas of the South Lake also sported this same weed crop and all held fish on a regular basis over this same

The Snags.

period but unfortunately you can't fish everywhere at once.

Another area that was always worth a look from the boat was The Snags. Situated up a small overgrown channel between two of the Dredger Bay islands, there was a large tree that had toppled and was now half-submerged in the water. Completely inaccessible with a rig from any point on the lake, it offered total sanctuary to the fish. As an observation point it was second to none, and many hours were spent huddled amongst the branches just watching big old mirror carp gliding effortlessly in and out of the snags at my feet. To get to these snags involved a row out to the margins of Ten Acre Island and docking the boat on the opposite side to the tree. The island, although fairly overgrown, was still relatively easy to get across and as I neared the spot, I would then crawl slowly on my hands and knees making my way stealthily to the base of the tree. With a careful piece of manoeuvring, I would inch my way along the fallen bough until I was directly over the fish. At times they would lay so close to me that I could have quite literally reached down and touched them. On one occasion, I was lying prostrate along the bough, feeding an unknown thirty pounder with Chum Mixers by dropping them down a mere eighteen inches to land one at a time only a foot in front of his nose. As he confidently took them while facing straight at me I could watch their progress as they disappeared down his throat! With a swift move I could probably have put my finger in his mouth before he'd even noticed.

On another occasion, one hot summer's day, I parked the boat just off the branches and took photo's of the fish as they came and went at will, totally ignoring my presence. At times they were so close that I didn't dare move to point the camera. I saw fish that day that I'd never seen before or since. I did manage to get a few half decent photo's, in spite of the fact that I didn't have a polarizing lens with me. Unfortunately, while climbing back out of the boat and onto dry land in the Dredger Bay, I slipped and fell backwards into the pond, taking the camera with me. The photo's still came out but with a surreal green-glowing effect, a bit like a laser beam had darted across the lens. Only in this one area could you become so intimate with your quarry, they knew beyond a shadow of a doubt that they were safe from anglers whilst in the sanctuary of The Snags.

One thing that did surprise me was the lake bed below the tree, it was dark, almost black, and covered with a light coating of weed that looked as if it had never been disturbed. Not a single clear area could be seen anywhere in the immediate vicinity. It was as if they never fed here, preferring to use it purely as a safe house. Occasionally, they would leave their refuge in the snags, and follow the island margins into The Basin. The Basin is a large depression in the contours of the Ten Acre Island, actually within the Dredger Bay. It forms a shallow bay, three or four feet deep, lined with overhanging branches and snags. To fish this area involves a long cast from the swim to the left of the Dredger, but, due to the lack of depth, the weed can make it pretty well unfishable in the height of summer. It was also a favourite haunt of the Fungus Mirrors, who frequently all

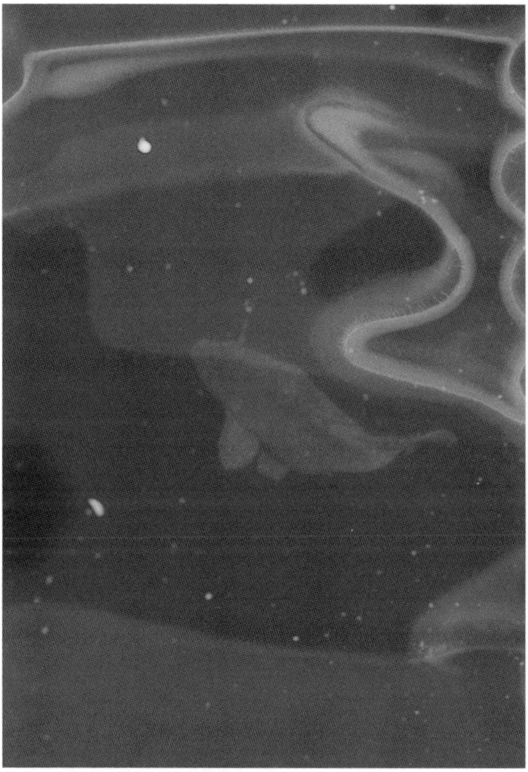
Like a laser beam had darted across the lens.

hung around together under one small bush at the back of the bay.

On one occasion, I was fortunate to spot a few of the big original fish cruising into the Dredger Bay late on in the afternoon. It had been a very humid and oppressive day, threatening storms all afternoon but never quite producing the goods. The odd fish cruised out from the snags and down the channel into The Basin and by climbing up a tree I could just make out a handful of bigger fish hanging around near the bushes at the back of the bay. Walking back around to the South Lake and collecting my gear from its secret stashing in the bushes, I opted to use the boat to row it all across. That way I'd have the boat for an emergency if I needed it. There was a lot of weed between me and the fish, not to mention the snags and the dredger on either side so I figured it was better to be safe than sorry. Within an hour, I was set-up and ready to angle there for the night, but casting up against the island proved to be a bit of a nightmare. Every mis-cast brought back half a hundredweight of weed with it on the retrieve. Although I was reluctant to take the boat out there, as the fish were clearly visible cruising around The Basin, I soon realised that even more harm could be done by thrashing the water to a foam from the bank. I put the rod down and sat on the deck pondering the Catch 22 situation before me. Eventually, deciding on a course of action, I rowed out to the actual Dredger and tied the boat up alongside then, by clambering up onto the roof, I could survey the entire scene. Standing up there like Captain Pugwash, I could clearly see the large belt of weed that isolated The Basin from the rest of the bay. It was this weed that was presenting the problem. Also, from my vantage point, I could make out the clear areas at the back of the swim. It was obvious now, looking at them from here, that I would be extremely lucky to land in a two foot square hole with twenty casts, let alone one or two. I finally decided to take the rods out in the boat as far as the belt of weed, and then gently flick the baits out the last ten yards into position. This plan, I figured, would cause the least upset to the fish, the band of weed acting as a barrier between them and the boating activity.

Once out there, and standing up with Polaroids on, I could see the bottom clearly and the biggest problem was going to be not spooking the fish. At that moment they were swimming around happily, only a few yards in front of me. I could make out two thirty pounders and a few twenties mixed in with the inevitable Fungus Mirrors that were

High hopes in Dredger Bay.

mainly very low doubles. An overhanging tree on the corner of the island marked the edge of The Basin, to its left in the shallower water was a small gravel bar with about four feet of water over the top. On the right hand side of the tree, as the bottom sloped away into six feet of water, the weed had grown to within two feet of the surface. One small bald spot in the weed, about fifteen feet from the tree, revealed a two foot square area of soft silt. Into this hole I flicked one bait with about twenty free offerings around it. The other rod was plopped on top of the gravel bar but, due to the camber off the bar, any free offerings that I introduced slowly trundled off the spot and into the surrounding weed. I took about twenty baits and broke them into odd shaped pieces before flicking them out onto the bar. They sunk at a more sedate pace and I watched their descent, spinning over and over like pennies in a wishing well, coming eventually to rest neatly on the exposed gravel and sand. Paying out line as I went, I carefully rowed back to the bank and set the rods in position for the night. As the air pressure mounted and the temperature rose I was convinced a storm was on its way, but only the occasional peal of thunder in the distance could be heard throughout the night.

By mid-morning the level of fish activity had increased and I couldn't believe that I hadn't received some form of action. As is often the case in this swim, around lunchtime the fish drifted into the sanctuary of The Snags, and I took the opportunity to go out and check the baits. Straight away it was apparent that something had occurred. Only two baits remained on the silt spot, and the bar had been totally cleaned off. A closer inspection revealed that my rigs had been tossed aside to make room for the dinner party that had obviously followed. Right! The gloves were off. If they wanted to play rough then so be it. I changed the leads over to three ounces and, using the handle of the oar, I buried them deeply into the lake bed. If they could pull those suckers out without getting hooked in the process I'd eat my own ear wax! I'd just got the job finished and was drying out back in the swim when the first fish of the bunch started to leave The Snags on their way back to The Basin.

Throughout the course of the evening, I saw Mary and a couple of lesser beasts drift into the swim as well, making their way in from the Finger Bays to my left. So, when the rod on the gravel bar ripped off in the middle of the night, I thought I'd cracked it. Unfortunately, after a brief tussle, a nineteen pound common turned out to be the culprit, and amazingly it was a fish that I recognised from two previous captures earlier that year. This was typical of Wraysbury, the same few fish get caught again and again while others evade capture altogether. At first sight the swim looked totally different, only a handful of the Fungus Mirrors remained and the biggest of these was only about mid-doubles. I think the commotion with the common in the night must have put the cat amongst the pigeons, and by nine o clock I was loading the tackle back into the boat. I decided on a slow drift through the Finger Bays and around the island to see if they'd moved onto the shallows in front of the Douglas Lane point.

I drifted down into the Finger Bays and standing up whilst punting the boat along allowed me to see down through the gin clear water. The day was already hot, although it was only mid-morning, and it was one of those still and tranquil days when the slightest of sounds seems to amplify and carry across the calm waters. Although I was trying my hardest to remain quiet, every dip of the oar seemed to shatter the ambiance of the morning. I reached the gap that led through into the South Lake, this being my intended route, but I hesitated on the edge of the small piece of water at the bottom of the bay. Poets Corner we'd named it, a mere fifty yards long and twenty yards wide and, at the moment, totally choked with weed. I'd never taken the boat in there before and I'm not sure what possessed me to do so on this particular morning but it looked strangely inviting and, in my mind's eye, visions of monumental mirrors lurking unseen below the weed drew me in. I pushed the boat through the blanket of floating milfoil and Canadian pondweed, searching for any signs of carp sheltering under the canopy of greenery but only the odd perch or jack pike skittered away from the intrusion of the boat. Suddenly, the silence was shattered by the tortured screech of an animal, clearly in its death throes, a horrendous scream gave way to a whimper and then cold silence as a rabbit or similar became a statistic of the food chain.

The bank in Poets Corner is about six feet above the water so, from where I stood in the boat, I could almost see ground level. Almost but not quite. The kill sounded as if it had taken place just a few yards in front of me so, straining up on tip-toe, I struggled to get a better view. I could hear the scrabbling about of the unseen hunter with his now lifeless prey but, try as I might, I couldn't quite see him. Just then, almost as if a sixth sense, one that I was previously unaware of, came into play, I instantly knew I was not alone in my observations. As the hairs on the back of my neck stood to attention I turned to see an adult male fox standing twenty feet away to my left. He was as engrossed in the proceedings as I was, so much so that he seemed totally unaware of my presence. As I stood there, a rare and privileged onlooker to one of Mother Nature's spectacles, I saw the fox's tail stand out erect behind him and as his ears pointed the way, he launched himself forwards, graceful in the extreme. I heard a loud squeal, and through the bushes, heading straight for the lake, came a stoat. In a split second, from hunter to hunted, he dashed along the sloping bank in front of me. The fox, lacking the agility of the stoat, raced along the higher bank above his head, and nearly had him as he made a desperate dash for freedom across the path to my left. As the stoat crashed his way through the bushes at the other side of the path on his way to freedom, the wily old fox sauntered up to the still twitching rabbit corpse and, lifting it carefully between his jaws, trotted off into the woods.

I made my way slowly around into the South Lake, reflecting as I went that it was a harsh old existence being a stoat but an even harsher one being a rabbit. I was just grateful for being at the top of the food chain. Even so, I was going to eat my Chinese

tonight as quickly as possible as you could never be too careful!

The fish had started to appear in the South Lake quite regularly by the end of June and, after sighting a few one afternoon near the central island, I set-up for a session in the White Fence swim next to the Douglas Lane car park. The island is about one hundred and twenty yards out and a small sand and gravel hump sits five yards in from its snag-lined banks. I'd found the area quite by chance, one day when the water clarity was at its very best. It sat three feet proud of the bottom in seventeen feet of water, and I could clearly feel the difference now as the lead donked down on the hard gravel top. It took a while to get both baits positioned perfectly, and when I was eventually satisfied they were fishing properly, I put on the kettle for a much needed cuppa. No sooner had the steam started rising from the spout than the rustling of the bushes heralded the arrival of my first visitor. I'd been expecting a bit more activity on the 'social scene' seeing as how I was set up in such close proximity to the car park, but I was still amazed and delighted to see Little Robbie from Horton. This was a rare sighting indeed!

"Bloody hell, Raver," he said. "That was handy, I thought I'd have to walk for miles."

"I set up here especially for you," I lied, as I topped up the kettle.

We sat chatting and drank endless cups of tea until, eventually, we watched mesmerised as the sun sank behind the island into a sea of molten reds. The calm surface of the lake mirrored the spectacle perfectly, and Robbie announced that I was definitely going to catch the 'big fella' tonight, before he bade his farewells and made his way off through the bushes. I could still hear the engine of his car making its way up the Douglas Lane when the first bite came. It was a drop-back on one of the island rods and it had me winding down and striking as hard as I could. Well, Robbie had been right about me catching but I don't think a five pound stockie could possibly constitute 'the big fella.' More annoying was the fact that it was now too dark to reposition the bait, so I was down to just one rod on the main spot. Another hour later, an even smaller stockie in the landing net meant that I was no longer fishing the island at all, so I re-cast it out into the middle of nowhere alongside the other rod and retired to bed in disgust.

Just as I was drifting off to sleep, I became aware of noise in the background, and when I listened harder I could clearly hear the roaring and crackling of a fire. Thinking somebody had set-up in the Root Nightmare, I whistled Tench Bloke over from The Point swim and made my way across the grass car park. As I approached, I couldn't believe my eyes, the fire was raging, not in the car park as expected but on the end of Bryants Point. My swim must have been three to four hundred yards away from Bryants but I'd heard it as clearly as you like. The flames danced a clear twenty feet off the ground and lit up the whole bay. Tench Bloke appeared with a, "Bloody hell, what's going on over there?"

We set off at a flat run to try to get there in time to minimalise the damage, only by the look of it we were going to be a bit late. As we passed Dutch Bloke's garden, we found him furtively pacing the bank looking more than a little worried. "Have you seen that fire?" he asked. "I didn't do it you know," he added quickly.

"Nobody said you did Dutch Bloke," I replied, shooting T.B. a knowing look. "But you can help us put it out, eh?"

The three of us legged it round to what was left of The Point. When we arrived the truth became instantly apparent. A whole new swim had been hewn out of the trees and bushes, the resulting log pile had been torched and the flames now threatened to engulf the surrounding trees. The heat being chucked out was frightening, and great plumes of smoke and steam gushed upwards as we dampened the edges using water scooped out of the margins. For half an hour we battled to control the flames, dragging the largest logs out of the fire and plunging them, hissing and spitting into the lake. Finally, with the fire back in hand, we turned the edges in, burning all the small bits of branch and twig that littered the ground. Throughout the whole affair Dutch Bloke kept repeating, "I can't imagine who could have done this," and "I just looked out and saw it burning."

By pure coincidence, the very next weekend Dutch Bloke's own nephew was sat angling in the newly hacked-out swim! When we were eventually sure that everything was in order we strolled back to the Douglas Lane, my skin felt as if it had been sand-blasted and black soot was ingrained into every pore, but at least there were some trees left standing on The Point.

Chapter 18

Long Session in Root Nightmare

During the next few weeks, I travelled around the lake at an alarming pace, fishing a new swim almost every day, but the main sightings always seemed to be in the South Lake.

The weed in the huge centre section had flourished and made an ideal area for the fish to hide out in, it had the advantage of being out of range of all the usual bankside disturbances as well as holding an incredible amount of food, including massive beds of daphnia that would appear like swirling red clouds in the otherwise clear water. Fish spawn was also present in large quantities and a marker left out there for a week could be retrieved absolutely encased in natural tapioca. The occasional band of fish would leave this safe haven and move off through the Dredger Bay, en route to the North Lake or even the Finger Bays, but by far the most consistent area, for sightings at least, was the middle area of the South Lake. There were only two swims that you could reach this area from, although if not for the out of bounds fence of the sailing club, there could quite easily be three. It was apparent throughout the summer that the fish were not travelling overly far from The Root Nightmare, in fact they were seen there regularly, and often at extreme range. At the opposite end of this middle section lies Mary's Point and the carp would alternate between the two. Out from Mary's, at about one hundred yards, are a pair of islands connected by a very shallow bar and the fish would invariably cross this wall of sand and gravel on their way up or down the pit. From the back of these islands, stretching out into no man's land, ran a series of three or four bars, one of which was very shallow and constructed of the type of stone-encrusted solid rock that, at Wraysbury, constituted a very poor feeding area indeed. The other two or three were slightly deeper, sand topped, and prime ground for intercepting a Wraysbury whacker. Unfortunately, there were no swims within even a half sensible distance of this forgotten area of water, at least there never used to be until I had the idea of constructing a jetty next to the out of bounds fence of the sailing club. Originally, the only method of fishing over the fence and out into no man's land, was to weave a bankstick into the top of a six foot, barbed wire topped, chain link fence and this obviously put most people off. It also had the disadvantage of leaving your lines six feet above water level at the entrance to a very active sailing club, which in itself is a recipe for disaster. Using The Shootist's boat, I rowed all around the waters of Wraysbury and collected up all the old discarded railway sleepers and large lumps of timber that I could find. Stringing them together on a rope from the stern, I slowly dragged them back to the fence and, with the use of some scaffold poles, sandbags, and an old trout fishing platform that I liberated from Horton, I constructed a serviceable fishing stage that allowed you to fish with your rod tips around the end of the fence. The front rod rest was a scaffold pole sticking out of the pond a good six feet from the end of the jetty which made the use of a boat an absolute necessity, even just to turn the alarms on or off.

The Wraysbury bug had well and truly gotten hold of me by now and I was returning home less and less as the summer progressed. I was only living in shared digs with a few mates, so I had very few outgoings or responsibilities, which suited me just fine. Every so often when the need arose I would brave the real world and return to Crawley to spend a day or so putting all my affairs in order so as to give myself the maximum time available for searching out the hidden monsters of Wraysbury.

It was one of these necessary excursions that had torn me away from a swim full of carp on the South Lake to sort out my finances, among other things. I hadn't wanted to go and was now wishing I'd not bothered. The whole affair had been a disaster! The Volvo overheated twice on the way home and, when I finally arrived back, instead of a

My swim 'The Fence'.

cheque on the mat as expected there was a two day old letter summoning me for an appointment that was only ten minutes away! A quick change of clothes and a splash of water later and I found myself sitting in a dole office staring blankly out through the window. I was working out where the fish were going to be feeding today, while some jumped up little jobs worth, with a terminal case of acne, bleated on about re-evaluation and such-like. Eventually, after I'd promised them the earth, he begrudgingly handed over the giro. In the same split second that he released his grip, I was out of the door and away as fast as my little legs would carry me. Unfortunately, I turned up at the post office moments after the arrival of a bus load of OAP's and I stood in line, hopping from one foot to the other in frustration, for what was surely the longest half an hour in living memory. After stocking up on food and bait on the way home, I paused briefly to transfer the bills from the mat into the bin, and then I was back on the motorway. All my tackle had been left with Tench Bloke, who was fishing on the Point Swim in the Douglas Lane and I couldn't wait to re-acquaint myself with it. Fate hadn't quite finished with me for the day, though, and halfway up the M25 the traffic ground to a standstill and, for as far as the eye could see, all three lanes were blocked up solid. It was absolutely frying in the Volvo, so I turned off the engine and waited. One hour later found me sitting cross-legged on the tarmac in the middle of the motorway, with the Coleman cooker blasting away merrily. I was busy making tea for all and sundry. People roamed freely among the parked cars chatting to each other in an attempt to stave off the boredom. Fat Sam had found the only piece of shade available and had curled up in the middle lane half tucked underneath a Suzuki jeep, with the occasional motorbike weaving its way slowly between the cars, carefully negotiating Sam's fat bum as it passed. According to a workman on the central reservation, a lorry carrying chemicals had overturned five miles ahead, and I had the dubious honour of being a part of one the longest queues ever seen on the M25! Eventually, after almost two hours, a gallon of water, and half a box of tea bags, we were finally on the move again. Driving as fast as the old Volvo could manage, in a vain bid to make up for lost time, I eventually reached junction 13 and turned off for Wraysbury. With sanctuary within my sights I sped up the Douglas Lane but, unfortunately, I omitted to slow down for the heavily-pitted section next to the gate and, as the rear wheels bounced down a pot hole, the exhaust caught briefly on the ground tearing a hole in the back box. The noise was incredible. Volvo's are not renowned for their silent running at the best of times but with a shredded exhaust pipe it was audible for miles. A few minutes later Tench Bloke appeared out of the bushes to find me methodically kicking a hole in the front wing, not much of a remedy for a broken exhaust I'll admit, but incredibly satisfying nevertheless!

Nothing of note had occurred during my absence and T.B. was up for a move of swims so, eventually, we decided to set-up in the car park swims, those being the Root Nightmare and the Little Root. Whilst here, we could rip the old exhaust off and, after a trip to the local breaker's yard, hopefully we could fit another one. Abandoning the car at the back of the swims for now, we set-up camp and laid a few plans. The odd fish had been seen in this area lately, but a high percentage of the recently stocked small commons seemed to reside here as well. These were all like peas in a pod and were around the four to six pound mark. Quite why Wraysbury needed an injection of one hundred of these zero character pasties was beyond me, but they were in there now and that was that. We decided to bait quite heavily with particles, as well as boiled baits, to see what we could get interested. I was still a bit dubious about end tackle after having my rigs moved so easily in the Dredger Bay and vowed to keep a very close eye on any activity around the bait from now on. The first thing we needed were a few clean areas as the weed reached the surface over most of the two swims.

From the tree to the left of the Root Nightmare, Tench Bloke found a small sandy hump just a few yards out. The odd stockie could be seen browsing over it and it seemed like a good starting point as it could be checked regularly without the need for the boat. After much searching, I located just two spots, both were small sand bars, one at thirty and one at fifty yards range. I had a sack of dry hemp with me which we set about cooking up and as each batch cooked it was spread evenly over all three spots. By that evening we were set-up and angling. The odd fish had rolled and we were feeling confident. That first night, produced two stockies to T.B.'s rods and one to mine. Up until now only a couple of these small commons had been caught at all, and although they were not what we were after, it was an encouraging sign to have something feeding in your swim. Maybe the activity would draw the bigger fish in to investigate? More bait was cooked up and, as soon as it went in, so the stockies started to come out. By dawn the next day we'd had four each and were both already sick of the sight of them, so most of the day was spent underneath the Volvo. The exhaust had welded itself together and we ended up having to heat up the pipe, using two Colman cookers, to get it apart. Half way through this rather absurd scheme, and just as our petrol reserves were running out, a car pulled up behind us and out jumped Phil. Just arriving for his weekend session he was full of enthusiasm as usual, convinced that he would find The Pug, a pug-pug-pugging around somewhere and bag him.

He was as surprised as we had been about the stockies and a conversation about the ethics of barbecued carp followed but after deciding better of it, we relieved him of his shiny new green can of petrol and bade him good-bye as he strolled off to find that Pug. His parting words were, "mind the can, Tench Bloke, it's brand new."

Sometimes Phil has a sixth sense about these sort of dangerous situations involving his belongings, especially where Tench Bloke or myself are concerned. I scuffled back under the car with the one full cooker and continued heating, and clouting the exhaust with the jack handle, while T.B. filled the other Coleman to cook up some more hemp. True to Phil's pessimistic prophecy, I'd only been under the car a few moments when I heard a loud WHOOSH! A scream made me leap up, cracking my head on the hot pipe as I did so. Tench Bloke was hopping about maniacally, stomping the ground all around him, most of which was quite convincingly alight! The source of the fire lay nearby and through the still spewing flames, I could make out Phil's not-so-new-looking green canister fully ablaze. Snatching up a piece of old carpet that had been covering one of the many exposed roots in the swim, I braved the flames and gingerly smothered the spout of the can. Luckily, the fire in the can went out quite easily, which is more than can be said for Tench Bloke's little inferno. Even his feet were smoldering now. The more he stamped, the more the flames danced about so we settled, in the end, for handfuls of dirt scooped up and hurled over it, and this seemed to do the trick.

When Phil turned up later, T.B. dutifully returned the black, charred, and partly melted can, complete with the lid that no longer fitted, and suffered the abuse as a consequence. At least he had managed to fill the cooker first and, eventually, after much blood sweat and tears the exhaust came free.

Friday afternoon wasn't the time to be off looking for a new exhaust, so I decided to stay put until Monday. I piled a load more bait in, chopping up a few kilos of boilies and mixing it in with hemp and tigers and, following its introduction, small carp could be seen topping all evening. In the night a couple of much larger fish crashed out, giving us the confidence to stay put for a while longer. In the end we stayed put in those two swims for most of a two week period. The more bait we put in the more we caught. Stockies, tench and bream, queued up to get at it and most days at least one or two proper carp were spotted over the baited areas. Tench Bloke even caught an eighteen pound common one morning. One thing was becoming apparent, and that was the stockies ability to learn from their mistakes. By halfway through the second week, all the bait would be eaten and just the hookbaits would remain. It seemed that they had been taking lessons from originals in avoiding the hookbait. Neither of us particularly wanted to catch these bait-robbing stockies, but if our rigs were not capable of hooking even them, then what chance had we with the larger and more educated fish? I took to going out in the boat to bait up every afternoon and would regularly find just the two hookbaits remaining, even after putting three or four kilos of bait out there the day before. Still the bigger fish showed, and eventually the question had to be asked, were they getting away with it as well? Were they out there feeding regularly and leaving our hookbaits whilst clearing up everything else that we threw at them? If this was the case how did we ever catch them in the first place?

Deciding that a bit of rig experimentation was called for, I jumped into the recently repaired Volvo and popped over to Horton. Once there, I perused the many brimming tackle boxes on display, to see what I could liberate in the way of advanced rig components. After a walk round, involving a few beers and the odd sympathetic ear for my rig problems, I returned to Wraysbury, my pockets overflowing with flat leads, square

leads, fly hooks, sky hooks, bolt beads, shrink tube, and every kind of hooklength material known to man. I dumped the whole lot at Tench Bloke's feet and said, "Right then, how the bloody hell does this lot work?" After a few hours of trial and error, an impressive assortment of wonder rigs adorned the ribs of the brolly. All that remained was to try them out. By the next afternoon, it was obvious that we'd actually found one that worked. One of T.B.'s rods was catching stockies and tench regularly, while all others failed. But when he showed me the rig I couldn't believe that anything in its right mind would fall for such a monstrosity. It comprised of a long shanked fly hook with a small boilie tied tight to the eye, this was attached to four inches of dacron and a four ounce square lead! It looked absolutely, bloody ridiculous, but three stockies and a tench so far disagreed with me. Figuring that if the other fish could fall for it then maybe so would the proper carp, we tied up half a dozen and before long all our rods were sporting one. Instantly the bites returned and, although no better fish were hooked, a couple were once again heard jumping in the night. We even saw one in silhouette against the night sky. It slid straight out of the water over T.B.'s baits before toppling over with a mighty crash. Unfortunately, I had to return home for a couple of days the next morning, and just as I was loading up the Volvo, a large mirror carp thrashed on the surface over my furthest spot.

Tench Bloke bags Mallin's.

As soon as was humanly possible I was driving back through the Douglas Lane gates, only this time a bit more slowly. I could see the carp sack hanging from the tree in triumph as I bumped across the grass towards the swim.

"How big?" were my first words as I stepped out of the car.

"I've 'aaadd one," replied Tench Bloke in a perfect impersonation of The Plumber.

"I can see that," I replied. "How big?"

Mallin's fish at thirty eight pounds twelve, it turned out, and apparently the fish had been leaping non-stop ever since I left. It obviously goes without saying that they stopped as soon as I set foot on the bank!

The next morning T.B. had another take that was unquestionably another proper carp. It was an absolute run from hell, and was followed by the most amazing boat battle amongst the weed that I've ever witnessed, let alone been a part of. The boat we were using left a lot to be desired as well, it started off stable enough but a slow puncture limited our time spent afloat. Three times in all we had to abandon the fight and return to the bank to re-inflate the dinghy. Most of the fight, for me, was spent with my head under the water trying to free the weed from the main line. Looking through the mask I could see what appeared to be the lake bed ten feet under the boat, strewn with weed, but the water here was in the region of sixteen feet deep which left an awful lot of weed. The fish utilised this to his full advantage, and every time that I managed to unbury him and shout to T.B. that he was back in control he would simply charge back into this subterranean jungle again. After about an hour I noticed that Steve Allcott, who was fishing at the other end of the South Lake, was also out in a boat playing a fish. Unfortunately, the weed had got the better of him and I could almost feel the dejectedness of a lost battle exuding from the little inflatable as he paddled back to shore with the now lifeless rod. After approximately two and a half hours, we finally had the fish circling under the boat, unable now to reach the weed again, I'd already had a few very good looks at it through the mask and knew that it was a big old kipper. The problem we had now was the boat. It was almost flat but the fish was almost beaten, if we slackened off now to return to shore we'd have to start from scratch again.

Then the cavalry arrived, just in the nick of time as always. General John 'Custer' Cross rode in, astride his trusty white charger called 'Transit' and saved the day. Seeing our predicament, he pumped up his own boat and bringing our pump with him, he rowed out to re-inflate us mid-battle. Shortly after this kiss of life operation, the carp must have decided that enough was enough and, realising that we were never giving up, he threw in the towel. Somewhere in the region of three hours were spent, from bank and from boat, with various poles, tree sections, and diving mask to land one very angry carp. When we eventually looked in the net, though, we knew why. It was Mary's Mate. Undoubtedly, the angriest-looking carp there is. This one weighed in at thirty nine pounds and completed a brace of personal bests for a very happy Tench Bloke.

Later that night Steve and Del turned up to see if we might like to wander over the road to The Perseverance, to celebrate Tench Bloke's capture and listen to Steve's tale of woe, regarding his lost fish.

Due to the ever-present risk at Wraysbury of returning to your swim to find your tackle has been liberated by pikey's, I'd started to employ a few anti-theft ruses. The best of these was the 'false body in the bed' ruse. Whenever I left the swim after dark, I would

A brace of personal bests for a very happy Tench Bloke.

stuff the sleeping bag with clothes, pillows, and the dog bed, then sculpt it on the bedchair into the form of a sleeping person. By taking the baits off and flicking the leads into the margins, I could clip on the indicators and give the impression of an angler lying next to his rods. As a finishing touch, I'd put Sam's dog bowl on full view in the middle of the swim just to add a bit more uncertainty for the prospective thief. With this task completed we set off for a slow stroll through Bryants Bay to the pub.

Apart from the aforementioned fishy tales, one of the many topics of conversation that night was the near plague proportions of earwigs and damsel fly larvae that were about. The larvae trudged relentlessly up the bank and slowly climbed up into the ribs of your brolly to dry out and hatch, while the earwigs and spiders ran around merrily eating all the casts that were left behind. Although everyone was suffering from them, nothing could have prepared me for the sight that greeted me on my return. Shining the torch in the doorway at the false 'me' that was lying there, I saw about thirty crawling slimy things running up and down what would have been my back and legs. Startled by the beam, an earwig that would have rivalled the British record, reared up at me from atop my false head waving its many arms menacingly. It took ten minutes with the Coleman cooker to purge my bivvy of alien life forms, and for the next week I slept with the sleeping bag pulled firmly up over my head. It really doesn't do, to know what comes visiting while you sleep!

We stayed on for a few more days and I was convinced I'd get a take eventually as, although the main activity had ceased, the odd fish still showed around my furthest marker. On what was supposed to be my last morning of the session, two weeks after first setting up here, I finally got the pick-up I'd been waiting for. I'd just taken the brolly down and was standing, staring blankly at the bomb site that was my swim, when the long rod leapt into action. There was no doubts about a stockie or tench being responsible and the spool emptied as something large charged off through the thick weed. With the clutch screaming, I held on to the bucking rod, waiting for the first run to subside and eventually he stopped, solid in the weed. After a few minutes of stalemate, the tip suddenly pinged back a couple of feet and I had a horrible feeling that the battle was lost. Not wanting to put any further pressure on, just in case, I rowed out to the spot and found my main line wrapped around and around a large weed bed. The rig was nearby also heavily weeded but the fish was long gone. On my way back to shore, I paused next to my marker and peering down through the depths, I could see that every single grain of bait had been cleared, probably long before the run occurred. The bottom shone from all the attention it had received over the last two weeks. Two whole weeks of effort and sacks and sacks of bait, only for it all to end in tears! I suppose you have to lose some battles though, if only to make the eventual victory that much sweeter, my time would come. I cancelled all my other plans and set the brolly back up, determined to even the score. But it was not to be.

The Root Nightmare died a bit of a death after this marathon session, although I'm sure the fish still visited the areas and probably still fed there as well, but with a level of caution that defied belief. So, after a few more days of trying, we packed away and left for pastures new. I decided that now would be a good time to try out the newly created Fence Swim or even Mary's Point, as the fish seemed determined to stay in the South

Persevering in The Fence.

Lake all summer. A lot of time and effort went into this swim but unfortunately, it seemed that I had made myself a bogey swim. Apart from the inevitable stockies, I never managed to get a single take from here.

Mary's Point was a considerably more comfortable swim to fish from and, should it be free, I would much prefer to fish the island bars from here than The Fence. When I first started to pay some attention to the bar that linked the two islands there was weed covering most of the shallower marks along the top and sides, although a small spot about three feet across had been cleared on the very top of the bar. Due to the lack of depth (about two and a half feet) I opted to bait lightly with tigers and hemp so as not to attract the attentions of Mr and Mrs Coot. Unbeknown to me, Steve Allcott had also been baiting the same spot, hence the original clearing. Between us over the next couple of weeks we had managed to create a large feeding area. I was never to reap any benefits from this swim but Steve and a number of other anglers made this one of the most productive swims of this period. Every time that I would vacate the swim the fish would instantly move in and the lucky angler sat there would reap the rewards. Steve's results in this swim, though, brought together years of hard work and dedication at Wraysbury and came as a well deserved reward for some very fine angling.

What follows is a brief account of Steve's Wraysbury adventures and has been written by Steve in his own unique and distinctive style, I have long been a fan of Steve's writings and as soon as I made up my mind to create a book about Wraysbury, I knew that it would be lacking without the following chapter. I hope that you enjoy reading it as much as I did.

Steve's Story

What's that smell? The smoke from Compo's barbecued hot pot drifted across the pond. Wraysbury rabbit, carrots, and spuds were dish of the day from the Dredger Bay. I stared into the skies, admiring in awe the sight of a thousand ring-necked parakeets en route to roost on Ten Acre Island. It was just the perfect evening, Mary was due out and it was to be John or I who caught her. We were at opposite ends of the South Lake and we both felt that we had an equal chance to bag her that week.

The sun had risen to around the ten o'clock position when I saw Compo rowing through the gap towards me - I knew!

"John needs you, I'll see you around there in half an hour."

With the camera kit in hand, I made my way to the other side. I was elated for John, a tad of envy maybe but he had paid for it more than I. We weighed her in at 49lb and the word awesome was invented that day in the flesh. She was not as big as everyone had presumed - but she was big enough for us. If ever there was a carp that no picture could ever do justice to, then that fish was truly it.

Time had passed and I had taken a shine to the little swim that is now called Mary's Point. It's just one of many lovely little parts of Wraysbury. It gives a view over half of the South Lake and most of No Carp Bay. It's one of those secret swims where you can fish a few rods here and a few rods there, if you get my drift. So many ideal-looking spots. The two best and, if you look, the two most obvious are the shallow bar between the two distant islands and the margins of the smaller close island. It is not that this was particularly a better swim than the others, it was just where I'd decided to sit and wait through the glorious sunrises and sunsets that the swim offered. The bad point about Mary's Point was the yachts. Let's not forget the yachts! Sometimes you couldn't even have a line out there for the whole day. Leaving your gear was out as well, as the hooligan swim in No Carp Bay was always full on a hot day. When the evening comes, though, the yachts drift away and so do the kids, and then it's a quiet carp lake just like any other that you'd sit and watch. Often the tench would dance at dusk, but you rarely saw a carp and if you did you knew that you were 'on'.

Another year had passed by and I had a week's fishing holiday, which eventually turned into about nine days. I fished one night in one swim and then a couple in Mary's and then off again for another night before returning to Mary's for a couple more. I fished in this fashion for the whole session, and I saw absolutely nothing, not until the very last stop. I was opposite Mary's near the sailing club and from somewhere they had all appeared. I watched about eighteen large carp for a couple of hours until about tea

A shallow bar connects the islands.

time. Really, my session was over and for me to go back to Mary's Point, I would have to motivate myself for the two long trips back to the swim I left that very morning. I drove around to the Douglas Lane stopping for some refreshments along the way. T.B. and Dave were there and were glad of the thirst quencher. They had also hunted the pit all that day and we'd passed each other a few times.

Dave asked, "Seen any then Steve?"

"Have you?" was my reply.

"One fish," they said, and they were on their way round there to angle.

"Well, have you?" they asked. I took a slow deep breath, "All of them - and more."

We went to have a look.

"You are going back in aren't you?" Dave asked.

"Silly not to," I replied, even though really I'd had enough, plus they would have given me so much stick for bad angling if I hadn't. A couple of hours later, I was set-up and angling once more, just in time to see the fish swim off into No Carp Bay! With no action and no fish seen, I went back to work the next day. The week passed slowly, most evenings I spent dreaming that I was on Mary's Point. With the curtains open, I watched the hot July sunrise, that Friday feeling, back to the pond and hopefully Mary's Point.

I only had weekends for quite sometime. With this in mind I knew I had to make the most of any situation that arose. The way the other half live! Sometimes I envied them. Total escape from reality as we know it. Dave said to me once, "Nothing is more precious than time, you can't buy it and you have to sacrifice to make it." I can't do that, I won't be without. I've already had everything and although I may be spoilt I'm accustomed to my luxuries. The passion is strong, though, and ambition drives me on

"If you're happy and you know it - have a drink!"

the same today as it drove the boy who caught his first carp 25 years ago.

Eventually, I was back on the pond and obviously the first thing was to see who was on Mary's Point. Yippie! There's nobody on there, I can't believe my luck. I found Dave and T.B. at the Douglas Lane end, they had been working for most of that week. T.B. had done a night in Mary's, but had seen nothing. I ventured forth anyway, as it was simply the only place in the world that I wanted to be, fish or no fish. In the dregs of daylight, I had a fast take on the distant bar, using tigers buried under a bucket of mega-hemp in shallow water, my favourite summer method. The battle took place from the dinghy and it fought as hard as any bank-caught carp. The fish christened Three Scale, with a very large tail, lay in the bottom of my landing net. It hadn't been out for four years and was part of the pack that we called the 'Odd-Uns', Wraysbury carp that put in very rare appearances. He weighed 25lb, as he always has done, and after a few flash and low speed shots my first Wraysbury carp went back home to sulk. I just managed to re-bait the trap before it became dark. If you're happy and you know it have a drink. So I had a cup of tea with two sugars, like I would!

Eagle-eyed, I watched the sunrise and as the water warmed, so the dorsal fins appeared. Through the channel from the Dredger Bay, big black backs glistened in the heat. Floaters today or hemp on a shallow bar? More hemp was coming, big blocks of ice in bin liners filled with mega-hemp. The rigs were set and covered up as before with no apparent sign whatsoever of a trap. 'Away she blows' and off I rowed, she fought hard and deep, the water magnifying her magnificence. Could it be Mary, Cluster or Mallin's? I'd just have to wait and see. She fought hard and then fought some more, from weedbed to weedbed with me in tow.There was extreme excitement as the odd card came up. Cluster, a once a year at the most job. I danced in the dinghy under the red hot sun, a truly great moment for me at 36lb. Dave and T.B. were waiting at the shore.

"Good morning gentlemen," I began. "Would you like to see Cluster my friends? I had a wonderful starter last night with Three Scale at 25lb." When it eventually comes you have to roll with it.

I really like this swim. The day got very hot and as the yachts came out, in came the lines.That evening saw me re-trapping the bars with a view to a kill. Surely no more would come my way? Sunday at six thirty a.m., my double Grange bait was picked up from the side of the island margin. From the start I had no control. The speed of the take was making it impossible to raise the rod into test curve. The accelerated power was so immense that the beast had passed the island and was getting behind it. With some kind of sideways test curve locked in she held, and then the hook broke at the bend, the first time ever. It was gone! Was it Mary? After all it was one of her favourite little spots. Oh well, another day!

Time ran out and the real world beckoned, but eventually Friday came around again. No one on Mary's Point? Surely not? But there wasn't. Dave and T.B. had moved

A truly great moment at 36lb.

on there after I'd left, but had retreated just as quickly. Six large gypsy caravans had moved into the field behind the swim. They were the roughest of the rough. Real scum-types and would steal the petrol from your Coleman. Dave and T.B. were plagued by them from the onset. The gypsy blood in me must have sent them! I couldn't pump the dinghy up quick enough, and I was angling by tea time when the first one arrived.

He was about thirteen and covered in fake gold and attitude.

"Giz a go on your boat mister, giz this, giz that, what's this, what's that?" "Gold for your boat mister, please giz a go - you can have me sister."

A big dragon fly swooped into the swim. I said, "Be careful, get down and don't let it bite you."

I deciphered some Irish mumbo-jumbo type slang into," What is it? What is it?"

"If it bites you, then you'll need to go to hospital," I said. "You'll be on a drip for a couple of days, and they give you injections in your butt twice a day."

I kept ducking and diving, making him really nervous. He was looking all around him, really scared. It hovered in front of him, and he ran and ran without any loot. I heard a lot of shouting from the caravans and an hour later they were leaving, which they probably were anyway! I told everyone that I'd seen them on their way - quite!

Almost dark and Plumb Bloke appeared in his boat, opposite me in No Carp Bay - now that's a tad unlucky I thought. In the morning I caught a really old-looking common of around 14lb. Plumb Bloke came round and told me that he'd caught Mary and a couple of passing tench anglers had witnessed, weighed, and photographed her for him, and she'd gone back for no-one to see. He told me of a small fresh tear in the other side of her mouth and with mine being the only recent loss I could only deduce... Oh well! Perhaps she's not big enough for me yet! By eleven thirty a.m., the big black backs were out again, and so were the yachts. I had to wind in for the day.

Now here's a memory. A big leathery-looking carp cruised straight up to the bar and disappeared. I sat there in anger, gritting my teeth at the yachts, hardly breathing. I watched in silence. Fifteen minutes later, she rose up again and rolled over before cruising off. There was just no way that I could go out there, Wraysbury sailing club were having an open day, and there was tuition and races all day. In the evening my dinghy turned into a hovercraft, as I raced to the spot. It was polished cleaner than clean. Oh, what could have been! The evening was very close, odd fish were still about and I was very confident, as you can imagine, who wouldn't be? Mary's Mate had rolled that day. I'd wanted her even before I'd known she was in the pond. She was just my kind of carp. Three feet long, a long lean fighting machine, just like the old Savay Leney's that I knew so well.

Time escapes me... I just knew that it was early, no air, no breeze. The birds were still asleep but my buzzer was wide awake and telling the world that something was happening. My boat was soon being pulled against the wind. I turned her and gained a bit then lost a bit more. It was seventy yards from the take position that I landed her. Without looking I knew, the length was hint enough. Thirty eight and a half pounds, and one of my best carp. It became very difficult (why I'll never know!) to get on Mary's Point again that season. I did manage to get a weekend in the middle of August on

The length gave it away.

there, and I hooked a big carp on a double Grange bait. After several weedbeds the hook pulled. I baited heavily throughout the autumn, just for someone else to catch her mid-week. But such is life! The original spot was the size of a house brick, just big enough for a rig. After 50 kilos of mega-hemp and a large portion of tigers the whole bar was polished. The swim hasn't done a fish now for two years, they prefer safer spots elsewhere in the pond. It's lost its appeal and nobody bothers to go around there any more.

I've just started baiting the bar!

Long time carp angler and fashion guru, Steve Alcott.

Chapter 19

A Feeling of Déjà Vu

During the period of Steve's results, I'd been persevering with The Fence swim and also fishing at range from the Root Nightmare, where numerous humps and short bars littered the bottom amongst the myriad of weedbeds.

My rigs had been altered to counter the super-wary mood that the fish seemed to be in of late, and much heavier leads were employed to hopefully make the rigs less disposable. The thinking being that even if the fish cleared out the spot of bait and rejected the rig, it would still be left in a position where a fish may find it at a later date and hopefully make a mistake or fall foul of the sheer greed factor. I am firmly of the opinion that a high percentage of takes fall to a single hookbait long after all the free offerings have been polished off. The hassle with using large leads at range over heavy weed comes into play when a fish is hooked. They tend to drag deeper into the weed and snag up with alarming regularity. To combat this I started attaching them by means of a short piece of silicon tubing pushed on to a running swivel. Into this, I'd push the eye of the swivel enabling them to pop off under strain. Obviously, they could not be cast out, but for boating they proved invaluable.

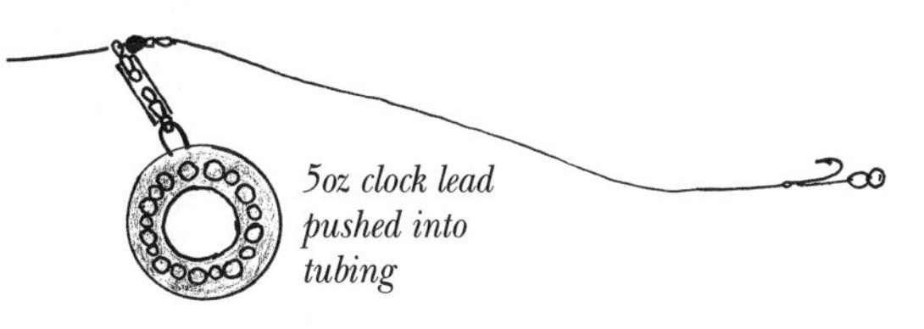

An added bonus was found when reeling in through heavy weed at range as, without the added encumbrance of a lead, the rig could simply be skimmed across the surface collecting no weed and also causing zero line twist. The only downside to this method was the price of leads and the need to carry a mountain of them around with you at all times. Cheap old 'clock' leads from the sea fishing department of my local tackle shop eased the problem, and offered excellent holding properties. However, a friend who had been fishing, until

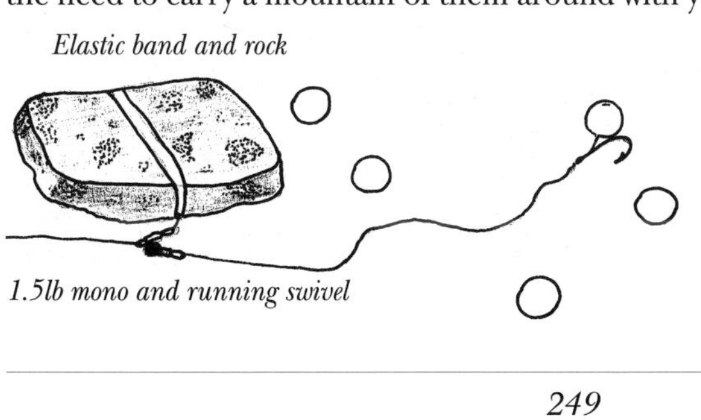

recently, a nearby pit brought with him the perfect solution. Jacko, who had been using a similar method on his pit, had utilised the various shaped rocks that lay scattered around these gravel pits. By attaching one to the running swivel by the use of a short piece of very light line, he had created the Running Rock Rig. After a great deal of experimentation, I found that any line over two and a half pounds breaking strain was practically unbreakable over any significant range and the ideal line was around a pound and a half, to this an overhand knot was added to further weaken the line. A palm-sized rock would be wound with an elastic band and three inches of the weak line would attach this to a running swivel. Usually, a flat rock of about twelve ounces or more would be ideal. Lowering these onto a spot without snapping the weak link could be a bit tricky, but once in position an amazing amount of strain could be put on them from the bank, far more than you could ever put on a four ounce lead without moving it. Couple this with a bait that has the ability to resist the ravages of time and various fishy attentions, and you have a set-up in which you can be confident that your hookbait is properly positioned and 'fishing' at all times. It was not until I started using a boat that I realised to what extent fish can move rigs and leads, without the angler receiving any indication whatsoever. This problem is further compounded at range when the considerable stretch inherent in monofilament lines also comes into play. Over a distance of one hundred yards, there is so much stretch in a normal mono line that the lead can be moved literally yards before any indication is registered on a normal bite indication system.

Long shadows fell across the water.

The only problem with fishing in this style is that once the rigs are set and fishing, all that really remains to be done is wait. There are, of course, more interesting ways of waiting than sitting on your butt staring at motionless indicators, and I took to fashioning various items of tackle out of sticks and branches and before long my fishing gear had started to become one with the surroundings.

Rear rod rests were lovingly carved from willow, and storm rods quickly followed, along with a mug tree and tackle tree and a wonderful pair of golf clubs. Tench Bloke had suddenly taken to fancying himself as a bit of an Arnold Palmer, so we decided on a little tournament. Flags were made out of T-shirts and, of course, Wraysbury sticks and with holes dug using even sharper sticks, we were soon looking at a four hole golf course with a longest drive of almost seventy yards. Over the following day, we managed to complete three full rounds before the formidable water feature claimed the last ball. The final result? Let's just say Arnold Palmer was having an off day!

Towards the end of the month, I started to bait the long distance bars that lay on The Root side of the middle. I used large quantities of mixed particles and liberally coated the tops of these bars a few times a week. I would still move around hoping for an instant result in other areas but by keeping a constant supply of bait going in to The Root, I hoped to create a regular feeding area. I marked the spots with tethered pieces of buoyancy foam, as the weather was starting to break, and the less time spent out on Wraysbury in a boat when the wind starts cutting up rough, the better. These markers were to prove my own undoing in the end, when on one particular afternoon at the beginning of October I moved out from The Root and rowed down to the bottom of Bryants Bay for a social with Tench Bloke, dumping off a fresh bucket of bait as I passed the markers. Just before dark, as we sat there drinking tea and watching the long shadows falling across the water, a set of headlights appeared in the Douglas Lane car park and made their way across the field to The Root. Before long, the unmistakable form of Plumb Bloke appeared, paddling out in a desperate attempt to drop the rigs on clear spots before total darkness fell. Time, however, was not on his side. Before long we could only just make out the bare outline as he made his way back to the bank.

Imagine our surprise when, about one hour later he wandered up and announced, "I've aaad one!"

At first, we steadfastly refused to believe him but, eventually convinced, we followed him back to the Root Nightmare and he recounted his tale along the way. My heart sunk further with every word. As it transpired, he had indeed been beaten in his race against the inevitable darkness and, unable to see the bottom through a mask, had noticed a fixed marker. Assuming, correctly, that it must be marking something worth fishing on, he lowered a bait next to it and within half an hour he had a take that after a short scrap produced a very large Wraysbury mirror. He was convinced that he had landed the much sought after Olive, who had been on the missing list for a good few years. As he placed the sack on the mat I ran my hand along the back and even through the material I was able to identify the unmistakable scaling of Cluster. The weight surprised us all, and at thirty nine pounds fourteen ounces she looked superb. The empty sack was, unsurprisingly, full of my particle mix.

The next day a decision had to be reached. Plumb Bloke was obviously still installed in The Root, and the fish were just as obviously feeding out in the middle. The point to my left (Bryants) offered the best available choice for a shot at the middle. and the weather overnight had changed into the ideal conditions for this area. A drastic drop in pressure and gathering cloud cover had pushed a strong westerly windflow coursing down the pit. By mid-morning white capped waves charged out of No Carp Bay and whipped the water in front of Bryants Point to a lather. By lunchtime, I was battling against those waves in an attempt to locate two small bars that I knew rose above the thick weed at a range of at least one hundred and twenty yards! The nightmare that followed took up the rest of the day and resulted in me being soaked to the skin and freezing cold, having had to thrust my head under the waves with a mask on and battle to drop markers and rigs with some degree of accuracy. The water was too rough to allow the use of the Running Rock Rig, so I opted for four ounce leads and short nylon hooklinks, with two mini Grange boilies on each. Loose bait was out of the question in these conditions. The speed that the boat moves as soon as you stop rowing against the wind, means that you are always

"More than any other!"

trying to hit a moving target. Every time you overshoot with the hookbait there is no alternative but to bite the rig off and row back, to start all over again.

By late afternoon, I had managed to get two rigs in a position that I was happy with and I considered even that a right result. Stripping off my sodden attire, I clambered into the sleeping bag to dry off. A hot meal and change of clothes later, I was sitting behind the rods rubbing my hands together as the white horses continued to gallop into the corral. If ever there was a perfect night for fishing out in the very middle of Wraysbury then this was surely it! Somehow, the fish managed to resist the temptation until nine o'clock the following morning when the furthest rod bleeped once before ripping into life.

It would have been a hard enough job holding a twelve foot carbon rod upright in the wind as it was, but with the added impediment of a large, and enraged carp on the other end it was practically impossible. The fish fought like an absolute demon and it was a full half an hour before I could eventually persuade him to join me on dry land. Once there it was like a meeting of old friends as, for the third time in two seasons, I'd crossed paths with Mallin's.

When I originally joined Wraysbury, I'd said that I wanted to catch this fish more than any other, but I hadn't meant it quite this literally. At a few ounces under forty pounds he was at an almost identical weight to our last meeting when he formed part of the brace with Mary's Mate. Re-captures are not something I usually relish anyway, but on the third capture it all starts to become a bit too familiar. Such though, is the nature of Wraysbury, where certain 'bait' fish form the bulk of the captures. Putting

Hovering.

the bait back out was a repeat of the previous day's trials and tribulations but, eventually, after yet another soaking, I was happy that it was fishing once again. My original plan had been to pack up and leave as I had other commitments to attend to back in Crawley, but I knew beyond a shadow of a doubt that, come nine o'clock the following morning, there was only one place on this planet that I'd be and that was sat right here with my hand hovering over the rod butts.

I decided to leave the rod that had gone unmolested out there for another twenty four hours, as the severe weather conditions did not warrant poncing about risking my life just to drop it back in the same spot again with a fresh bait on. As it turned out, it couldn't have deterred the carp one iota. At exactly nine, the following morning that rod absolutely melted away. I was so expectant of the freshly cast bait to produce that I almost struck the wrong rod, even though I had been staring at the bobbins when the take came. In fact, I'd been staring at the bobbins since six o'clock in the morning and I'm sure that sheer will power must have played a vital role. If the previous day's fish had fought like a demon then surely this fish was the devil himself, I was never in the slightest bit of control. The wind had refused to relent throughout the night, and the north sea could not have looked more foreboding. From the first contact, line was torn from the clutch and only stopped when numerous weedbeds had been defiled. The very last thing that I wanted was to have to go out in the boat to land him, as I was totally alone and unsure as to what advantage it might offer in such adverse conditions.

In my swim were two life jackets, the first a normal foam-filled life preserver, and the second an army issue compressed gas job that practically turned into a life raft when you pulled the rip cord. I opted for both, putting the army one on and kneeling in the front of the boat on the other one. Before I left shore, I firmly lashed Fat Sam to a nearby tree in case she was stupid enough to try and follow me out there, as she had done once or twice in the past. Getting out to the fish was no hardship at all, it was stopping that proved a near impossibility. On the first attempt, I overshot the line's point of entry by at least thirty yards! Rowing a boat on your own into the teeth of a gale is no picnic at the best of times, but attempting it one-handed whilst clenching a rod between your knees and reeling in with the other hand is bloody near impossible. Eventually, I had to lie the rod down with the bale arm open and dig the oar deep into the swell with two hands just to stop myself being blown backwards. After an eternity of white-water rafting, I was back in position over the fish. As soon as I stopped rowing to pick up the rod, the wind crushed the waves into a black seething monster that smashed into the boat and sent me hurtling backwards again. The clutch was screaming as line was ripped from the reel with the speed of my sudden departure. This pitiful exercise was repeated time and again until my hands were completely numb from the cold and wet. At one stage, after over half an hour of trying, I managed to persuade him up to the top but as I picked up the net it acted like a sail and I was suddenly a serious contender for the America's Cup. I could see the carp lying on the surface as I was forced away from him at breakneck speed, backwinding like crazy as I went, eventually he awoke and dived back down into the jungle below. Unable to think of a solution, I struck out for a nearby life buoy and tethered the boat up to that, for a much needed rest. I tried pulling him out of the weed from my new position, but everything was locked up solid again. I even tried beating the surface of the lake with the oar and calling it a bastard, but even this failed to produce a result! Eventually, I just buried my head in my hands and sulked profusely.

I remember when I was a young lad and on a caravan holiday near Hastings with my Nan. On a trip to the pier, I saw a second hand multiplier reel for sale in a small fishing tackle booth. It was only £4, but this was still way out of my price range. That evening I phoned my dad and told him about this wonderful piece of kit that would enable me to cast to the moon. Kindhearted soul that he was, he arrived at the pier the very next day and the little green reel was mine. I stood on that beach at Winchelsea with my very first proper sea reel attached to my trusty broomstick of a rod and hurled a four ounce lead out to the horizon, but unfortunately after only the first ten yards of its journey, a tangled bird's nest of line wrapped itself around the rod and the lead crashed into the breakers. After a painstaking half an hour untangling it all I tried again. The second cast fared no better, nor the third, nor any of of the subsequent thirty or so attempts until eventually, hours later, I sat dejectedly down on the beach. With my head in my hands I wept tears of frustration at my total and utter inadequacy.

I had that exact feeling once again now, as I sat there in that little rowing boat staring into the face of adversity, being tossed about by a force far greater than I. Knowing I had a big old fish on the other end but having absolutely no idea how I was going to land it, until I noticed an inflatable dinghy set out from the Douglas Lane with Jacko at the helm paddling like the clappers in an attempt to reach me through the waves. My knight in shining waterproofs had arrived! How the hell he managed to row against the wind in an air-filled boat all the way out to meet me I'll never know, but without him I'd probably still have been sitting there now. We lashed the two craft together and I helped Jacko clamber into the more sturdy rowing boat before setting off to do battle again. Even with the two of us the task was bordering on the unachievable and another half an hour elapsed before I finally dragged the fish into the net.

Poor old Jacko had been rowing flat out most of this time in an attempt just to stay in one place and was, at the moment of netting, embracing a large pink buoy like a long lost cousin. Not only had I beaten the carp but I felt like we'd taken on the

The same brace!

Tench Bloke cradles The Pug.

Mary's Mate, the angriest fish I have seen and (below) Mallin's.
Background: The sun sinks into a sea of molten reds - another night starts at Wraysbury.

Above: Persevering in The Fence swim. Below: Checking the spots!

might of Mother Nature and somehow scraped through ahead. On looking in the net, though, I must admit to being a little disappointed at yet another re-capture. Mary's Mate lay on the foam matting in the bottom of the boat.

Over two days I'd taken another Wraysbury brace and incredibly it was made up of the same two fish as before! Once on the bank, the scales showed the weights to be almost the same as in the spring, thirty nine and a half pounds of pure muscle.

After a suitable rest and few gallons of tea, I plucked up the courage to drop another bait out there in the vain hope that one of the true Wraysbury 'Oddun's' may be lurking about, and I postponed my arrangements for yet another twenty four hours. It was, as it turned out, all in vain as the fish having had enough for one session had moved off. I wisely decided to do the same and packed up all my sodden kit and headed off for a much needed hot bath and the unashamed luxury of dry clothing.

The winter was soon firmly installed once again and Wraysbury began to lose some of its appeal. As a result, I made a few social trips to Horton, and occasionally I even got to cast a line out! Winter fishing is not a pastime that holds a great allure for me any more. It wasn't long before I was once again hanging up the rods and dreaming of the warm spring days ahead.

As it happened, I missed nothing and not a single fish was landed during my absence.

Chapter 20

Mary from the Sunnymeads Tree

Before I knew it the cold months had once again slipped past my guard, practically unnoticed. This could be, in part, due to the fact that I spent the vast majority of them propped against the bar of the Maid of Sussex, purely to be sociable of course!

I'd visited Wraysbury on the odd occasion, hoping beyond hope for a repeat of the events of my first winter, but it was not to be. April arrived and, with it, came enthusiasm and great expectations for that first decent spell of hot weather. I was unsure if the fish would revisit Sunnymeads this spring after their little upset the previous year, when they found not only the usual free bait but the addition of two of my rigs. Time of course would tell, as it always does, and the clock was ticking steadily towards the onset of warm weather. I knew that this year I would have to be extra vigilant, and ready to drop everything and go at a minute's notice, as there were obviously other eyes keeping watch over Sunnymeads this spring. I knew that Tench Bloke had been hoping to get camped up in there and await their arrival and, with unlimited time at his disposal, I knew that I had to play my cards close to my chest for a while. As it transpired the heatwave came early that year and caught everybody on the hop, but with a lot of effort and a large slice of luck I was once again the first angler of the spring to beat a path through the bushes to the Sunnymeads tree.

I knew that one look from the tree would either confirm or negate my suspicions. One look could have me charging about like a headless chicken in an attempt to get a bait in the water, or skulking off with my tail between my legs in search of a likely looking spot to blank in for another week. With trepidation, I scaled the lower branches and at first I saw nothing, but when I reached the highest bough I could clearly see three large, dark shapes picking their way along the right hand margin. It seemed that not only had I picked the right spot at the right time, and beaten all the other anglers to it, but I'd narrowly beaten

One look from the tree. . .

the fish there as well!

After the aforementioned impression of a recently beheaded fowl, I set about the familiar but still treacherous task of lowering the rigs from the tree. The spots were a lot less defined this year and obviously today was the first visit that they had received from the fish. Although the three carp were still thirty yards or so from the back of the swim, I knew from past experience that they would soon be circling below the very tree that I was struggling to climb with the rod dangling from my teeth. Due to the angle of the sun and the clarity of the water, I could see the bottom over most of the swim, but only two spots really interested me. The first was last year's hot spot that still had a small area of gravel poking through the encroaching weed. It was a comparatively easy task to lower the first rig onto it and sprinkle a few of the Extract mini boilies around it. The second spot lay off the further most trailing branches and required a more trapeze-like stance to enable me to flick the small lead onto the tiny yellow patch of sand that glowed at the bottom of a small drop off.

After setting up the rods on alarms I took a last peek from the tree to confirm that only the three fish were present, before sneaking around to the path to watch their progress. I'd filled my pockets with various baits before I'd left and carefully sprinkled a few under likely-looking bushes as I approached the spot, where I could just make out the 'tenting' of the water as three large backs lifted the surface film as they glided slowly along. As quietly as possible, I picked a path through the brambles until I was able to climb the very tree that they were currently lying in the shade of, and after climbing only a few feet I could clearly see The Three Amigos.

It had been exactly two years since I last set eyes on the Big Leather but here he was now with his two bodyguards in tow. The Pug was there and I still had an old score to settle with him and, of course, The Fat Linear. I'd already made his acquaintance. Slowly they

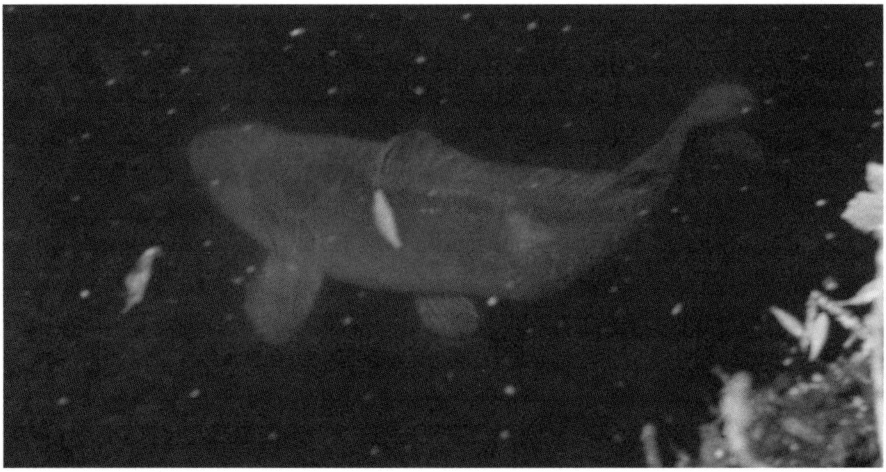

Sunnymeads mirror.

made their way from bush to bush, ignoring all my carefully placed free offerings along the way. The Leather stayed low and slightly to the rear of the trio but occasionally, as the sun's rays slanted through the foliage, I would be rewarded with a brief but awesome sighting. There was now only ten yards left before they made it to the boundaries of my swim and I crept around a large willow to await their arrival at the other side. As they appeared, like grey submarines, I noticed that The Leather had momentarily disappeared, and as I searched through the branches for a glimpse of him I saw somebody making their way along the dog walkers' path towards me.

Not wanting to spook the carp with the sound of voices, I stood back from the water's edge and awaited his arrival. Dave, 'the other Tench Bloke,' came wandering up and asked if I'd seen anything and I could barely control the words as they came blurting out of their own free will.

"He's here, the Leather. He's in my bloody swim, mate!" I stammered. "I might even catch him in a minute."

Once again the two lesser beasts hove into view, their backs creasing the surface as they left the bushes to our right and drew ever closer to the traps waiting in the corner. The Leather was still out of sight. As we walked around the corner to the swim for a cuppa, I thought I heard a noise. It was a mechanical type of whirring noise that had no place in the other sounds of nature that surrounded us. I asked Dave, "Did you hear that? It sounded almost like the clutch on a reel."

I ran the last few yards and, sure enough, I'd forgotten to turn the bloody alarms on once again. The bait that I'd put under the branches had been picked up and the spool was emptying rapidly. As I bent in to the fish, I tried to figure out what had happened. I could still see the two smaller fish on the right hand margin, which, seeing as there were only three to start with, meant I must be attached to none other than the Big Leather!

The puzzling thing was, though, that he must have left the other two and practically bolted over to the corner to grab the hookbait as I'd seen him only minutes earlier under the bushes, a full twenty yards away! Whatever was on the end certainly felt massive. There were no doubts on that score, and I was soon missing sixty yards of line before he eventually slowed and I began the long job of coaxing him back into the corner. The more protracted the fight became, the more convinced I became that I was actually going to land the uncaught monster, that was until Phil arrived. Suddenly, appearing on the path where I had been standing a few minutes earlier, he announced, "There's three more fish over here, Dave, and one of them's absolutely massive!" Instantly my heart sank, for I knew what Phil could see and the Leather was obviously still there. Out of frustration, I piled on the pressure and soon had my fish swirling off the end of the tree. From up the tree Dave gave a running commentary as the fish approached the net, upgrading the estimates of size every time it rolled until there could realistically only be one candidate, and sure enough, five minutes later, Mary rolled into the outstretched net. Mixed emotions swam over me as the retreating bow waves from the path heralded the departure of The Three Amigos.

There at my feet lay the biggest carp in the lake and possibly the whole country. I had dearly wanted to catch that Leather, and, thinking for a while that it had eventually become a reality, had jaded even a capture as fine as this one. I soon came to my senses, though, and we weighed in the biggest carp that I had ever caught at fifty pounds and five ounces. The sheer bulk of that carp on the bank stunned everybody present into silence, save from the occasional gasp. She behaved perfectly for the cameras and, with the minimum of fuss, was soon gliding effortlessly away into the rapidly warming waters of Wraysbury.

So, once again I had managed to sneak in and do the damage, before either carp or anglers had realised what was happening. Unfortunately, the weather did not hold long enough to tempt any more monsters into the swim. In fact, the conditions deteriorated rapidly and spring retreated once more behind winter's coat tails.

Back into the crystal waters she goes. . .

Chapter 21

First Wraysbury Twenties and The Pug Finally Submits

According to the calendar the date was May the eighth although, looking out of the window, you could be forgiven for thinking it was the middle of October. A howling wind blew from the north east, biting savagely into the less sensibly dressed. This time last year I'd ended up swimming, during the saga of Tench Bloke and The Pug. I had no intention of repeating that little caper this year! This weekend, as indeed this time last year and countless years before that, was to be spent in the celebration of yet another of Phil's Thirtieth Birthdays. Last year we journeyed back to the place of his birth, Windsor, drinking the town dry and in the morning that memorable battle between T.B. and The Pug merely postponed the hangovers. What wonders lay in store for us this year? As I loaded all my gear into the van I checked it over for thermal jackets and spare jumpers, plenty of dry socks etc, and then satisfied that I had everything needed for a British springtime session, I set off once more for Wraysbury. I got as far as Gatwick this time before realising I'd forgotten the bait. Although frustrating, it was too much of a common occurrence to get overly wound up about. Over the last season in my mad panic to get back to the lake as quickly as possible I had forgotten a wide variety of essential items. One week I realised, on arrival, I'd omitted to bring my bedchair, another time my landing net, countless bags of bait, water bottles and food parcels have spent the entire session at home on my kitchen table. It was just one of those things. Half an hour and a fifteen mile detour later, I was back en route and, eventually, I pulled into the Douglas Lane car park early in the afternoon.

Tench Bloke's funny little van was there already and there were no prizes on offer for guessing where he'd be angling! Taking as much gear as I could carry and with the carp dog trotting on ahead, I made my way down to the bottom of Bryants Bay where, as expected, sat Tench Bloke. We sat chatting for a while, drinking tea and musing over the level of celebration that Phil would go to this year. Who would end up in which bush? Would anybody get to see the same Chinese twice? Where to have the bonfire? One thing was for sure, it was a bloody sight colder this year than last so wherever we ended up making the fire it was going to be a big'un!

After some deliberation, I settled on Bryants Point. These type of conditions, with the low pressure and big winds, especially north easterlies, sometimes congregated a few fish out in the vast middle section of the South Lake that lay in front of the point. It was conditions almost identical to this that had furnished me with a brace of thirty nine pounders last October. Also it was nice and close to the pub and the Chinese take-away! The scene that greeted me as I walked into the swim was a far cry from the comparative serenity of the bay where T.B. sat. Great white horses charged relentlessly in from my right, ending their stampede from the Douglas Lane Point by smashing themselves to a foam at my feet and bringing with them an assortment of flotsam and jetsam from the North Bank.

I set to work pulling out the largest of the branches from the turbulent margins, each one hung with weed, a sure sign of problems ahead. The first cast with a plumbing rod was grabbed in mid-air by the cross wind and hurled around to my left, landing a clear country mile off its intended target. After retrieving my line from thirty yards of bankside bushes, I wound down to find half a hundred weight of Canadian pondweed hanging on the end. The next cast was no more successful. I knew from previous boat trips with the mask that among the weed, at distances of forty, eighty, and one hundred and twenty yards, lay ridges of comparatively clear bottom. These ran parallel to the bank like miniature mountain ranges, between two and six feet off the bottom. Some of the tops of these bars are covered with weed or dark muddy silt, others are comprised of 'ironstone', sharp pieces of stone and flint set in a solid clump. Apparently these configurations, some of which are up to fifteen feet in diameter, were left behind during gravel extraction due to their tendency to collapse on their removal from the pressures of the deep. Although these humps feel the absolute business with a plumbing rod, I've learned through experience that a bait could happily sit on there unmolested until the cows came home whistling Dixie.

I knew that dotted about along the tops of these ranges lay the favourite areas for a hookbait. Small areas of clean sand could be seen in the right water clarity, cleared by the grubbing around of fish. A bait dropped onto one of these spots, sometimes only two or three feet in length, would offer the very best chance of a pick-up. The conditions for boating were far from ideal, the side wind was likely to push you through the swim far too quickly to drop a bait with any accuracy, but as I was getting nowhere fast with the more traditional methods it was still worth a try. The Shootist's house was only across the bay and I knew his solid fibre glass boat would be under the big willow in the garden, so off I set back around the bay. I stopped off at T.B.'s swim on the way to enlist the help of my long suffering boating assistant. Tench Bloke's job consisted of paying out the line as I rowed the baits out, making sure I didn't drown, and, most importantly, making the tea.

I've found the best method in windy conditions is to take three markers out first, dropping them just beyond the spots and then to drift through on the inside with the wind. By looking down through the mask as the bottom flies past your vision, it's possible (just) to quickly drop a bait on the money as you sail past. This tenuous operation relies heavily on timing and a large slice of luck. It's hard enough bait dropping accurately in calm conditions without the added disadvantage of a gale force wind. I was fairly confident, though, that by having the bait hanging on a long line under the boat as I approached the spot, I could drop it on target. That was the theory but as is quite often the case, the reality of the matter was something entirely different. Tench Bloke declared that I had totally lost the plot. What did I care? Carp or bust.

On reaching the eighty yard mark, I stuck my head over for a look and instantly began to have doubts about my own sanity. For a start it was almost impossible to keep my head under due to the pitch and toss of the boat in the swell. The waves were crashing down the back of my neck, and the vegetation on the bottom was charging past my vision like the bushes viewed from the side window of a car belting up the motorway. Eighty yards was definitely the range I was after, though, being the deeper of the marks. It took a good ten minutes to get out there battling against the breakers, and about ten seconds to get back without even rowing! As if putting down the markers wasn't torturous enough, taking the baits out was a veritable nightmare! At one stage I looked up to see if I was nearly on the mark, only to find myself almost fifty yards away, and although Tench Bloke was out of sight behind the bushes on the point I could hear the laughter as clear as a bell as it was carried on the wind.

By the time that I eventually clambered out of the boat, happy that all three rigs were fishing as well as they possibly could, I was soaked to the skin. Even my underpants were sodden. My hands were numbed by the cold and two hours had been stolen from my clock. All that remained to do was to build a big boy scout fire to warm up next to. I was under no illusions about the temperatures that would arrive hard on the heels of the setting sun.

Just behind my swim there was a large pile of cut bushes and branches that had been cleared from one of the gardens and dumped on the bank just begging to be burned. I surrendered to the temptation of my one complete change of clothes, planning to dry the others over the fire. As darkness arrived, it was greeted by showers of cherry red sparks as the fire between us roared and crackled. It was warm enough for beers as we sat there in the glow, so we cracked a can or two and sat long into the night reminiscing days gone by while Sam slept on oblivious on her little blanket by the fire. Periodically she'd wake and, thinking nobody was watching, try and sneak so close to the embers that the hairs on her nose would smoke in her attempt to get as hot as possible before T.B. or myself would unceremoniously drag her back to the blanket. The clothes drying didn't exactly go according to plan, resulting in two socks totally devoid of feet and a T-shirt with a bloody great hole in the back. At least they were dry. Finally the log pile dwindled away to nothing and it was time for some serious carp angling.

It was one of those strange dreams that has an annoying phone or alarm clock ringing incessantly in the background. Eventually, though, the screaming of my bite alarm battered its way through into my subconscious and I shot bolt upright in bed. The swim was illuminated only by the red glow of my left hand indicator and line was disappearing off the spool with a vengeance. I tried to leap out of bed, but the sleeping bag became tangled around my ankles and I did a perfect nose dive into the mud beside the rods. Wrestling free, I bent the rod into the darkness where, somewhere out there, an angry old carp kicked back in defiance. I managed to get him under control fairly easily considering that the wind was even stronger than yesterday's hooligan, making it hard to feel exactly what was happening out there. In spite of this I was soon leading him back towards the net with the rod tip bucking and wrenching in the darkness as he shook his head from side to side in a vain bid for freedom. Before too long, big inky black flat spots appeared on the surface just a few yards out as he rolled, unseen, in the early morning gloom. The skyline in the east was just beginning to crack open into shades of morning, as a big old mirror carp slid into the waiting arms of my landing net.

Any angler will know the feeling of absolute relief as you finally close the battle. I sat on the ground holding the net handle and let the tension flood out of me and it was a while before I even looked to see what I'd bagged, preferring to have a quiet moment and appreciate just how much I loved this carp angling game. When I did finally get it together to gather the mesh and heave my prize up onto the unhooking mat I couldn't believe my good fortune.

Now, to an angler who spends his whole life in pursuit of the biggest carp or indeed fish of any species that reside in their chosen lake, the concept of my delight at the size (or rather lack of it) of this old mirror carp may be hard to grasp. I could see at a glance that he was under thirty pounds and, as I've pointed out before, these are the elusive 'Oddun's' of Wraysbury. I'd wanted for so long to bag a twenty pound mirror from this pit and now here he was. Only once before had I the good fortune to gaze at this dumpy little fellow on the bank. That was last summer when Tench

Bloke landed him from the swim he now occupied at the bottom of Bryants Bay. The Finger Bay Mirror we'd called him, due to his fondness of lazing under the branches of a certain overhanging tree at the bottom of the Finger Bays. Deep in body, being almost round in appearance, he bore the marks of old spawning rituals along his flanks, a mottled colouring to his skin and an abundance of small red marks on his belly. Although we did not know it at the time, it became apparent later on the next year, after looking over old photographs, that he was once known as Measles, and in his youth came unstuck occasionally to some of Wraysbury's early rods. All in all, a true character of a carp.

I slipped him into a sack which I secured in the deep margins to my right. The hook, a size six Super Specialist, still seemed sharp enough for the job. Even the long two pound hair had stayed intact throughout the fight so I slipped two fresh ten mm Grange baits on and secured them with a lucky piece of twig. It was still far too dark to put the rig back out, so I plonked it in the rests and brewed up a nice cup of tea. As soon as the light was good enough for photo's, I started on the near impossible task of rousing Tench Bloke to do the honours with the camera. Being reluctant to leave the rods, I went into the small swim on the right of the point where I'd sacked the fish. It's only a few yards away but looks out in the other direction down to the bottom of the bay where T.B. slept on oblivious to the morning's events. I shouted and screamed at the top of my voice, so loud that bedroom lights were springing to life all around the bay in the adjacent houses. I could see the recumbent form of Tench Bloke clearly from here but not a movement in sight. Just as I was about to give up the ghost who should appear but Phil and Dave. As they made their way down towards T.B. they came to a point opposite me and I shouted across the mouth of the bay that I'd had one and told them to check that Sleeping Beauty was still breathing on their way round.

Feeling generous, due to my good fortunes this morning, I thought I'd make some tea and toast ready for their arrival. I was just pumping up the cooker when my middle rod launched into life. This was your original run from hell. The clutch on my poor old Cardinal 55 threatened to go into meltdown. Sending the cooker flying, I grabbed the rod and bent into the fish as hard as I dared. It didn't seem to make a jot of difference to his mission to reach the sailing club on the far bank in record time. I could feel the grating and ripping sensations being transmitted up the line as he tore through the weedbeds until, eventually, he came to rest somewhere right out in the middle beyond the buoys. Just then the others arrived.

"I thought you'd already landed it, Dave," said Phil.

"I've landed one of them, this is the second," I said trying hard to keep the smile from totally circumnavigating my head.

Looks of disbelief disappeared from all three faces simultaneously, as I pointed to the wet unhooking mat and redundant rod still lying in the rests.

"I've got the Finger Bay Mirror sacked up and this one's solid in the weed about two miles out."

After cups of tea all round, and when every known method of fish freeing known to man had been exhausted, Dave volunteered to row me out there.

We figured that we'd have a better chance of landing it if we took up the battle at close quarters and, although the wind was still howling down the pit into our faces, the white horses had abated for the time being and Dave soon had us out over the top of the weedbeds beyond the one hundred yard buoys. The line wove an elaborate web in and out of large clumps of Canadian pondweed and when we eventually came across the lead encased in a ball of weed, it gave us a few problems swinging six foot off the rod tip. Once to hand, the lead was easily removed to give a more direct line to the still unseen carp.

Most of the problems with landing fish in heavy weed are down to the lead snagging up in one place while the fish charges about on a long leash in another so, when rowing out baits, I attach the lead to a swivel running on the mainline by utilising a small piece of silicone anti-tangle tubing. It can then be removed easily during the fight should a problem occur.

Once out of the way, we followed the remaining line back towards a large pink buoy that was being tossed around in the swell. Dave was doing a sterling job of holding the boat steady and before long I was in direct contact with the fish. Straining my eyes down through the murk, I could see an orange belly twisting and turning as its owner begrudgingly gave ground and allowed me to pump him ever nearer the surface. The problem now was that every time Dave put down the oar to pick up the net, the boat was propelled off across the surface by the wind leaving me frantically back-winding so as not to pull the hook out. Eventually, I screamed through the howling wind at Dave to try and get us alongside the buoy where we could tie off the boat and concentrate on landing this fish as it was all beginning to turn into a bit of a farce. Once we'd managed to get the boat secured, the job in hand was made considerably easier and I lead what was obviously yet another mid-twenty pound mirror into the waiting net. Dave scooped it out at the first attempt and rowed us back home to the hoots and hollers of the small but enthusiastic crowd.

Back on the bank, I couldn't believe my luck. All those nights sat extolling the virtues of the elusive Wraysbury twenty pounders and here I was with two on the bank at once. The old London bus syndrome was working true to form. This second fish was also slightly familiar to us although nobody present had ever seen it on the bank before. Known as Three Scale, it was the first fish that I had ever seen swimming in the waters of Wraysbury almost two years ago. Unbelievably, I hadn't set eyes on it again from that day until now. It is an absolutely stunning carp, a real wood carving.

To be privileged enough to hold two magnificent Wraysbury mirrors in a brace for the cameras made this one of the top days of my angling career.

I'd invested in one of the pre-paid type of slide films from Kodak, as I was trying to put a new slide show together, and we were soon putting it to good use on the incredibly rare spectacle of a Wraysbury brace. After the weighing and photographing ceremonies were completed, and the brace of twenty six and a half pound mirrors were returned to fight another day, we set about a small celebration

A rare Wraysbury brace.

of this most momentous of occasions. Phil was in fine fettle and getting some serious practice in for his birthday the following day and, while he and Tench Bloke resurrected the fire, I got two more baits out just in case there were any more fish about that were feeling unusually gregarious.

This obviously involved another two trips out in the boat thrusting my head under the water with the mask on. The water had started to colour up a bit now which made positioning the baits even more tricky than before. By the time I'd finished, I'd totally soaked all my dry clothes and had to resort to the charred remains of last night's laundry. No sooner had we got settled in around the fire and cracked open a celebratory can, than one of the recently cast rods roared off. Unfortunately, the battle was short-lived as the hook pulled out whilst trying to pull him up short of a buoy at the far right hand side of the swim.

Oh well, three runs in a day at Wraysbury was still a major occurrence even if only two ended in success.

The weather had deteriorated even further and standing there looking at the wind-lashed water, I couldn't bring myself to suffer another boat trip so, chucking the rod in the bushes behind the bivvy, I beat a retreat to the warmth of the fire. I still had two rods out there and that would just have to do. The rest of the day passed in a celebratory huddle around the flames, drinking lager and re-running the events of the previous few hours. Many an excursion was made to top up the log pile and, as darkness fell, we sent out for some extra hot curry to warm us from the inside out as well. Then, about ten o'clock that evening, just as I was considering turning in for the night, a loud clanking sound heralded the arrival of The Shootist bearing gifts of lager for Phil's birthday. Making his apologies in advance for his absence on the day, he handed out cans with gay abandon. Consequently, by about half past eleven, I was more than ready to reacquaint myself with my sleeping bag so, leaving Phil, Tench Bloke and The Shootist by the fire, I wandered off to bed.

At eleven forty five, after a whole fifteen minutes' kip, I was rudely awakened by the sound of a screaming alarm complimented by the Three Stooges behind me also screaming, but more abusively and generalised around my level of good fortune whilst casting aspersions on my parenthood. With all the grace of a three legged cow, I tumbled out of bed and attempted to make some impression on one very powerful fish, my fourth carp hooked in just eighteen hours! If I'd woken up then to find that it had all been some crazy dream I wouldn't have been in the slightest bit surprised, although the pounding in my head and sub-zero wind chill did seem to indicate that this was in fact real life!

All my best efforts however, seemed to have no effect on my adversary. The harder I pulled, the more determined he became to rip the rod from my grasp. In and out of weedbeds we battled, and a good hour had passed before a large grey lump rolled over the net cord as I screamed down the wind in triumph. Over a year had passed since that unfortunate disaster when I lost The Pug in Sunnymeads Corner but now, at last, revenge was mine.

There he lay in all his magnificence, thirty six and a half pounds of battle-scarred warrior on the safety of my unhooking mat.

Every dog has its day or so they say, if that holds any truth then I was having all mine for the foreseeable future rolled into one. As if a brace of mid-twenty mirrors wasn't enough for one day this really was the icing on the cake. We sacked him up for the night in the deep swim, Phil and T.B. wandering off to bed and promising to return at first light to do the photo's.

After they'd gone, I sat by the dwindling fire for a while trying to take it all in. Eventually I kicked some cold ash over the flames and floated off to bed absolutely exhausted. True to their word, the gruesome twosome turned up for the photos in the morning although, thankfully, not at first light. Everyone felt a little fragile which we put down to the fumes from the fire. Phil excelled himself with the photo's, managing to cut my head off in ninety percent of them. He later blamed it all on a new camera, but thankfully I ended up with a few decent shots. I'd given my camera to Tench Bloke who happily clicked away using up the rest of the slide film. After I'd returned the old warrior to his watery domain, I reeled in and trotted off with Phil to help in the arduous task of the birthday celebrations. This was after all why we were there in the first place, wasn't it?

It's worth noting that after waiting two weeks for my slide film to be returned, I phoned Kodak who informed me that they had no record of ever receiving it. It eventually transpired that somehow, after posting it off in the pre-paid envelope for development, the good old post office had lost the bloody film. Eventually, after a couple of months, they admitted liability and sent me compensation, a cheque for twenty five pounds!

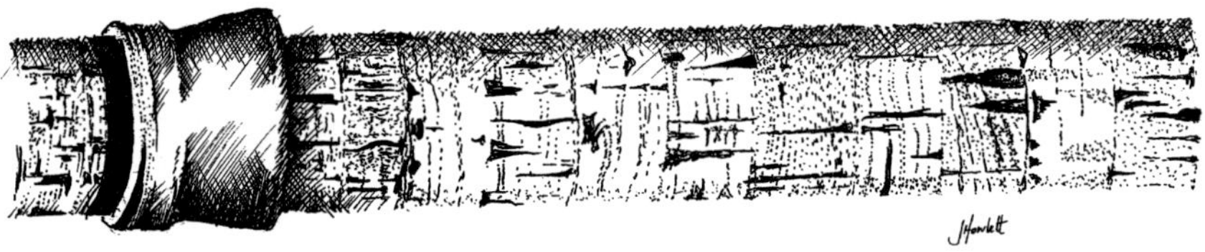

Above: Right, how the bloody hell does this lot work? Below: The immaculate Three Scale.

Mary at fifty one pounds - 'nuff said!

Above: The Pug, one of 'three in a day' from Wraysbury. Below: Chilly with The Long One.

Chapter 22

Another Close Encounter with Mary's Mate

The fish once again went to ground for a while and sightings became a rarity. The fish did visit me a couple of times but they managed, once again, to clear me out without picking up the hookbait.

Although, thinking about it afterwards, I'm sure that they probably picked up and rejected the hookbait an alarming amount of times, only without registering a bite. The tench were by far the most adept at this manoeuvre and could strip an area bald in no time and transfer your rig to the nearest weedbed practically at will. The inherent stretch in over one hundred yards of monofilament, did not help matters either. I only wish that I'd thought to try some form of braided mainline when boating out baits at range. My rigs were changed around and around, until, eventually, I lost sight of what it was that I was trying to achieve. In frustration, I switched back to my original rigs. At least I was confident that fish could be hooked on them, if only I could find them in a confident feeding situation. I kept to the big lead or running rock, though, to minimalise rig movement. We found that the old clock leads, produced for sea fishing, held the bottom wonderfully, although they took a bit of tarnishing to get rid of the hideous shine that they had when new. I used these on the same principle as the running rock, attaching them via a piece of very light line.

It was now the middle of June, and I turned up at the lake after a short break at home, determined to try and find a few fish before I set up to angle. Most of the morning was spent rowing about the lake, checking out the weed growth and hoping to see a couple of fish, or at least a sign of one, but even with the weather being hot and still there was nothing to be found. I'd been right around the far bank of the North Lake and down into the shallows at Sunnymeads Corner, then off around the islands and back up across the plateau in front of the shallow sandy point on the East Bank. Everywhere looked dead and uninspiring.

A light northerly breeze had sprung up while I'd been out so I drifted down with it towards the entrance to the Finger Bays and, putting on the mask, I leaned over the edge of the boat and peered down through the deeper water as I went. It was eighteen feet deep in places here, but still clear enough to see the Canadian pondweed taking a hold almost everywhere, in its relentless struggle for the sunlight filtering in from above. Within a few weeks, a lot of areas would be practically unfishable. The knowledge gained from little sorties like these would become invaluable when looking for clear areas from the bank should an actual fishing situation arise. Just a few shoals of perch held court, the larger ones terrorising the smaller juveniles.

Before long, the battle for this year's Wraysbury Record Perch would begin. This usually entails a handful of jaded carp anglers maniacally thrashing the water to a foam with a bizarre collection of lures and spinners at every spare moment. If you take into account the length of time between takes, results in enough thrashing to put Wendy Whiplash to shame. Last year's record perch was somewhere in the region of 12oz, with the average being about 6oz. It is amazing to what lengths boredom can drive a man!

I made a mental note of some of the more 'perchy' areas in case I needed to pull a few strokes at a later date and then made my way into the Dredger Bay. My plan was to cut through in front of the sailing club and check out No Carp Bay and the shallower bars at the back of Mary's Point, fishable from the Over the Fence swim just on the exit of Dredger Bay. My plans were thwarted by the sailing boats out in force on the South Lake so I moored up to the large yellow buoy in the bay and waited for the intrepid sailors to bugger off for tea. As I sat there, however, splashing water over the sleeping fat dog to keep her cool, I started getting that feeling. The more I looked around me at this sunny sheltered little bay the stronger that carpy feeling grew.

I unshipped the rope, rowed ashore and, standing there looking out, I half expected to see a fish hurl itself out by the far island. Remembering a bar I'd seen in the gap between the first and second island, I started to imagine carp down there, sniffing about looking for an easy meal. Maybe I was suffering sunstroke as, after all, this was the swim I'd fished to death over the last season and not had a single sniff for my efforts. I'd even declared it a 'shit hole' at the end of my last session and vowed never to return. There I was an hour later fully installed!

I cast one rod to the bar at about seventy yards, and another under the bushes sticking out from the island to my right, the third and final rod I cast all over the bay finding only weed. I even tried tight up against the Dredger hoping the shadow cast by it might have held back the weed growth but all to no avail. Eventually, I put on the mask and life jacket and went out for a look. The entire left hand side of the swim was a lost cause with the exception of a very small spot tight to the island, the shallowest part of a little gravely bar that had been cleaned off. Whether by ducks or fish remained to be seen as only about two feet of water covered the exposed area of stones. I put ten baits on and around it and a double mini bait offering on the hook. It reeked of Duck Surprise - probably at some time in the dead of night when you really don't need it! However, options were at a premium so out there into Duckland it went.

Dave the Tench Angler had set up next door, so I put my house up and popped round for a chat and a few cups of tea, eventually turning in as darkness fell. Amazingly, there had been no sign of Mr Coot and family all evening. So confident was I of his imminent arrival that, when I was rudely awoken at three in the morning by a two inch drop back on the shallow rod, I responded, not with the usual panic-stricken mad scramble for the rods, but a more sedate affair resulting in only minor cuts and bruises on impact with the flint and gravel laden ground. I stared out at the island margins through the gloom and although I couldn't make out any ripples coming back, I couldn't make out much of anything so, after five minutes, I put it down to the bird life and limped off back to bed. An hour or so later, another two bleeps on the same alarm had me back out of the pit and hovering over the rods. Although the bobbin hadn't moved, the line seemed tighter than it should be. I sat there on the stones at the water's edge, the rod in my lap, feeling the line for any movement and watching the tip in the moonlight. Slowly, I pulled the rod round until I was sure the lead should have moved. It had not, so I wound down and heaved the rod round into what I was now convinced was a crafty old coot that had somehow dragged my rig into the overhanging branches of the island. Sure enough everything was as solid as rock. I was still on the unbreakable 12lb mono, so I started bouncing the rod on a tight line as hard as I dared then pinging the line back on an open bail arm and striking it up tight again. Nothing out there in the darkness was moving so, after about three quarters of an hour of trying everything I could think of, I moved

The Dredger Bay Gap.

the alarm up next to my bedchair and put the rod back on it with the clutch slackened off. I got back into bed.

I was sure there was nothing on the end but rather than pull for a break, which I never do, I thought the best plan was to sort it out in the morning. I woke up a couple of times over the next few hours, checking the rod both times, but there was still no change.

Dawn arrived, made me a cup of tea and biscuits, then disappeared into the mist - strange girl!

Leaving the carp dog snoring away in her little bone print bed in the back of the van, I put on the life jacket and loaded the net into the boat, just in case, and started to reel myself out to the island to retrieve my rig from the tree.

As I got about twenty feet short of the tree, I saw that the line, instead of being on dry land, disappeared down into the weed. I positioned myself directly over the top and pulled for all I was worth, which was about four pound fifty at the time! Heave as I might, still nothing gave so, carefully standing up and spreading my feet apart for balance, I put the butt in my stomach and bent into the rod in a come out of the sea style. The rod held still at full compression and then, ever-so slowly, the tip inched back up as a very begrudging dead weight rose painfully slowly from the bottom. It seemed to take forever to haul it up the nine or ten feet from the bottom of the bar, but slowly it came into view. A weedbed almost as big as the boat rose up. With the multi-tendrilled underside waving about, it looked like a giant green jellyfish. It even had a piece waving out of one side of it that looked just like a fin! The more I looked, the more like a fin the fin-shaped thing looked. Finally, I could see the bloody great big fish shaped thing that it was attached to!

It was at least three feet long and carrying about three quarters of a ton of weed on its back, which it suddenly decided to utilise to its full advantage as it set off on a totally unstoppable plod around the bay. Periodically, it would sink down to the bottom, from where I had to risk multiple hernias pumping it back to the surface again, only to have the fish turn and dive again taking his weedy home with him like some sort of giant aquatic mutant snail. This fiasco went on for bloody ages, until a large section of the weed eventually

Sam snoring in the back of the van.

broke off and, with much struggling and even more swearing, I was able to cram most of the fish and some of the weed into the net and drag the whole lot up onto the boat. I started ripping lumps of weed out of the net hoping beyond hope to see a new fish, or at least one that I hadn't had yet, lying in among this bed of green. As the scale pattern showed through, Mary's Mate lay there before me in all her splendour. Lovely as she looked, I'd have gladly swapped her for a fish half her size that I hadn't seen on the bank before. This was the third time she'd graced my net, albeit under slightly strange circumstances this time.

As I rowed her back to the shore I began to wonder if we would ever get among the 'Odd uns' of Wraysbury, or would we be doomed to catch the same few fish over and over?

A bit later on that morning, however, when I held my prize up in the morning sun for a photograph, she still managed to take my breath away. A more classic-looking mirror carp it would be hard to imagine. Long and solid, armour plated with big thick linear scales glistening down her flanks, I stood and gaped as she glided off back into the depths of the Dredger Bay. At last I'd caught something from this poxy swim, after all the time and various disasters I'd endured in here, I'd finally put one on the bank. I fished on for another night in the bay but the coots came home and raped me as soon as it got dark. In fact, I never managed to fish that spot duck-free again.

The next week Phil and I spent the whole of Friday walking circuits of the lake under the frying sunshine in a fruitless search for carp. Eventually, beaten by the elusiveness of our quarry and the extreme conditions, we decided on a little social visit to Horton where we knew Keith and Chilly were trying their hand. After a stop off at the Thresher off licence to stock up with ice cold lagers, we arrived in the car park to find Chilly just in the process of setting up in the Plateau Swim nearest to the lodge. Conditions were absolutely perfect for this area and the carp were blatantly evident, cruising around the surface over the shallow bar. The events that followed made for one of the most entertaining weekends that I'd had for a long while, but, not wishing to steal Chilly's thunder, I shall let him tell you the story himself in his own military style. Before I hand the reigns over, though, I feel it only right that I first try and let you know a little about the man who will be wielding them. Chilly first came to our attention when Keith made his acquaintance at an army lake in Aldershot. He returned home with tales of a six foot paratrooper with the thirst of a camel but, unfortunately, the tolerance of a field mouse!

Many a drunken night was spent over the ensuing year, until Chilly eventually procured a ticket for Horton, and with it the chance to angle for the fish of his dreams. To add the required ambience I suggest you imagine the voice of a classic Windsor Davies style sergeant major to narrate the following piece.

Chilly's Story. . .

Having just banked my first Horton carp in the shape of Polly at 20lb 14oz, stalking in the Weedy Bay, Keith and I decided to do a little more stalking. We collected up a few bits and pieces and went for a walk. Passing Sir Pete in the Plateau Swim, we could see that there were a few fish in front of him. I asked how he was doing and he informed me that things were a little slow and that he would be leaving at about 1400h that afternoon. Not being one to miss such an opportunity, I moved some of my kit behind the swim, thus saving it, ready for the midday move that Keith and I had planned, the pair of us then continued our little stroll.

We hadn't seen a thing until we reached the Church Bay, whereupon we spied some carp, and not small ones at that! I left Keith drifting some Mixers out into the bay and continued my walk into the back of the bay. Imagine my surprise when, whilst peering into the back of the bay, I spotted Jack grubbing about in the margins. At the time, I thought I would never get a better chance to bag her. Having presented a bottom bait right in her anticipated path, I thought it was all over bar the shouting. However, it seemed that brain cells had been in short supply in the Darenth Valley that day, as one of the newly joined Darenth Bad Bloods, sent his 3oz lead across the bay, landing within inches of Jack's nose. She wasn't standing for that and soon disappeared from sight. Thank goodness for locked gates and barbed wire fences, they prevented Horton's first murder! Still frothing at the mouth, I made my way back round to Keith who somehow having managed to calm me down then decided that now was a good time for the planned midday move.

As I moved into the Plateau Swim, two of my latter day heroes, Dave Lane and Phil Thompson, arrived fresh from another sortie at Wraysbury. True to form, Phil got the beer out and Dave climbed up a very tall tree just to the right of my swim, from which he could clearly see the plateau some 50 yards out into the lake. Now, at this stage of the game I would love to tell you how I sussed it all out for myself, but I can't. Dave and Phil took charge. From his lofty vantage point, Dave could see that most of the Horton carp were now sunning their buns atop the plateau. He could make out individual fish and was giving a running commentary as to what was going on. Although I could certainly see that a floater would probably be my best chance, I was content to sit back and let my two mentors sort it all out for me. With Dave's commentary raining down on us from the tree, it was down to Phil to decide which tactics I should employ. It just had to be an anchored floater according to Phil - two Chum Mixers on a ten foot hooklink. Fair enough, I thought, and set about the task of tying it all up. By now Dave sounded more like a horse racing commentator as the Grand National was coming to a very close finish, and, in accordance with the frenzy he was whipping up, I grew ten Cumberland sausages for fingers.

"Settle down my old son," were Phil's calming words. "Here, have a slug of beer."

The man is a genius and the old nerves began to settle down a little. Dave, still up the tree and sounding more like a colony of howler monkeys by now, insisted that I got a bait out there pronto. Enter Keith and the multi-talented mug. Let me explain. Have you ever tried casting a ten foot hooklink, a 2oz lead and three foot of lead core? Impossible. Keith coiled up the hooklink into the mug and stood behind me facing the lake. I got into position and launched the whole lot out into the lake - without the mug! Result! It landed dead centre of the plateau first time. Now that was worth celebrating all on its own! Dave, still up the tree, informed the now growing mass of anglers below him that the bait was visible and in amongst the fish so I put the rod down on its rest and switched the buzzer on. Phil slapped me on the back and slapped a can of lager in my hand.

"That'll be away in a minute," he said. I'd have to save the beer until later!

I grabbed my binoculars and sat looking out at my bait bobbing in amongst the glistening backs of carp out on the plateau. Trap set.

If I thought Dave had been excited before, then he was just about to take it to a new level.

"They know it's there, boy. They're using it as a roundabout... Yeah!"

Cheers Laney!

"There's Shoulders, he's right behind the bait!"

"Please, shut up and get down from the tree," I thought. My nerves were in a mess. "Please God, let me catch one... I need a beer!"

Dave eventually got out of the tree and I could concentrate on staring at the bait through the bins. Although I could see loads of fish out there, they seemed a little reluctant to come too close to the hookbait. It was a real surprise when, twenty minutes after the bait had hit the water, and whilst I was looking at the bait through the bins, a back broke the surface and the Mixers were gone. I threw the binoculars down and, as the buzzer gave a single bleep, I wound down and swept the rod over my shoulder for all I was worth. Fish on!

The gathering hordes gave a cheer, and I settled down to do battle with what I was convinced was 'a small one' and I informed Keith and Dave of this. The pair of them gave me a withering look and told me to grow up, which I did immediately. In fact, I was ageing rapidly. The fish kited away to my left, away from the plateau and into open water, seemingly intent on reaching the far end of the lake. Steadily it slowed, and I felt I had some sort of control for the first time. The same could not be said of my bowels, things were definitely getting out of control there as the fish started to grow rapidly as the battle continued. Steady pressure soon had the fish heading my way when, about thirty yards out, the fish rolled on the surface. I saw the flash of scales, as did everyone else.

Up went the shout, "Jack!!"

Now, as a paratrooper, I have been involved in some very hairy and sometimes life-threatening situations, and sometimes I have wondered when I would feel that heart-pumping, adrenalin-rushing moment when your very life depends on what you are doing at that precise moment in time.

Well, I was there, I had never felt so alive, the adrenalin highlighting every twist and turn that the fish made. I can honestly say that I have never felt so frightened in all my life. Keith, aware of how I felt, took control of the net, gave me a reassuring wink and made his way to the water's edge. Phil, cool as ever, just looked on. Dave, however, became a gibbering heap. Now, here is a bloke who has caught fish that us mere mortals can only dream of, and in quantity too.

"Get it in the net, no, no leave it, let it go in the weed, someone get the boat, no no just get it in the net."

On and on he went. At the time it did terrible things to my state of mind. One of my heroes and he was twice as nervous as I was! Looking back though, don't you think it is wonderful that a bloke with all that experience can still get like that over the capture of a fish. Anyway, Keith was manning the net and advising me just to keep it moving, which I managed to do. I never saw the fish go into the net. The long hooklink meant I had to walk back from the edge of the water and, as I did so, the crowd moved in front of me. Next thing, a roar went up and I knew it was all over. I dispatched the rod into the bushes and went absolutely nutty. Once I had calmed down a little, I found that the lads had been getting the fish ready for weighing.

Some had thought that she would be over fifty pounds but it mattered not a jot that the scales settled a little shy at 49lb 4oz. Oh, deep, deep joy! We sacked her in the deep water off the end of the pontoon and I was glad to see her come to rest in the shade that the pontoon offered. Half an hour later Gary Bond retrieved her from the water as Dave and I sorted out the unhooking mats and the gallery of photographers that had gathered. She had seen it all before and behaved impeccably as we posed together. After the compulsory 'author returns' shots, Phil and I ended up having an early bath!

Having just bagged Britain's largest surface caught carp, and with Jack being my second Horton carp in only a few hours, there was only one thing left to do. Carp party! Dave, being the world's greatest party organiser, had begun to dispatch people to various places for supplies. In a total daze I managed to dispatch two hookbaits back into the general area of the plateau, both pop-ups off the lead. They both came to rest in the thick weed that abounded in the area. I was happy anyway. Keith, Dave and I organised the furniture from the lodge behind my swim. We were now ready to party.

First though, I had a few people to ring. Most importantly, my wife Lynn, she has suffered so much in the past few years with her battle against cancer. Through it all though, she has encouraged me to, "get out there and bag a whacker." Well, I had, and she could not have been more pleased for me. My mate Stu McDermot was next, he simply downed tools at work and headed for Horton via the off licence. Nice one, fella. And so the party began.

There were a few calls of "Angler Down!" that night! Much later, most of the revellers had gone their merry ways which left Keith, Dave and myself sitting under my bivvy. " 'Tis the company not the carp which maketh the feast," someone famous once said, and I couldn't think of two guys I'd rather be sharing this moment with. Good company, good friends and a bloody good time! Eventually though, even these masters of the drinking art retired to bed. Dave to the lodge, where he and Fat Sam, the faithful carp dog, curled up on an old sofa on the verandah, and Keith to his swim, two up from me. I managed to get to sleep myself somehow.

The next thing I remember was standing, somewhat unsteadily, doing battle with yet another Horton carp! Just to make me suffer, this fish went absolutely bonkers. The best hangover cure I have ever come across! A deft piece of netting by Del in the margins away to my left and the Long One was mine. Even in my delicate condition, I was able to let out the old battle cry, loud enough it would seem to wake the dead, as 30 seconds later Keith and Dave stumbled into my swim. It was 0800h in the morning, a little early for these two, but again they couldn't have been happier for me. Keith warmly shook my hand and wished me Happy Birthday, because indeed it was. Up on the scales and she went 28lb 12oz and an absolute stunner to boot.

Photo's done, it was time for Dave to get back to Wraysbury and for Keith and myself to look back on what had been, for me, the best session of my life.

Finally, for Jack, thanks for the memory and may you rest in peace.

Chilly with the legendary Jack.

Chapter 23

The Hoover from Douglas Lane Point

With renewed vigour at the incredible sight of Jack the previous week, and armed with some new Response Pellets to try out, I bounced the old jallopy through the Douglas Lane gates once again.

After stashing my gear on the Ten Acre Island in the morning, I set out with the express intention of spending most of the day afloat. The weed had really taken a hold now in the South Lake and it was necessary to find some new clear areas, and also to find out the general state of play in the North Lake.

Checking the spots.

The first half of the day was spent out in the middle area from the Douglas Lane up to the sailing club. This is one of the deepest parts of the lake, although you wouldn't have known it by looking over the edge at the moment. The weed reached within a few feet of the surface over at least fifty percent of the entire area, and the actual clear and fishable bits were limited to half a dozen small spots. I marked up a couple of the better ones and slowly made my way down towards No Carp Bay where Terry Hearn and Wayne Dunn were angling. Now, going without tea for any length of time is not exactly one of my strong points, and long before

I reached the swim, I was standing up tilting my hand to my mouth in the internationally recognised gesture of tea drinkers everywhere. Taking the long route round so as not to disturb their fishing, I docked at the side of the Round Point just as the steam started to rise from the spout.

The first cup barely touched the sides and we chatted about this and that as I badgered Terry to put the kettle back on for another. I noticed as he filled the kettle, that the bottle looked a bit green, but, being no stranger to the old algae bloom in the water container syndrome myself, I thought nothing more of it. On closer inspection, just shy of the third cup however, it turned out that it was the actual water that was green and not the bottle.

"What's this then, lake water?" I asked

"No, it's just been in the motor for a while," he replied. "It should be all right though."

I passed up on the kind offer of another cup and went for a walk along the peninsula with the faithful carp dog in tow. The day was turning out to be a real scorcher, the sort of day where you might see a few fish lazing in the snags in the Dredger Bay. Returning to the boat, I set off for the afternoon. The snags held only stockies so I resorted to the original plan of mapping out the weed growth.

By the late afternoon I'd started to feel a bit queasy. At first I put it down to too much sun and not enough food, but half way back to the Ten Acre Island things took a turn for the worse. I was standing up punting the boat along when a loud gurgling noise emitted from my lower back area and I could feel a strange bubbling sensation deep inside. It stopped as quickly as it had started and, shrugging it off, I carried on towards the island. The next one was so loud that even Sam, who's half deaf, looked up accusingly at me. The island was only fifty yards away now and, knowing that I had some food in my rucksack, I struck out once more with the oar.

Suddenly, a pain tore through me as if I'd been shot. I doubled over clutching my stomach in agony. After a few seconds it subsided and I gingerly carried on, realising now that I had to get to dry land straight away. A few yards short of the island, and with cold sweat pouring off of me, I was struck by another wave of pain, this one deposited me in the bottom of the boat writhing and moaning. The second that it had passed, I paddled the last few feet and ran up the bank of the island, disappearing into the bushes and not re-emerging for a considerable time. I was in a terrible state and I knew it was all down to that bloody green water of Terry's. For the next hour, I ran relays in and out of the bushes, until eventually lying down on the ground, totally exhausted.

I stayed there for a while trying to decide what to do and, in the end, unable to face the row back to the bank, I dragged out the bedchair and collapsed onto it. I felt like death, I was sweating and shaking, alternately boiling hot and then freezing cold. Every time that I thought I'd got my bowels under control, I was sent charging back into the bushes again. Eventually, at sometime during the evening, I must have drifted off to sleep, as the next thing I knew it was the middle of the night and Fat Sam was curled up under a bush snoring her head off. I was lying out in just shorts and a T-shirt and consequently being eaten alive by mozzies. I tentatively stood up and discovered, to my delight, that I felt a little better. A fresh breeze had sprung up from the south west and I went and sat by the water's edge, taking in great gulps of air to clear my head. It was too late now to find anywhere to set up camp so, dragging the sleeping bag out, I curled up under the stars on the island for what remained of the night.

I awoke about nine the next morning and the first thing that struck me was how hungry I was. I hadn't eaten much the day before and anything that I had eaten was certainly long gone now. Deciding it was best to leave the tackle where it was for now, I set off to the shops to get some breakfast. I rowed across to the Douglas Lane and stashed the boat in the bushes, pulling a few old branches over the top for good measure. Rather than drive, I took the scenic route, walking around Bryant's Bay and returning an hour later to the Douglas Lane Point, armed with rolls, pasties, and various other sell by date-challenged items. While the fat dog and myself struggled with Mr Patel's finest fare, out on the plateau in front of us a fair amount of activity was going on.

Small splashes and bow waves peppered the surface over the weed at the left hand edge of the shallower water. They were too small to be carp, more likely tench or stockies, but I resolved to row back via the plateau on the way to collect my tackle, just in case. Just as we were preparing to leave, the morning flight of Concorde ripped a hole in the skies above us, and the water erupted over the plateau. What were now evident to be tench scattered in all directions in a blind panic. Fetching the boat, I set off for the island. I made a wide birth of the plateau and drifted in towards it on the gentle breeze. As I approached, I could see a huge shoal of tench chasing each other around in a spawning frenzy. There were far more fish present than I'd even thought existed at Wraysbury in total. Akin to a shoal of sea bream or reef fish, they rotated in tight formation, smashing the weedbeds all around them to a pulp. I'd seen tench spawn before, but never in this number or with this intensity so I carefully manoeuvred the boat into a position from where I could observe without getting in the way. I stood spell-bound as the smaller males thrashed repeatedly into the sides of the heavily laden females, oblivious to me or anything else. The boat was parked in the centre of the weed and the action was occurring off to my left. Then, out of the corner of my eye, I noticed something larger move around the boat from the right.

As it came into view, I could clearly see a common carp of about fifteen pounds make his way towards the tench. After a quick look as if to check every thing was in order, he turned and went back the way he had come. I followed his progress around the front of the boat, not daring to move in case I spooked him off as he made his way into the weed behind me. I turned to get a better look at where he was headed and almost fell out of the boat in surprise. There, sitting directly behind the boat, also watching the tench spawn, were at least ten clonking great mirror carp! They were just milling about on the periphery, in the expectant hope of a free meal of fresh spawn, no doubt. So close to me were these fish, that with a single glance I could put names to most of them. The Pug was there along with The Egg and Mallin's fish, a couple of the elusive mid-twenty commons were also present.

One particular fish got me really excited. In just over two years of fishing Wraysbury I'd never set eyes on him before, but I recognised him instantly from an old photograph that Pete Springate had shown me over a year ago. The photo had been of Johnny Allen holding a Jurassic-looking twenty nine pounder, and, without a doubt, this was the fish that I was now looking at. Big half-moon scales adorned his sides and he gave an impression both of age and nonchalance, as if he knew the effect he was having on me and revelled in his aloofness! I'd show him, somehow!

I was in a bit of a strange position. I'd finally found the fish but standing up in the middle of a weedbed, in a boat, surrounded by them wasn't the ideal situation. My tackle was on the island about fifty yards directly in front of me, but I was too scared to breathe let alone start rowing. Luckily, Fat Sam had curled up to sleep in the bottom of the boat so there were no extra disturbances from her. The words of an old song kept drifting in to my head, how did it go?

"Tench to the left of me, mirrors to the right, here I am, stuck in the middle with you."

Eventually, I decided to gently propel the boat forwards between the two groups of fish and head straight for the island. On my way past I carefully lifted a piece of weed with the oar to mark the clear strip that meandered through the otherwise solid weed, and then headed for the tackle. Just as I cleared the weedbeds and made it into open water, two more fish appeared from between the islands heading straight for me. I stopped punting and stood, stock-still, as Mary and her mate cruised casually under the boat reappearing behind me moments later on their way to join their friends. I gathered up all my tackle as quickly as was humanly possible. I hadn't had a definite chance like this for bloody ages and my heart was hammering on my ribs as I rowed the long way back around the Railway Lake. I kept thinking that, at any second, someone would appear, walking their tackle along the point. I don't know what I would have done if they had? Probably beaten them to death with the oar and hidden the body in the bushes and then fished there anyway!

Dragging the gear out of the boat, I opened the rucksack and rod bag and unceremoniously tipped the whole bloody lot on the floor in a big heap. With no time for searching about, this way I could instantly find everything that I needed, and before long I had two baited hair rigs ready to go. The lifted piece of weed marked the spot perfectly, and with an easy forty yard lob, both baits were soon in position. Rods were laid on the ground with the clutches slackened while I organised the rest of the kit. I kept having to stop and climb the big oak tree on the right to remind myself it was really all happening and that I was definitely going to catch one. The morning drifted slowly into the afternoon and still the carp milled about in and out of the weed, it could only be a matter of time now. Every time an exceptionally low plane passed over, a chain reaction would start with the tench and result in an all-out eruption of fish on the plateau. I couldn't sit still and, as a result, most of the afternoon was spent wearing a trough through the middle of my swim. Occasionally a single bleep on the indicator from drifting weed would threaten me with a cardiac arrest. The drifting weed problem grew steadily worse as the wind picked up throughout the afternoon. By the evening, I'd had to lift both rods twice each and painstakingly flick clumps of weed off the line as it hung at all distances.

Just before darkness fell, a rustling in the bushes heralded the arrival of The Shootist.

"Hello Dave, have you bagged any?" he asked.

"Not yet, Shootist, but it's imminent," I replied.

"Well I've had a right result," he countered. "Can you take a couple of photos for me?"

Then, after a short struggle with the cord on a large and dubious-looking hessian sack,

"There you go, look at that lot," he said, tipping his right result on the ground at my feet. Rabbits and crows littered the deck. Shaking my head in incredulity, I rummaged around in the bivvy for the camera - and people think carp fishing is a bizarre pastime! I let him arrange the carnage accordingly, and then took a couple of trophy shots. He rewarded me with a couple of cans of warm lager, which thankfully hadn't shared the same sack as his spoils of war. After recounting the gory details of his day's sport, he wandered off leaving me to continue my pacing of the banks in anticipation.

Spoils of war!

Just after dark, a large splash over the plateau was followed a few moments later by a short burst from the left hand buzzer as a fish, realising it had slipped up, dived into the sanctuary of the weed. On striking, I was horrified at the amount of weed hanging off the line. It had practically braided itself to the mainline making reeling in a nightmare. The new diameter of the line would not physically fit through the rod rings. I could only gain ten feet of line at a time before laying the rod down and ripping off a fresh batch of weed. This tortuous method was so painfully slow that for the first fifteen minutes, I had barely even felt the fish at all. The light had totally faded into night now so I couldn't really see what was happening either so, by the time I'd got into direct contact, the fish, if it was still on, was totally solid in the thick weed. As I held the rod high I could see, silhouetted against the skyline, thirty yards of weed-encrusted line and knew that the boat would offer a much better chance of a result. After half an hour afloat, I started to doubt the wisdom of this method as well. I was knee-deep in weed with coils of line laying spaghetti-like all around me. Thankfully, though, and after a lot of perseverance, I had the fish thrashing on the weed in front of me. By stripping the line down through the rings by hand, in a fly fishing style, I managed to bundle him unceremoniously into the net. All the way back to the bank I prayed for it to be Johnny Allen's twenty nine, but the old carp god couldn't have been listening as there, encased in weed in the bottom of my net, lay The Hoover. It was like a meeting of old friends as I unhooked and weighed him in at thirty three and a half pounds. After slipping him into a sack, I wound in the other rod, as it was festooned with weed anyway, and set off in search of somebody to do the photographs for me.

A quick tour of the lake (by car) revealed that I was in fact the only angler on the pit and as I didn't want to keep the fish sacked up overnight, there was only one thing for

A meeting of friends.

it, so I drove over to Horton and dragged an unsuspecting Barry over to do the honours.

Not without a considerable amount of struggling, I managed to get both baits back out there somewhere near the mark. I think that all the palaver involved in landing The Hoover had destroyed my chances of any further action, and, come the morning, all I was left with was two washing lines liberally hung with weed. In fact, they were so badly weeded that I was forced to cut both the lines at the tip and hand line them in!

I stashed the gear in the bushes and set off on yet another tour of Wraysbury to see what surprises a fresh day would hold in store for me.

Like washing lines hung with weed.

Chapter 24

Battle of the Pikeys

It was now late August and I suppose I'd been living on Wraysbury for pretty much most of the summer. As a result of which I'd seen a fair few goings on among the local non-fishing fraternity. The night's events about to unfold before me would knock the rest into a cocked hat.

I'd spent the previous four nights fishing in four different swims. I just couldn't seem to settle anywhere. The fish had stayed elusive throughout and I'd walked right around the pit at least once a day. I'd fished in the most likely-looking swim each night, but I remained fishless for my efforts. This particular day I'd seen a 'maybe' at the mouth of the Dredger Bay, so a move into the right hand swim had seemed like a good idea. It was a good spot to hopefully intercept any fish that might be passing through into the North Lake.

Since my capture of Mary's Mate from here a month previously, my enthusiasm had returned for the Dredger Bay. It was, however, to be short-lived. Having totally lost track of days, I didn't realise it was a Friday until I'd already set-up and got my baits out. I usually gave the peninsula swims, of which this was the end one, a miss at the weekends, as the level of nuisance activity from the kids swimming, partying, and generally loitering with intent could be a bit off-putting to say the least.

I'd managed to pull the van out of sight behind the bushes and there were a few other anglers around me. Most of these were in positions more likely to draw any flak, as it were, so I made up my mind to stay put. I was in the right hand deeper swim of the Dredger Bay and recently set-up in the left hand swim, which was separated from me by a small marshy copse of trees, was one of the new members and his girlfriend.

The afternoon had passed quite uneventfully, and most of the time had been spent unsuccessfully trying to scare the living daylights out of the local coot population that always presented such a problem in this swim. With all the far banks being made up of three islands they could hole up quite safely. They would wait for you to lose interest in them just long enough to send out a raiding party, grabbing another half a dozen boilies, before scurrying off for cover from another futile hail of projectiles emanating from my bivvy.

Just on dusk, a crashing in the bushes to my left heralded the arrival of one very flustered-looking Irish youth. In between furtive looks over his shoulder he blurted out, "Oim being chased by some big blokes. Dere troiying to foking kill me dey are!"

This was all I needed! In the distance, I could hear the bellowing of death threats and general abuse.

"Can oi pretend oim fishing wid you?"

I could hear the shouts getting closer and there were obviously more than one or two of them.

"What have you done to upset that lot then?" I asked.

"Oi never did a ting, oi only went out wid his daughter," he said. "Oi was wid me mates but they legged it through the woods."

I couldn't see me convincing a baseball-bat wielding lynch mob that matey was a carp angler. Besides, it was none of my business, so I told him his best bet was to hide somewhere in the woods. I wanted nothing to do with any of it. No sooner had he disappeared, than another much bigger bloke came panting to a halt at the back of my swim. "Have you seen a little fokker with curly hair come past here?"

"I dunno mate," I said trying to be as diplomatic as possible. "I heard someone crashing about in the bushes earlier."

He shot off in hot pursuit. I decided to retire into the bivvy until the whole lot of them had disappeared. After half an hour of hollering and shouting, the chase seemed to drift off to another part of Wraysbury. A few minutes later my neighbouring angler popped round to find out if I had any idea as to what the bloody hell was occurring. According to him, the lynch mob had been at least twenty handed and armed with a various assortment of blunt instruments. As we sat there chatting, I heard a twig snap in the bushes to my right. I knew there were no other anglers down there and the only other swim was the half finished Over the Fence that I'd built myself and I'd have seen anyone arriving. So, taking Fat Sam with me, I set off to investigate. In the back of my mind, I knew what I was going to find before I got there and sure enough there he was, down by the water's edge smoking a fag.

He practically left his skin when he looked up and saw me standing there.

"Oh Jezus. I didn't hear you coming, I thought it was them, you nearly gave me a heart attack."

"They've long gone mate," I said. "Best you skidaddle before they get back," I added, desperately wanting rid of him as soon as possible. After a few minutes, he warily made his way back down the peninsula towards the gate in search of his mates. I followed behind at a distance keeping to the shadows and out of sight until I was sure he was on his way.

By the time I got back to my swim, matey from next door had trotted off back to his rods, so I brewed up a nice cup of tea and, setting up the low chair, settled down to enjoy the eventual peace and quiet of the night. No sooner had I got comfortable, than I heard voices returning and having already had more than enough excitement for one night I picked up my tea and backed into the shadows of the trees from where I could see without being seen. Three people rounded the corner leading into my swim, two of them had torches which they shone at the car and on the back of my bivvy as they approached. I stepped a little further back keeping another confrontation as a final option.

"Hello, is anyone there?" boomed a voice. "This is the police."

I felt a bit of a prat emerging out of the pitch black of the bushes drinking a cup of tea, but I tried to act nonchalantly regardless. There were two coppers and they had the Irish kiddy secured firmly between them. It transpired that the girl that he'd been with earlier and her mate had legged it during the family feud, or something like that, and the law had been called in to find them, as they were only fifteen. Eventually, they left saying that if they'd had no joy by midnight they may have to consider a helicopter search of the area, and if this should happen could I please stay in my vehicle for easy identification.

Now, it was obvious to me, and by the look on his face obvious to the young kiddy, that the two girls had legged it round to a friend's house, too scared to face their dads. They were at this very moment probably concocting matching alibi's and blissfully ignorant of the full scale search being launched on their behalf, but I suppose nowadays you can't be too careful.

So it was that, about one o'clock in the morning, just as I was finally nodding off to sleep, I heard the approaching 'wokker, wokker, wokker' of the police helicopter as it started its search at the base of the peninsula, and within a few minutes using a heat-seeking camera he was hovering noisily above my bivvy. Then came the spotlight. I thought it was going to melt the top of my brolly it was so bright. I climbed back out of bed, resigned to a night of no sleep, and went and sat in the car like a good boy. After a while, my thirst got the better of me and I decided to make a cup of tea. The helicopter was still directly above me which meant for the first time ever I didn't have to search in the dark for the lighter and tea bags. In fact, I was considering putting on some sunblock. Two different coppers arrived and asked me all the same questions as the first two had and, eventually satisfied that I wasn't two teenage girls, they radioed through to the helicopter and away they all went. Any slight chance that may have been left of catching a fish that night soon disappeared, as the chopper did a quick circuit of the bay in front of me, illuminating the bottom with his mega spotlight and whipping up the surface in the down draft from his rotor blades.

By about two thirty in the morning peace descended once more over Wraysbury, so packing away the low chair and locking up the van, I climbed into the sleeping bag intent on salvaging some amount of sleep from this nightmare. But, once again, Mr Reality had other plans for me and before I'd even zipped the bag up I heard the all too familiar sound of footsteps approaching. I tried pretending to be asleep, but it is easier said than done when six feet of copper attached to three feet of sabre-toothed Alsatian is standing in your doorway coughing politely.

Sam, who'd slept on oblivious up until now, suddenly smelt the other dog and flew out from under the bed growling and barking as she came. Luckily, she had the good sense to hold back on the actual attacking part or I'd probably still be picking bits of her out of the trees now. All the same questions were repeated, had I seen? Did I know? Who, what, why? He seemed satisfied with my well rehearsed answers and finally wandered off to quiz someone else. The sky was just beginning to turn a deep blue around the edges as I eventually clambered back to bed. I'd already made up my mind that as soon as I woke up the first thing on the agenda was a relocation.

If this was a typical Friday night on the peninsula I certainly didn't want to know about Saturday.

Chapter 25

More Encounters with The Pug and a Decision Made

The next weekend, rather than suffer a repeat of the previous Friday's disaster, I opted for a social session over at Horton. I still held an honorary ticket, and this meant that I could just pop over and use the showers or bogs whenever I wanted and on the odd occasion I would angle as well, although to be honest it was always just an excuse for a good 'jolly up'.

Due to one thing and another, by the time that I arrived it had been dark for about an hour, but I soon found Reggie's bivvy, set up in the Ski Slope swim. After a quick rummage through his cool bag which he had inadvertently left outside, I decided it would be a sound idea to set-up in the swim immediately to his left. I had recently acquired another Carp Dog as well, in the form of a black collie cross, called Joey. He belonged to my girlfriend, Sue, and somehow I had been volunteered to become a two dog angler. Now, Sam knows the ropes and is more than a little sedate in her approach to angling, whereas to Joey it was all still a great adventure. Charging around like a lunatic seemed to be the order of

Joey.

the day, and by the time I had set up camp next to Reg, Joey had whipped himself up into a frenzy and could hardly even breath properly. When everything was set I went next door to surprise Reg. I hadn't heard a sound from his dome tent and I assumed that he must have been asleep. Grabbing the front of the dome in both hands I started shaking it about and yelling through the door, "Yo Reg, put the bloody kettle on then!"

How was I to know that he was in some form of compromising position with his fair lady Kate? I couldn't understand why they seemed so upset at seeing me? I thought it would be a nice surprise! Eventually when they realised that I wasn't going away, the door was unzipped and the two dogs and I spilled in through the doorway. Kate was less than impressed at sharing a double lilo with two slavering hounds, but I somehow managed to convince her that no harm would come of it, or so I thought! I'd just talked Reg out of a can of Stella when an all too familiar retching sound emitted from Joey's corner of the bed and, before I could reach over to evict him, he threw up all over the duvet! For some strange reason, I was the only one who found this little episode side-splittingly funny and, by the time I had cleaned up the mess, and consumed a couple more of Reggie's beers, I thought it best to retire under the withering stare of Mrs Reg.

A burst of gold - Reg with his thirty five pound common.

By the morning, all of the previous night's mishaps had been forgotten and my neighbours had resorted to their normal cheery dispositions. Breakfast was a glorious affair but I had to remember to feign surprise when Reg pulled eggs, bacon, and mushrooms out from the cool box! We were just tidying away the dishes, with the help of the two voracious hounds, when the unthinkable happened and Reg actually had a take. We gazed in shock and disbelief for a split second, before Reg sprang into action, striking into what appeared to be a very large fish. Reg is one of those anglers who refuses to put even the slightest bend in a rod whilst playing a fish and, as a result, the fight was a very protracted affair. Time and again we saw the form of a very large common carp, materialising from the depths, only to power away again at every glimpse of two shabby-looking blokes, standing on the bank waving a net about hopefully!

Reg managed, eventually, to bore the fish into submission and he let out a whoop of delight as, with a burst of golden scales, it rolled into the net. At thirty five pounds it was, by far, his best ever common and we celebrated the event accordingly. After a while, though, my feet were beginning to itch for Wraysbury soil and so the next morning, before daylight had fully installed itself, I was, once again, treading on her hallowed turfs.

Whilst I had been loading up the boat with all my tackle, and settled both the dogs into their respective positions, a south westerly wind had sprung up as I was packing away my gear, ready to leave the scene of the 'Battle of the Pikey's' in the Dredger Bay. By the time that I'd loaded the boat and set off towards the North Lake, it was blowing quite convincingly.

Unlike most lakes where a strong south westerly would push fish in to the north east corner, there's an abundance of north east corners to choose from. I started off by boating across the Dredger Bay and out through the smallest channel, stopping for a look in The Snags on the way. Only a few of the Fungus Mirrors could be seen gliding in and out of the branches along with one slightly better mirror, around twenty two pounds in weight. Emerging from the channel in front of the Douglas Lane point, I drifted on the wind into the Railway Lake, but it didn't look particularly 'carpy', so digging the oars deep into the now quite choppy water, I struck out for the back channel that would lead me through the Finger Bays and ultimately out into the North Lake.

As soon as I entered The North I knew I'd made the right decision as it looked absolutely prime. The wind was pumping into the corner formed by Springate's Point and the Rocky Barge. Rowing the boat there couldn't have been easier as I simply lined myself up and drifted in on the wind. I tipped out most of the tackle into the Rocky Barge swim, leaving only the rucksack as a balance weight in the back of the boat. After getting Sam comfortable in her little bone bed, I left her to guard the gear as I set out to try and find some clear areas among the weed.

I knew from recent trips that this area of the North Lake was a veritable jungle of milfoil, and as I peered down through the mask, I half expected to see Tarzan swing past with an aqua-lung strapped to his back. After an hour of searching, I'd only confirmed what I already thought, just three spots were fishable in the entire swim. Now, from the Barge swim there is an awful lot of water in front of you to angle in, so to only find three spots meant that the weed was practically at its worst. The spots were small sand-topped humps about six feet in diameter, two of which were situated in the middle of the lake level with the big island. The other was forty yards out, slightly to my right and, although it was usually hard to find, on this occasion the sailing club had placed a buoy ten yards to the left of the spot, marking it perfectly. Over each of the three areas I tipped a small bucket of hemp (about one kilo) and a scattering of chopped up boilies. I had to chop them in order to stop them rolling off the spots. As I was dropping the last of the baits, I caught sight of somebody setting up a bivvy on Springate's Point. This seemed a bit of a strange move, as I was obviously already angling over the majority of the water on this side of the point.

After setting up my brolly, I ventured round for a chat with the new arrival. As it turned out it was Wraysbury Two as he'd become known. He was a little miffed as he had walked his gear right around the pit to fish in this area before even noticing that I was already there. He decided to do the night here before moving off again in the morning, so I left him to it and wandered back to my swim to cook up a bit of grub.

Hemping it up.

After a short while, the sound of clanking aluminium dragged me from an afternoon siesta and I stuck my head around the brolly to see a grinning Phil laden with ice cold lagers. After congratulating him on this feat of "bloody good angling," we set about our favourite Saturday afternoon pastime, apart from catching carp of course! As the day grew darker and the carrier bag in turn grew lighter, Phil made his way back to his swim. He'd elected to fish in the Grassy Point, which was directly opposite my swim although a good two hundred and fifty yards of water separated us. I sat back and watched as he positioned his baits for the night. As is nearly always the way with Phil, he merely flicked one into each margin. A few visitors came and went throughout the evening, and I noted what a different lake this was at the weekends. During the week barely a soul was to be seen wandering the banks, but come Friday night they all emerged like hungry mice from the woodwork.

As the sun started to set, I could see the massive flocks of jackdaws making there way up from Windsor to their nightly roosting place on Ten Acre Island. This was always a spectacle worth watching. As they drew nearer the squawks and screams of this most impressive invasion could be clearly heard and, as they passed overhead, the sky quite literally turned black as thousands upon thousands of birds raced to procure the best branches. Tonight though, they had decided for some unknown reason to settle in the woods that stretched from my swim into the Finger Bays behind me. Maybe they thought that The Shootist was lying in wait for them on the island? Akin to a scene from Alfred Hitchcock's The Birds, they swooped and wheeled overhead in such numbers as to be almost frightening. I stood still at the top of the small hill behind my swim as they settled all around me. Not fancying the idea of sharing my swim with a few thousand squabbling birds for the night, I waited until at last I was sure they were all settled, before moving quietly into the centre of the woods. In retrospect I should have carried out the next part of my plan from under the sanctuary of an umbrella, but unthinkingly, I brought my hands together in the loudest clap that I could muster. The trees erupted as legion upon legion of birds scattered in every direction, eventually settling back on the Ten Acre Island where they belonged. I emerged from the woods looking like a cross between the Abominable Snowman and the Birdman of Alcatraz! Shite and feathers littered the ground, but at least the peace of a Wraysbury evening had been restored once more.

The morning dawned bright and, with the south-westerly still blowing in, the swim looked absolutely perfect. Just then the peace was shattered by the sound of a screaming buzzer, but not mine! Peering through the bushes I could see that Wraysbury Two was bent into a good fish and after a short fight he slipped the net under Mallin's. This was down a bit in weight from its last capture but at thirty eight pounds it was certainly big enough to put a dirty great big smile on his face! As we took the photo's on the little lawn between our swims, he told me how he'd already

Waiting for the jackdaws.

packed up his bivvy and had only the rods left to go before moving!

I returned to my swim and sat there staring accusingly at the rods. I thought I was supposed to be in the prime position? As if in answer my right hand rod, the one near the buoy, stuttered into life. I was on it in a flash but the fish instantly made a bee-line for the buoy and I had to hold the rod as far right as I could whilst piling on the pressure. I only had to gain a few yards in order to bring him inside the buoy to safety, and then the hook pulled. It was over in a flash and, hurling the rod on the ground, I cursed everything within range before getting down to some serious sulking. I hadn't even given it that much stick, but I suppose you just can't land them all. I was still groaning and moaning half an hour later when three bleeps emitted from my left hand rod and, looking up to see the rod bent double in the rests, I grabbed it just as the baitrunner kicked in and line was torn from the reel, oblivious to the finger pressure I was putting on the spool. Before I could stop him he'd crashed into a dense weedbed and, sulking even harder than I had earlier, he refused to budge. All the heaving in the world would not persuade him to leave the security of the weed and, eventually, the boat seemed the only option.

With Wraysbury Two at the helm, we set off in hot pursuit. The weedbed we eventually found him in was only three feet under the surface but I knew the water there to be over eighteen feet deep! It seemed to take an eternity to coax him out. Every time we started to make some progress the wind would push us away and return us to square one but, just as we were beginning to think it was getting futile, a large grey shape rolled among the weed stems. I piled on the pressure, determined to keep him moving, and gradually I eased him up through the weed. Tantalisingly close, he turned and twisted beneath the boat in a last-ditch attempt to free the hook, the netting also hampered by the wind. After a few bottom-twitching moments, I drew him cleanly into the folds of the waiting net. As I lifted my prize onto the mat in the bottom of the boat, I really thought I'd captured Olive at last. But it was not to be, for there in between my feet lay my old friend The Pug.

Most of the fight had been hidden to Phil by the small island. In fact, he was totally unaware of my morning's events so, after sacking the fish, I stood on the end of Springate's Point and looking over into his swim, I could see he had a couple of visitors in the shape of Jacko and Tetley, lounging on the grass outside his bivvy. Taking a deep breath I hollered across the lake, "Yo! I've had The Pug!"

All three bodies jumped up and, after a brief discussion, gave me the thumbs up and Phil reeled in, but no one moved. After a few minutes of staring at each other blankly across the pond I tried again.

"I've had The Pug!" Only this time even louder!

"Good idea!" came the somewhat confusing reply. After even more open palm 'what the bloody hell's going on,' type gestures, Tetley eventually broke from the pack

Putting The Pug back.

and started to trot around the lake. Fifteen minutes later a very hot looking Tetley appeared at the back of the swim.

"I've had The Pug," I repeated.

"Oh, right," he replied. "We thought you said, I'm going down the pub!"

While he was there I enlisted his help in taking the photo's before weighing and returning The Pug. He weighed much the same as the last time that I'd caught him, around thirty six and a half pounds. Although I was obviously enjoying my time at Wraysbury, the repeat captures were starting to wear me down. With all the effort I was putting in I couldn't help thinking it might be best put to use on another water where all the stock would be fresh new acquaintances.

I decided to take Tetley up on the pub idea and have a serious think about my future at Wraysbury over a few pints of Guinness.

The more I thought about it the more I came to the stark reality that my days at the great Wraysbury lake were numbered and with this realisation came the urgent need to find another water to channel my enthusiasm into. I had assumed, on joining Wraysbury, that all the foreseeable years would be spent in tracking down just a few of its prized inhabitants. Fate, however, had once again dealt me a winning hand and allowed me an incredible nineteen captures over my two and a half year stay. It is 'the nature of the beast', though, that the moment you totally fall into tune with a water is also the moment to leave it behind you. Carp fishing, to me, is all about learning and every pit has its own idiosyncrasies and problems to learn and overcome, the time had arrived to move on.

I suppose I could have stayed on in the faint and desperate hope of The Leather or one of the true 'Odd-un's' but knew I could not tolerate all the recaptures along the way. I had a vague idea of where I wanted to try my hand next, but I also knew that it would present far more problems than Wraysbury ever had.

There was a pit that lay further along the valley that a couple of friends of mine had fished before, one of them up until fairly recently. It was about forty acres in size and held somewhere in the region of twenty carp, the largest of which had only been caught once but at an impressive weight of forty six pounds. You were not, technically speaking, allowed to fish there, but I knew people who were planning to. I thought "What the hell, what's food for the goose is food for the gander!" If somebody was going to poach there it might as well be me. Apparently, so I'd been told, it was incredibly over grown which I thought would probably make the whole thing a lot easier, so I promised myself a little visit at some stage during the next few weeks. I carried on fishing Wraysbury for the meantime, though, hooking and unfortunately losing a fish a couple of weeks later.

The circumstances were a bit unusual, but it showed me once again the clever reaction that fish show when they come into contact with our rigs. I was in the Dredger Bay and I'd found two fish lying up in the weed under a large snag tree that lay parallel with the water, just below the surface along most of its length, with the furthermost branches dipping further down into the pond. Both the carp were mid-thirties. One of them was The Pug and the other one I could not recognise. I could see it well enough to know that it was not one of the known faces which was obviously very exciting. I crept out along the base of the fallen tree for a closer look and planned my attack. The fish were tight on the back of the weed that had floated into the branches and a delicate approach was called for. So I set up with just a hook and a single swan shot pinched on the line about six inches back. In my rucksack was half a loaf of bread, so grabbing a couple of slices I crept back out into position and pinched a small piece of flake onto the hook shank.

The fish had drifted under the raft of weed and were now literally at my feet, separated from me only by the bough of the tree. I could just make out the odd bit of fin or scale through the thick canopy above them. This gave me the perfect opportunity to flick a bait the fifteen feet to the back of the weed to form an ambush for when they would next move out. The first cast fell short and, as I swung the sodden flake back to hand, it fell off the hook and landed a few inches from the bank in a foot of water. I pinched on another piece and crept forward to cast, but before I was able to, The Pug left the sanctuary of the weed and swam directly toward me. With an effortless flick of his tail, he crossed the tree trunk at a point where it dipped a mere foot below the surface. He had to turn on his side to do so but he still somehow managed to achieve it without causing so much as a ripple on the surface. To my amazement he swam straight up to me and, as I stood there not daring to breathe, sucked up the fallen piece of flake which lay only inches from my toes before returning once again to the weed.

I realised from this behaviour that the carp obviously had no idea that I was there, which put me in a very good position. The next cast landed perfectly, just behind the weed, and I could easily see the flake hovering a few inches above the silt and short weed. Both fish were concealed beneath the floating raft at my feet and I could see the occasional glimpse as they leisurely turned and twisted. I decided on a ploy, as I was wanting them to move further out in order to find my trap so, carefully rolling small pellets of earth about the size of a pea, I dropped them one at a time into the weed at my feet, not in order to spook the fish but hoping to ever-so slightly un-nerve them. As I watched the progress of the third or fourth pellet I could see the tail and dorsal of one fish but no signs of the other and on looking up I could see why.

The Pug had fallen for the method and was currently standing on his nose firmly hooked on the breadflake rig but, rather than bolt on feeling the hook he had opted to spin around and around in an attempt to shed it. With no lead to make him bolt away he was methodically trying every trick in the book to free himself. I watched for a few seconds, spellbound, before gently tightening in to him. On feeling the pressure, he bolted straight into the branches at my feet and with one scoop of the net he would have been mine. Unfortunately, just as I stretched to reach the net handle, I slipped on the damp tree trunk and fell backwards, spooking the carp back out of the snag. He then took full advantage of my predicament by charging off through every branch and root in the bay while I, lying flat on my back in the mud, struggled to gain control. Needless to say, he came out the victor by breaking the line against the sharp snags but, having already caught him twice he was obviously not the one of the pair that I was after, but nevertheless nobody likes to lose a fish.

This incident reinforced my thoughts that the chances of singling out the remaining few fish that I was after from Wraysbury, even when stalking, was not realistically an option. The catchable ones that I had already had would have to be caught time and again in order to be in with a chance of the occasional new face. With this in mind, I decided that now was the time to look at the new water, and so ended my time at the great Wraysbury pit.

I certainly had no complaints, as my results had far outreached my wildest dreams and expectations. When I'd originally started out I would have been happy with just the odd one or two fish, but in two and a half years I had nineteen captures under my belt. I'd enjoyed every minute of my time there and I knew that I would miss fishing Wraysbury more than I had any other water.

Chapter 26

In Conclusion

Wraysbury is, without doubt, an incredibly hard act to follow and the new pit, although holding some beautiful fish, went only part of the way towards replacing it. Restless as ever, I have moved on again from there and, although I still have whole reams to write about the place, my space is fast becoming limited.

Since April, I have been making the trip down to Kent once a week for a couple of nights at a time, in pursuit of a very elusive fifty pounder that, despite it now being September, has still yet to grace the banks. A lot of other waters have also been considered in the search for the perfect environment and a lot of idle gossip and rumours have been pursued to their eventual and fruitless conclusions along the way. I have heard of uncaught fifty pounders in most of the British counties and some of them, apparently, even originated there! There is also the obligatory big uncaught common. He, of course, feels like an old friend now that I have heard so much about him, and I suppose it would be an incomplete carp book that bore him no mention.

In almost every lake that I've ever fished the big common has lurked within the myths and legends that circulate late at night, and in hushed whispers. He always seems to be about five pounds or so bigger than the biggest known fish in the lake and, of course, has never been landed, although he has usually been lost under some bizarre set of circumstances, usually involving a punt that he just happened to be a foot longer than. In Frampton, for example, he almost tipped old Ted out of the boat.

"His head was sticking out of one end and his tail was poking out the other, eyes like tractor wheels he had!"

He was there again at Harefield. Forty pounds if he was an ounce. In another lake in the West Country recently he was spotted and reported as being, "big as a gurt pig."

Wraysbury was host to his elusiveness and even in the most well documented of pits he makes his appearance to tease and torment the hapless carper. Quite how he transcends from one end of the country to another is a mystery to me, unless of course, we are surrounded by uncaught monster commons! I think it more likely that he is, in some way, omnipresent and appears to all at the same time. It is my burning ambition to catch him one day. It wouldn't matter in the least from where he came, for surely he would be the incarnation of all the elusive 'big commons' that reside in every pond, ditch, or lake that has ever seen a rod and line. Long live the big common, I say, for he signifies the very essence of carp angling!

A lot of things have changed for me since my time spent on Wraysbury. The real world has finally tracked me down, and dragged me from my refuge. As well as angling, I now have a family to occupy my time, and there never seem to be enough hours in a day, or days in a week, anymore.

I would not, however, change it for the world and, although I enjoyed my existence as a full time angler, life moves on and I in turn must move with it, or get left behind in the rush.

Recently, I had the amazing gift of a small son called Conor, and before very long he will be old enough to make his first acquaintance with the parapet of a certain stone bridge. I have the necessary gaily-coloured float waiting patiently at the back of the drawer, and a five foot rod gathers cobwebs in the shed. I wonder if he will grow to share my obsession and, consequently, live out his life at one with his surroundings and in tune with the natural world?

Only time will tell!